BAJA BOATER'S GUIDE

VOLUME I -- THE PACIFIC COAST

The Definitive Guide for
the Coastal Waters of

MEXICO'S
BAJA
CALIFORNIA

BY
JACK WILLIAMS

By the author of
the best selling
MAGNIFICENT PENINSULA

Published by
H. J. Williams Publications
P. O. Box 203
Sausalito, CA 94966
(415) 332-8635

Printed by
Publishers Press
1900 West 2300 South
Salt Lake City, Utah 84119-0408
(801) 972-6600 (800) 456 6600

Library of Congress Catalog Card Number 88-050749

ISBN 0-9616843-1-3 (Volume I)
ISBN 0-9616843-2-1 (2 Volume Set)

A tuna clipper at anchor in Bahia Santa Maria

The information in this book is based on my own personal comprehensive, field investigations of the Baja peninsula by land, sea, and air. I guarantee it.**

Why should the author of a travel book make such a statement, and feel compelled to guarantee that he has personally seen what he is writing about? The reason is, that many travel books are based on little, inadequate, or outdated field investigations. This is particularly true in regard to the Baja peninsula. The result is that such books are often replete with errors.

Even the most prestigious Baja guides have been based largely on material gleaned from government charts and publications, and the works of previous authors. Some use the words "New & Revised" and "Completely New" on the covers of supposedly updated editions. Yet they report long out-of-date conditions.

For this reason, I decided that my books would be based primarily on my own personal observations. If I have not seen something about which I report, I will so state. Obviously, I am considerably indebted to preexisting literature for the chapters on History and Natural History.

The BAJA BOATER'S GUIDE is based on the following field investigations:

1 -- Four sea voyages to Baja in my ketch *La Patricia*. Two of these trips were complete "circumnavigations" of the peninsula and its adjoining islands.

2 -- A complete flight along the peninsular coast for the purpose of taking over 1,000 aerial photos.

3 -- Over 20,000 miles of travel on Baja's highways and roads.

The *Baja Boater's Guide* contains errors and omissions. This, I also guarantee. Anyone who would maintain otherwise, is both an egotist and a fool. Conditions are constantly changing in Baja, and my recommendations and observations are subject to the human frailties that beset us all. But this I pledge, "I went down and looked, and I done my damndest".

Jack Williams

** See statement on the back cover.

ACKNOWLEDGMENTS

Writing a book for a relatively limited audience such as the boaters visiting Baja California requires that one keep a watchful eye on the costs of production. To put it bluntly, one must become somewhat of a scrounger. So here is where I can pay a grateful tribute to those who have so unstintingly contributed their time and efforts to the production of the *Baja Boater's Guide*; Willing victims to *the touch*.

To *Alan Lamb*, my sole companion on the first circumnavigation of the Baja peninsula, and who joined the Pacific run on the second voyage. The performance of shipboard duties is of course essential for one's companion at sea, but Alan also brought along his brain. A true friend who uses his head is a rare commodity. ------ To Frank Gieber, who toughed out the entire second circumnavigation, its mechanical difficulties, and other assorted calamities. Many thanks.

Without aerial photos, this book's value would be substantially decreased. Airplanes are expensive. But how about the perfect plane, and the perfect pilot, for nothing but the trip expenses. My undying gratitude to *Lars and Carol Weseth* for the loan of their MAULE aircraft, and to *Jeromy Ainsworth* an Alaskan bush pilot extordinar. And to my long time friend *Bill Graham* who came to my rescue to put the whole deal together. What can I say.

As they did for *The Magnificent Peninsula*, June Siringer and my daughter *Barbara Williams Hitchcock* came forth with reviewing and editing. ------ to Professor *Burney J. LeBoeuf* for reviewing the Natural History chapter and elevating it to at least C- status ------ And the photo printing and developing; Muchas gracias to *Bob Tribble*. I paid him, but not very much; professional work for drugstore prices. He said, if you screw-up on the exposures, I'll save your ass in the dark room. And yours truly has a rear-end considerably in need of salvation. ------ Beware of Greeks bearing gifts, but Spiros Bairaktaris provided an outstanding cover design at minimal cost.

Every author thanks his wife for this and that trivial task. Perhaps it started that way, but I would have long since lost the above noted rear-end in total without the full-time assistance of *Patty* on everything from editing to fending off the tax collector. She won't set foot on *La Patricia* as she knows it will heal over and sink with the slightest breeze, but one can't have everything.

Thank you all. Without your generous help, there would be no *Baja Boater's Guide*.

DEDICATION

To the men and ships of the United States Navy, and to the authors of all previous guidebooks to Baja waters. Thank you for leading the way.

CONTENTS

The BAJA BOATER'S GUIDE got us here, now what do we do?

Get THE MAGNIFICENT PENINSULA

WELCOME TO BAJA

Even the fish know, NOBODY, goes to Baja without

THE MAGNIFICENT PENINSULA
By JACK WILLIAMS

THE MAGNIFICENT PENINSULA is the companion volume to the
BAJA BOATER'S GUIDE. It contains full chapter coverage concerning
CAMPING -- TRANSPORTATION -- HOTELS -- TRAILER COURTS
-- GEOLOGY -- WILDLIFE -- VEGETATION -- BAJA'S PEOPLE

248 PAGES -- 57 MAPS
100 PHOTOS -- 32 TABLES
HOTEL & TRAILER COURT LISTS

2,800 MILES OF ROAD LOGS
Highway logs tied to easy to
find roadside kilometer markers.

LOS ANGELES TIMES ———— "Credit Jack Williams for the excellent information in his guidebook. It's an in-depth presentation."

SAN DIEGO UNION ———— "The best description of the book is EXHAUSTIVE."

SACRAMENTO BEE ———— "It's pretty impressive."

LAS VEGAS REVIEW JOURNAL ———— "It's superior to any other offering."

LATITUDE 38 BOATING MAGAZINE ———— 38 calls it "The Magnificent Guide."

Get your copy from the BAJA BOOKSHELF in the Appendix

CHAPTER 1
INTRODUCTION
(ABOUT THIS BOOK)

IF ALL ELSE FAILS
FOLLOW THE INSTRUCTIONS

Most books have no moving parts and do not have to be assembled. Neither does this one. But it does have parts, parts of parts, gimmicks, policies, and techniques. It therefore requires a few instructions. This chapter, insidiously disguised as an introduction, is where they are deposited. It is, in effect, a chapter about this book. If you started reading in the middle and found yourself aground, perhaps as a last resort you are back here at the beginning. Regardless of how you arrived, welcome to the *Baja Boater's Guide. Volume I,* the book you are reading, describes the Pacific coast of Baja California. *Volume II* covers the peninsula's Sea of Cortez shore and numerous adjacent islands.

THE TARGET READER

A friend suggested that I name this book "The Baja Cruiser's Guide." He assumed that my audience was to be primarily the mariners who travel to Baja waters by sail and power vessels, and who engage in what is popularly known as cruising. In reality, these people form only a portion of the readers for whom this book is intended.

Even a casual acquaintance with Baja California will disclose that there are far more land-based trailer boats in Baja than there are ocean cruisers. And in recent years, the sport of ocean kayaking has grown substantially. At this writing, I am convinced that the number of kayaks in the Sea of Cortez at any one time is considerably greater than the number of cruising vessels. This book has been named the *Baja Boater's Guide* as it is intended for all of these recreational boaters.

Nevertheless, I am well aware that the skippers of ocean-going vessels will require more detailed and precise information than users of smaller boats. The cruiser's needs have thus set the standard for the material presented in this book; however, information aimed toward other boat users has also been included.

OTHER GUIDEBOOKS

In 1954, Wesley A. Bush wrote and published *Paradise to Leeward.* This volume touched only the high spots along Baja's Pacific coast, but it was the first privately produced guidebook for Baja waters. Since then there have been several others including *Charlie's Charts* by Charles E. Woods. Among the most respected is *Baja Cruising Notes* by Vern Jones. His book contains no photographs, and its charts are of the pencil sketch variety, but I have found his text to be accurate and to the point. With Vern's permission, I have referenced his views when they occasionally differ from my own, or where he cites an experience I have not had. His book is still in print at this writing.

Leland Lewis's *Baja Sea Guide* appeared in 1971. Leland's principal contribution was the publication of a *comprehensive* marine guide for the entire Baja peninsula. By comprehensive is meant that it included (1) sailing directions, (2) aerial photos, (3) charts, and (4) extensive historical and other background material.

The overwhelming shortcoming of the *Baja Sea Guide* was that large segments of its sailing directions were lifted more or less intact from the U. S. government's *Sailing Directions for the West Coast of Mexico and Central America..* Much of this material does little more than present a textual rendition of what is in plain sight on U. S. government charts and the book's aerial photos.

THIS BOOK IS BORN

In November, 1983, I signed an agreement with Leland Lewis to update and revise his out-of-print *Baja Sea Guide.* The winter of 1983-84 was then spent conducting a complete circumnavigation of the Baja peninsula in my 46-foot ketch in company with my good friend Alan Lamb. Copious notes, photos, and charts were turned over to Leland upon our return.

In joining with Leland Lewis to update his book I was unaware of its shortcomings. I had expected to find the need for corrections brought about only by man-made change. Instead I discovered scores of errors. It is my firm belief that Leland had spent little time field researching his material in Baja California. He apparently did take most of the aerial photos.

Leland advertised the planned new edition for sale through the mail, and collected a substantial sum of money, but as of this writing, has never produced a book. I received no compensation for my efforts and cannot even secure the return of my survey material. In the process, the relationship between Leland and me deteriorated badly.

Frustrated with waiting, I returned to Baja by land and drove thousands of miles over its roads and highways. The result of this effort was the publication in 1986 of *The Magnificent Peninsula,* a land-oriented book about Baja California. It has been well received.

As Leland Lewis's book still remained unpublished, I set about to produce my own marine guide. Two additional field investigations were required before this could be accomplished. These were (1) a low-level aerial reconnaissance flown in April 1987 during which some 1,000 oblique aerial photos were taken, and (2) a second complete circling of the Baja peninsula in my ketch during the winter of 1987-88. This *Baja Boater's Guide* is the result. As can be seen, I started out to be a Godfather to someone else's offspring but ended as parent of my own. Asi es la vida (such is life).

In spite of my sad experience with Leland Lewis, I owe much to my experience with him. It has led to a post-retirement activity considerably superior to haunting the pool rooms. And my trials with Leland have led to the policies that have governed the production of this *Baja Boater's Guide.* These are set forth below in the belief that readers should be aware of how this book was fashioned and understand both its strengths and weaknesses.

POLICIES

1 -- I endeavor to report only what I have seen personally. Only in isolated instances are items noted that do not meet this objective. In these cases, appropriate credit to the actual source is given, or the phrase "it is reported" will alert you to the fact that I am venturing beyond my own experiences.

In spite of this high ideal, remember that the Baja coast is over 2,000 miles in length. I have visited every anchorage noted in this book, some of them on several occasions. However, I make no claim to being an expert regarding any particular location. To accomplish this would require more lifetimes than I have available. Sea and weather conditions are constantly changing and

one needs to keep in mind that my observations do not encompass their full range.

2 -- U. S. charts and previous guidebooks frequently use the term *clear passage* when describing what is thought to be safe water lying between two bodies of land. In contrast, I will note that "I have found the passage to be clear" and give the water depths encountered. I make no guarantees as to what someone else may experience. Skippers should always be continually on the alert when traversing such areas and not be lulled into carelessness by clear passage advice that may be in error.

3 -- Charts and photos are allowed to speak for themselves. The text is designed to supplement, and highlight, rather than duplicate charts and photos. The term (See Photo) is presented in the text at the point where I judge it best for the reader to consult the photo of the area being discussed. Frequently the photo captions are of equal importance to the text and they should not be overlooked.

4 -- Only minimal space is devoted to land-oriented information. Forgive me for recommending that you reference my book *The Magnificent Peninsula* for details concerning, roads, hotels, trailer courts, and similar subjects. (See notice concerning this book at the beginning of this chapter.)

LAND, SEA, AND AIR

In showing this book's aerial photos to an acquaintance, I was asked, "How do you know for certain that the locations shown in the photos are really those places?" The answer lies in the fact that this book was produced as the result of extensive field investigations by land, sea, and air.

During the first circling of the peninsula by sea, there were occasions when there was a considerable degree of uncertainty about the vessel's location. I was not lost, you understand, but the coastline had become disoriented. These uncertainties were clarified during subsequent trips by road. The observations made during these land and sea trips then made site location a relatively easy chore during the aerial reconnaissance. Even the dullest witted of us get the lay of the land after we have seen it often enough.

The reliability of the aerial flight was further enhanced by having aboard the aircraft a complete set of highly accurate Mexican government topographic maps. The second sea voyage was then made in company with these topographic maps, the aerial photos, and drafts of this book's charts and text. Its objective was to field check all of these elements in order to produce a final product as free of errors as humanly possible.

BOOK ELEMENTS

BACKGROUND MATERIAL --Two chapters in PART I present material concerning the maritime history and various natural history features of Baja's Pacific coast. This full-chapter approach will allow you to obtain a broad overview of these subjects which would not be possible if this information were dispersed throughout the Sailing Directions in PART II.

More specific history and natural history items are included in PART II in conjunction with the area to which they apply. In most cases this background material will be enclosed within a box to clearly differentiate it from the Sailing Directions. Nothing can be more frustrating to the harried skipper seeking anchoring guidance than to find one's self immersed in the mating habits of the magnificent frigatebird.

CHAPTER ORGANIZATION -- The BAJA PACIFIC COAST Chart presented in Chapter 2 notes that this shore is made up of three reaches and three bights. The chapters in PART II correspond to these entities with an additional chapter on the group of islands near the peninsula's midpoint. Sectional breakdown within the chapters is based on some readily apparent difference between the sections such as a change from mountainous to level terrain. Each chapter and section is introduced with a summary description.

CHARTS -- The coastal outline of most of the charts in this book have been traced from a variety of preexisting sources using computer techniques. These include the U. S. maritime charts and various road maps. However, the great majority are based on highly accurate, Mexican government topographic maps. These maps are printed at a scale of 1 / 50,000; i.e., 1 inch on the map equals 50,000 inches on the ground. This scale results in 1 nautical mile equaling slightly less than 1 1/2 inches.

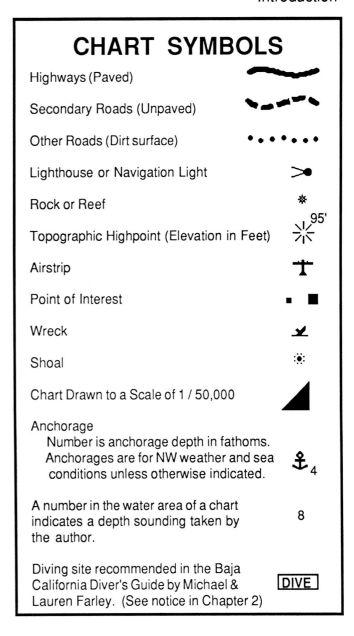

CHART SYMBOLS

Highways (Paved)

Secondary Roads (Unpaved)

Other Roads (Dirt surface)

Lighthouse or Navigation Light

Rock or Reef

Topographic Highpoint (Elevation in Feet)   95'

Airstrip

Point of Interest

Wreck

Shoal

Chart Drawn to a Scale of 1 / 50,000

Anchorage
    Number is anchorage depth in fathoms.
    Anchorages are for NW weather and sea
    conditions unless otherwise indicated.   4

A number in the water area of a chart indicates a depth sounding taken by the author.   8

Diving site recommended in the Baja California Diver's Guide by Michael & Lauren Farley. (See notice in Chapter 2)   DIVE

Most charts depicting specific coves, islands, or prominent points of land utilize this 1 / 50,000 scale. This standard has been used so that the size and shape of coastal features may be compared from one chart to another. Charts using this scale are delineated with a black triangle in one of the bottom corners. No such mark appears when other scales are used. The few charts which are based on my own pencil sketching will be so designated. (The symbols used on the charts in this book are shown in a box on this page.)

Because of the above-noted means of production, the charts in this book are far more accurate than in any previous Baja guide. They are not perfect, however, as they reflect the shortcomings of my mechanical drawing ability, and the limitations of producing maps on a computer. Nevertheless, the computerized process

has provided extreme flexibility. It has allowed the inclusion of far more detail than would have been possible if a human illustrator had been employed. Corrections and updatings are also easily accomplished.

AERIAL PHOTOS -- The aerial photos in this book were taken by me from a Maule STAL (short takeoff and landing} aircraft. Mr. Maule equips his airplanes with doors, but on the seven-day flight counterclockwise around the Baja peninsula, the right rear portal was removed to provide maximum picture clarity. As you may have concluded, I did not fall out. I did contact a ferocious cold.

Aerial photos are of great assistance to the mariner in obtaining an advanced bird's-eye view of places to be visited; however, they have their limitations. Primary among these is the fact that actual alignment of coastal features can be badly distorted by the angle at which the picture is taken. A cove with a substantial indent can be made to look virtually straight, and the most modest of bights can be depicted as being a well-protected harbor. I tried diligently to secure camera angles that present a realistic representation but was not always successful. It has occurred to me that this exercise is similar to the problem, or pleasure, facing a photographer who is endeavoring to enhance on film the physical attributes of a female model.

PLACE NAMES -- The names of coves, promontories, communities, and other features used in this book are those given in the latest editions of the U. S. government nautical charts. I am well aware that these names are frequently not the same as those shown on Mexican government maps, or as currently being used by local people. In effect, I am saying that this book often uses the wrong names. Many readers, however, will be using the U. S. charts in conjunction with this book, and it would cause considerable confusion if the two references did not agree. I overrule the U. S. charts only where there is an obvious error. Where no names

are provided by the U. S. charts I have used those shown on current Mexican government topographic maps.

MISCELLANEOUS -- A few final items:

1 - All compass directions are given in <u>magnetic degrees</u>.

2 - All mileages are in <u>nautical miles</u> except where they are referring to the distance between two places by road.

3 - Depth soundings are given in <u>fathoms</u> (6 feet = 1 fathom). The latest editions of the U. S. nautical charts have been converted to meters, but my mind and depth sounder are firmly entrenched in the past.

4 - Frequent use is made of <u>underlining</u> in the Sailing Directions text in PART II as is being done in this Miscellaneous Section. The use of this technique is somewhat at my whim, but for the most part it will call attention to place names, landmarks, anchorages, and other features which I believe should be emphasized.

FUELING UP AT GUERRERO NEGRO -- Alaskan bush pilot Jeromy Ainsworth fuels the Maule aircraft. The aerial photos in this book would not have been possible without this fine pilot and aircraft combination.

CHAPTER 2
THE BIG PICTURE
(ABOUT BAJA'S PACIFIC COAST)

Chapter 1 was about this book. Chapter 2 is concerned with Baja's Pacific coast. Here you will find an overview of the area, its weather, navigation, communications, and other items to consider before setting sail. The all important subject of anchorages is covered separately in Chapter 3.

BAJA'S PACIFIC COAST

It is a straight-line distance of over 800 miles from San Diego to Cabo San Lucas at the tip of the Baja peninsula. Considerable additional distance would be logged if one traversed all the numerous bays and coves.

REACHES AND BIGHTS -- Inspection of the BAJA'S PACIFIC COAST Chart will disclose that there are three sections with a relatively straight shoreline (reaches), and three indented portions (bights). The chapter breakdown of this book's Sailing Directions in PART II is based on these six sections of coastline. I have taken the liberty of naming them as indicated on this chart.

Two chapters are devoted to the Northern Reach because of the marked difference between its north and south portions. The north area is heavily urbanized. The south portion is not. One additional chapter describes a major group of islands (Islas Cedros, Benitos and Natividad) located near the peninsula's midpoint. The chapter and section breakpoints thus conform to physically distinct segments of the coast.

This organizational arrangement also conforms to the sailing patterns followed by most ocean cruisers. Many skippers will travel relatively close-in along the reaches, and will then set a straight-line course across the bights.

Fortunately there are good anchorages near both extremities of the three reaches. These make good resting points for use prior to crossing the bights. These crossings can involve night running for many vessels.

Most of the shoreline of the reaches is closely backed by steep and picturesque mountains. Along the bights, most of the highlands recede inland, and much of the actual coast is low-lying and relatively uninteresting.

LAGOONS -- Scores of miles of shallow water lagoons lie inland along the lower-lying sections of coast. These are concentrated in the Northern and Middle Bights. Most of these are long and narrow and are formed immediately behind the coastal barrier beaches. Others, such as Scammon's Lagoon and Laguna San Ignacio, project inland a considerable distance.

All of these lagoons have entrances to the sea. In some cases these channels are navigable by ocean-going vessels. Others carry water only in the event of rain. Most are fronted in the sea by dangerous breaking bars.

These lagoons are of little interest to the crews of ocean-cruising and sportfishing vessels as they should be entered only with considerable local knowledge. Many of the lagoons, however, are being discovered by kayakers and the owners of other small boats who launch their craft from the inland side. The larger lagoons are the winter calving grounds of the California gray whale. Observing their antics is a major attraction.

COASTAL COMMUNITIES -- Man is a social animal, and coming into contact with the people of another culture is one of the joys of foreign travel. May I recommend that this be one of your objectives in boating along Baja's Pacific coast.

BAJA'S PACIFIC COAST
(3 REACHES -- 3 BIGHTS)

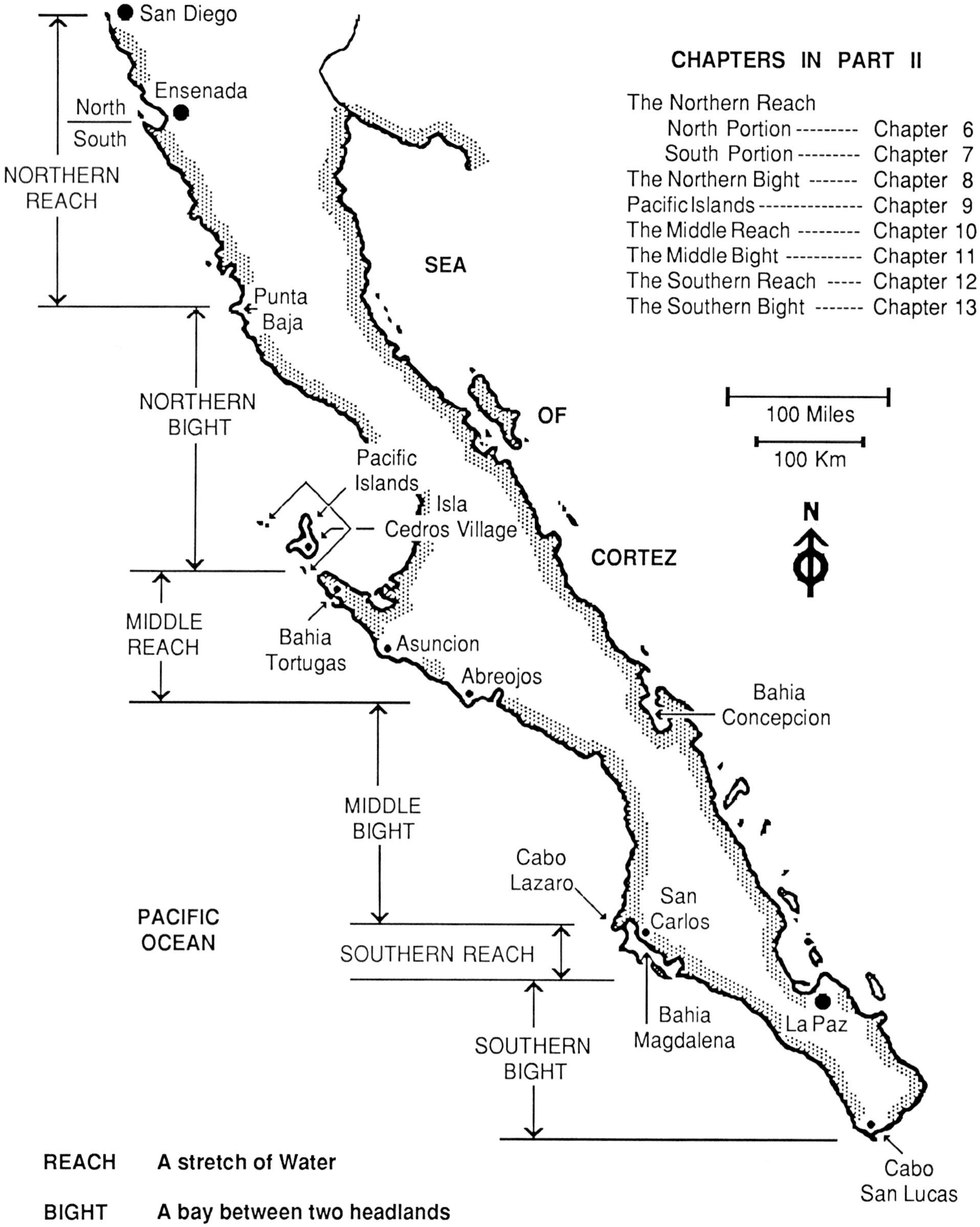

San Diego

Ensenada

North
South

NORTHERN
REACH

Punta
Baja

NORTHERN
BIGHT

SEA

OF

CORTEZ

Pacific
Islands

Isla
Cedros Village

MIDDLE
REACH

Bahia
Tortugas

Asuncion

Abreojos

Bahia
Concepcion

MIDDLE
BIGHT

Cabo
Lazaro

San
Carlos

PACIFIC
OCEAN

SOUTHERN REACH

Bahia
Magdalena

La Paz

SOUTHERN
BIGHT

Cabo
San Lucas

100 Miles

100 Km

N

REACH   A stretch of Water

BIGHT   A bay between two headlands

Ensenada is the only major city. The area bordering the harbor is heavily visited by tourists from north of the border, but it is a good place to break the cultural ice. It is also an excellent locale for shopping. It is far better in this respect than Cabo San Lucas.

Much smaller in size are six substantial coastal villages with populations in the 3,000-to-10,000 range. From north to south these are Isla Cedros Village, Bahia Tortugas, Asuncion, Abreojos, San Carlos, and Cabo San Lucas. (See BAJA'S PACIFIC COAST Chart.) There are smaller villages at Santa Rosalilita, Isla Natividad, San Roque, Punta Prieta, La Bocana, San Juanico, Puerto Alcatraz, and several other locations. Finally, there is the naval base community of Puerto Cortez in Bahia Magdalena.

Cabo San Lucas is heavily tourist-oriented with major hotels and all services. With the exception of the naval base, the others are strictly business fishing villages. Most of these have stores with a limited supply of staples. Beer and liquor are available in some places. To a large degree, one of these towns is much like the others, and when you have seen one, you have seen them all; but visit some of them. The best in my view are Isla Cedros and Bahia Tortugas villages. These are the largest and have the most services to offer.

Finally, there are the several dozen fish camps that are situated in almost every protected anchorage and landing not occupied by one of the larger towns. More correctly, these are lobster or abalone camps, as these delicacies are often the chief items sought by their inhabitants. They may be occupied only when these shellfish are in season. The camps consist of from one to a dozen shacks fashioned from plywood, roofing panels, and anything else that will cut the wind. Living conditions are primitive and constitute a marked contrast to what we know north of the border.

COMMERCIAL FISHING -- Mexican commercial fishing activities will be much in evidence to any boater plying the waters of Baja's Pacific coast. There are fish canning or fish fertilizer plants in El Sauzal, Ensenada, Isla Cedros, Bahia Tortugas, Asuncion, Abreojos, San Carlos, Puerto Alcatraz, and Puerto Lopez Mateos. Modern design, steel-hulled, fishing vessels in the 50-to-100 foot range will frequently be seen at these locations or trolling their nets in the coastal waters. These vessels are operated as part of Mexican government cooperatives. They put to shame most of the fishing craft seen in U. S. and Canadian waters.

Similar sized vessels rigged for shrimping may also be encountered in the shallow waters near the southern ends of the Northern and Middle Bights, and in Bahia Magdalena. The shrimpers frequently work in groups of several boats. These craft may be distinguished by the sizeable nets that hang from booms near the stern. Shrimpers also carry large flat panels of metal called flopper-stoppers. They are lowered into the water from each side of the vessel in rocky seas to, you got it, stop the flop. When not in use they hang in the air. Shrimpers often work at night. Thus, they will be seen at anchor during daylight hours, sometimes in the open roadstead where they will continue their patrol after dark.

Far more prevalent than the above vessels are the pangas. These 20-to-30-foot, fiberglass, outboard-powered craft were designed and originally built by an American named Maximillian Shroyer. The panga factory is in La Paz on the Sea of Cortez. Ten years ago, most of the small fishing craft on the Pacific coast were somewhat shorter and made of wood. A few of these are still in use. Most have been replaced by Mac's fiberglass product.

Mac advises me that panga is a Mexican word that refers to a small flat-bottom boat that would be called a skiff north of the border. The flat bottom is more stable than a round hull and allows the boat to be easily driven up onto the beach by the powerful outboard. The long narrow design gives the craft considerable speed. It is to heavy to be easily moved overland.

The presence of pangas is the universal sign of the fish camp or village. Many are drawn up on the beach. In places with protected anchorages they will be moored offshore. The mooring areas naturally occupy the preferred anchoring location, thus limiting visiting yachts to second best. A location adjoining the mooring area is usually a sound choice.

A Mexican Panga loaded with lobster traps.

Lobster receivers are also moored offshore from fish camps and villages. These are boxes made of wooden lath. They are used to hold the lobster catch prior to marketing. The receivers (recibos in Spanish) float just at the water's surface and may be difficult to detect, particularly at night.

FUEL -- Diesel and gasoline fuel is readily available at only four locations south of San Diego. These are: (1) dock side at the marinas in Ensenada, (2) gravity flow from barrels to end-tied vessels at the dock at Bahia Tortugas, (3) dock side at San Carlos, and (4) at Cabo San Lucas. At this writing, obtaining fuel at the latter location still requires ferrying your supply from shore in the tender, but eventually there will be a fuel dock. I hold not my breath.

Ensenada and Cabo San Lucas are at, or near, the extremities of Baja's Pacific coast. Fueling at San Carlos requires a roundtrip detour of about 40 miles into Bahia Magdalena. Thus, Bahia Tortugas is the only readily available fueling point along the central portion of Baja's Pacific coast. It is 340 miles from San Diego to Bahia Tortugas, and 460 miles from there to Cabo San Lucas. Reliable sailboats can readily span these distances. However, power vessels should not attempt the Baja Passage unless their fuel capacities are adequate. One would think that a 600-mile range would be the absolute minimum required to provide a margin of safety.

REPAIRS -- There is a travel lift at the Baja Naval Marina at Ensenada. This is the only place on the Pacific coast where a yacht can be taken from the water. La Paz offers the southernmost such facility in the Sea of Cortez.

Ensenada offers a full range of ship repair services. There is no other place where there is a repair facility specifically catering to boating needs. Various types of assistance are available at the larger communities noted above. The several fish canneries have machine shops as does the naval base at Puerto Cortez. Mexicans are very friendly and will generally go out of their way to be helpful, but be aware that obtaining specialized boat parts will be difficult and might require a trip to Ensenada, La Paz, or San Diego. The prudent skippers should assure that their vessels are equipped with a variety of hand tools and commonly needed spare parts.

TYPES OF VESSELS -- The most commonly seen recreational vessel along Baja's Pacific coast is the sailboat. The majority of these are aft-cockpit boats approximately 35-feet in length. There are also a substantial number of center-cockpit sailing vessels in the mid-40-foot range. A few are larger, and surprisingly, a few are smaller. On occasion one sees sailors braving the open Pacific in sailboats down to 25 feet in length. I don't recommend it, but it's done.

Powerboats, usually 40 feet and longer, also make the Baja Passage. During the winter cruising season they will be outnumbered in the anchorages by the sailboats 10 to 1 except at Cabo San Lucas. This is partly due to the fact that the powerboat skippers tend to turn on the motor at San Diego and don't stop until rounding the cape at Cabo San Lucas. There is also a a substantial migration of powerboats making the run to Cabo in the spring when the fishing off the cape is better than in the winter.

Some of the powerboats are well-fitted craft specifically designed for cruising and making ocean passages. Many, however, are the broad, aft-cockpit, sport fishers. I would personally rather go to sea in a kayak, but they seem to make the journey. Some carry extra fuel in barrels lashed in the cockpit, or in variously placed bladder tanks. I have witnessed such tanks being loaded with hundreds of gallons of diesel at the fuel docks in San Diego and then lashed to the foredeck with 1/4 inch line. God help them if they ever encounter a gale at sea.

Finally, I know of one individual who has twice traversed Baja's Pacific shore in a small open, outboard-powered, boat. One of these trips was in cooperation with a land party that transported fuel and supplies to prearranged points. Taking such craft into the open Pacific is fraught with considerable risk, but the challenge is there for the adventuresome soul.

It is beyond the scope of this book to present detailed counsel on outfitting a vessel to be taken into Baja waters. That is a book-length subject in itself. I do present several suggestions concerning anchoring in Chapter 3 ANCHORING AND ANCHORAGES.

Beyond that I have only one recommendation: equip your vessel with a depth sounder if you plan to anchor frequently. The anchorages along Baja's Pacific coast vary considerably in the deepness of their waters, and reefs of rock or sand of unknown depth frequently extend under water from promontories. One is simply flying blind without knowledge of how much water is below the hull in these places. The U. S. charts contain reliable depth readings, and a depth sounder can be effectively used to gauge one's distance offshore when approaching the coast. Many skippers go south without a sounder, but I suggest that they are failing to utilize one of the most inexpensive and effective safety devices that can be installed on a boat.

WEATHER

PREVAILING WEATHER -- The prevailing, non-storm-condition winds off the coast of Baja California are from the NW with accompanying NW swells. These winds will vary in intensity from day to day. Velocities will

BAJA BOATER'S GUIDE

VOLUME II -- THE SEA OF CORTEZ

BY JACK WILLIAMS

> **Volume II presents the same exhaustive treatment of Baja's Sea of Cortez shore as Volume I does for the Pacific coast.**

Volume II of the BAJA BOATER'S GUIDE provides the same type of detailed sailing directions, aerial photos, and charting as are found in Volume I. In addition, the location of boat launching ramps and other special materials needed by trailer boat and kayak enthusiasts are also included. Introductory chapters are directed at the Sea of Cortez area, with little repetition of contents found in Volume I.

Get your copy from the BAJA BOOKSHELF in the Appendix

frequently increase in strength to 10 to 20 knots in the afternoons. The wind is usually stronger the farther one proceeds offshore.

NW swells seem ever present. Their height often reflects the intensity of the wind thousands of miles to the NW rather than that of what is being experienced locally. It is these NW swells and winds that are the major factor in the selection of anchoring locations along Baja's Pacific coast.

The *U. S. Sailing Directions* reports as follows concerning currents: "The currents near the coast set in the same direction as the prevailing winds and vary in strength from 1/2 to 1 knot. Near the land the influence of the tides is also felt; and east set should be guarded against at all times. Between Punta Abreojos and Bahia Magdalena vessels frequently experience, at distances of 15 to 25 miles from the coast, a NW current with a velocity of 3/4 to 1 knot during the winter season. A strong inshore set has also been reported along this stretch of coast. "

STORM SYSTEMS -- Two circumstances dominate the climate of Baja California. As is obvious to any visitor, the peninsula is an arid land. Of equal but less apparent importance is the variability of the climate from one area to the other, from season to season, and from year to year. Most of the time the peninsula receives no storm-related rainfall because it lies outside the normal influence of any of the major weather systems in this part of the world. By a twist of geographic fate, it does

lie near the edge of several such systems. It is the occasional impact from these entities that creates climatic variability in Baja.

Two of these systems cause most of the storm conditions encountered along Baja's Pacific coast. These are: (1) weather fronts that originate in the NE Pacific (Gulf of Alaska area) and whose impact on the North American continent is controlled in large part by the presence of the Pacific High; and (2) tropical storms and hurricanes that form off the west coast of Mexico. Each of these is discussed below.

NE-PACIFIC WEATHER SYSTEMS -- Lying off the Pacific coast of North America is a persistent cell of high air pressure called the Pacific High. During the summer months this cell shunts weather fronts from the NE Pacific to the north. As a result little rain falls on either Alta or Baja California. The high migrates southward in the winter usually allowing frontal systems to deliver plentiful rainfall along the U. S. coast.

Baja lies south of, or at the southern edge, of these storms. Less and less rainfall occurs as one travels south. True desert vegetation starts near El Rosario only 200 miles south of the U. S./Mexican border. While these NE Pacific storms bring little rainfall to Baja's Pacific coast, their southern fringes do pass over the peninsula causing winds typically associated with such frontal passages; i.e., strong SW winds before, and NW winds following the passage. In summary, storm conditions experienced off the Baja coast in the winter are

AVG. NO. OF TROPICAL STORMS & HURRICANES PER TIME PERIOD BY 5 DEGREE SQUARE

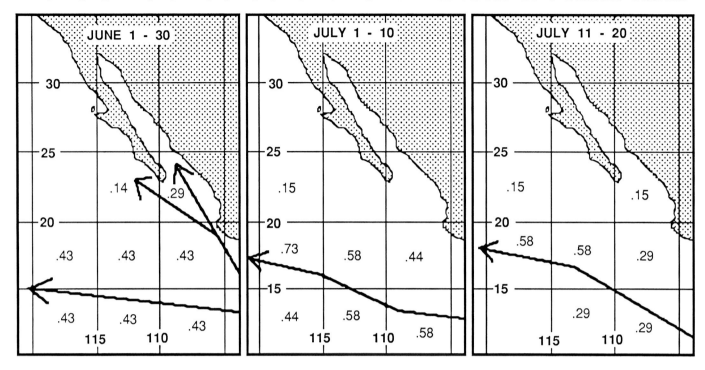

basically the moderate southerly extremities of the same systems that impact Canada and the United States.

TROPICAL STORMS -- Tropical storms are generated over warm ocean waters in six parts of the world. One of these is off the west coast of Mexico from about Puerto Vallarta south to the Guatemalan border. It is referred to as the Eastern North Pacific Area. While Baja is situated at the southern extremity of the NE-Pacific storm systems, it is at the northern fringe of this tropical storm area. The main storm season is from June to October, but with significant occurrences in May and November.

AVG. NO. OF TROPICAL STORMS & HURRICANES PER TIME PERIOD BY 5 DEGREE SQUARE

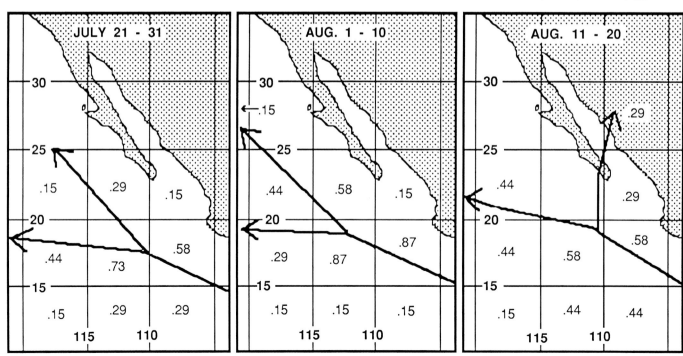

AVG. NO. OF TROPICAL STORMS & HURRICANES PER TIME PERIOD BY 5 DEGREE SQUARE

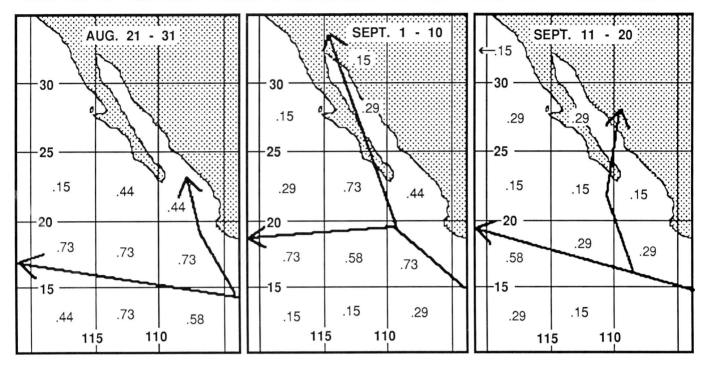

Meteorologists have established three intensities of the cyclonic disturbances under discussion. These are:

Tropical Depression -- Wind speed below 34 knots.

Tropical Storm -- Wind speeds from 34 to 63 knots.

Hurricane -- Wind speeds 64 knots or greater.

A table accompanying this discussion indicates the average number of tropical storms and hurricanes by month which have been generated in the Eastern North Pacific Area. Also presented are charts showing the average number of tropical storms and hurricanes observed for twelve time periods in the vicinity of the Baja peninsula. They reflect observations made from 1949 to 1970. These data are taken from *Mariner's*

AVG. NO. OF TROPICAL STORMS & HURRICANES PER TIME PERIOD BY 5 DEGREE SQUARE

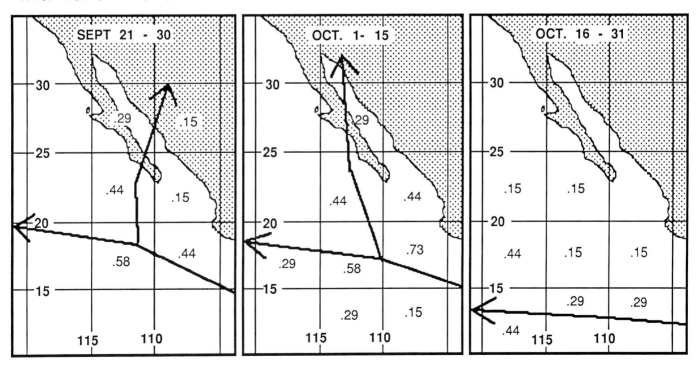

MONTHLY & ANNUAL AVERAGE NUMBER OF STORMS PER YEAR

	Jan	Feb	Mar	Apr	May	Jun	Jul	Aug	Sep	Oct	Nov	Dec	Annual
Tropical Storms (34 - 63 knots)	–	–	–	–	–	1.5	2.8	2.3	2.3	1.2	0.3	–	9.3
Hurricanes (Over 64 knots)	–	–	–	–	0.3	0.6	0.9	2.0	1.8	1.0	–	–	5.8
Tropical Storms & Hurricanes	–	–	–	–	0.3	2.0	3.6	4.5	4.1	2.2	0.3	–	15.2

Worldwide Climatic Guide to Tropical Storms at Sea, published in March of 1974 by the Naval Weather Service Command. Unfortunately, it is out-of-print at this writing.

Reference the chart for June 1 - 30. On the average, one could expect to encounter 0.29 storms with wind velocities in excess of 34 knots in the 5 degree square lying SE of the tip of the Baja peninsula during June. In other words, there is about a three percent chance of experiencing such a storm during June of any one year.

The arrows shown on each chart represent the most common storm tract for the period in question. The tropical storms formed off the Mexican mainland initially move westward and then poleward from their area of generation. Some of the storms then "recurve" eastward. It is this tendency to recurve which brings tropical storms to Baja California. Recurvature is readily apparent from August 11 until October 15.

Why all this concern with tropical storms? Perhaps it might save someone's life. In addition it is a key element in deciding when to visit the Baja coast.

WHEN TO GO ?

The answer to this question is a matter of your making informed judgments concerning the two types of storm systems discussed above. If you plan to spend a few days in the Ensenada area, simply make your plans in keeping with the latest NOAA weather forecast. Most boaters acquiring this book, however, will be doing so in contemplation of traversing the entire peninsular coast en route from San Diego to Cabo San Lucas, or beyond into the Sea of Cortez, or the west coast of the Mexican mainland. And the great majority of these people will be heading south from ports between southern British Columbia and San Diego, California.

The answer is simply: (1) leave home port prior to the onset of the winter storms coming from the NE Pacific, but (2) don't venture far into Baja waters until after hurricane season. And when is that? The Eastern North Pacific hurricane season is usually regarded as the period from June through November 15th. I don't venture south from Ensenada until the latter date, and then I take at least two weeks arriving in Cabo San

Lucas. When I arrive, it is obvious that many other skippers don't agree with my judgments because the harbor is packed with vessels. The same is true at La Paz in the Sea of Cortez. (The relationship of tropical storms and boating in the Sea of Cortez is presented in Volume II of this book.)

Many cruisers based north of southern California arrive in San Diego during October. They layover here until the now-famous, parking lot wine-drinking party sponsored by Pacific Marine Supply (usually the last friday in October). They then head south in droves.

I am not going to tell you when to go, and when not to go. I have presented my own views, and will stick with them. On one of my trips, a hurricane went ashore at Mazatlan (directly east of Cabo San Lucas) while I was halfway down the Baja coast in late November. In December 1981 a late, tropical storm visited Cabo San Lucas and deposited numerous yachts on the beach. I'm sure that most experienced Baja sailors will tell you that they have had no encounters with tropical storms. Just keep in mind that those who have had such experiences are probably not around to voice their opinions.

NAVIGATION & COMMUNICATIONS

CHARTS AND MAPS -- A discussion of the charts included in this book, and their method of preparation has been presented in Chapter 1. These charts have two positive attributes. First, they provide very good representations of the shape and size of bays, harbors, and similar coastal features. Second, their relatively large scale has permitted showing far more detail than is present on the government nautical charts. This book's charts should not be used for navigation purposes. This is primarily because they lack the underwater details that are shown on the nautical charts.

The U. S. GOVERNMENT NAUTICAL CHARTS illustration in this chapter shows the areas covered by charts currently available from the U. S. government. Prudent mariners will avail themselves of all the Golfo de California series indicated thereon. Chart 21004 from

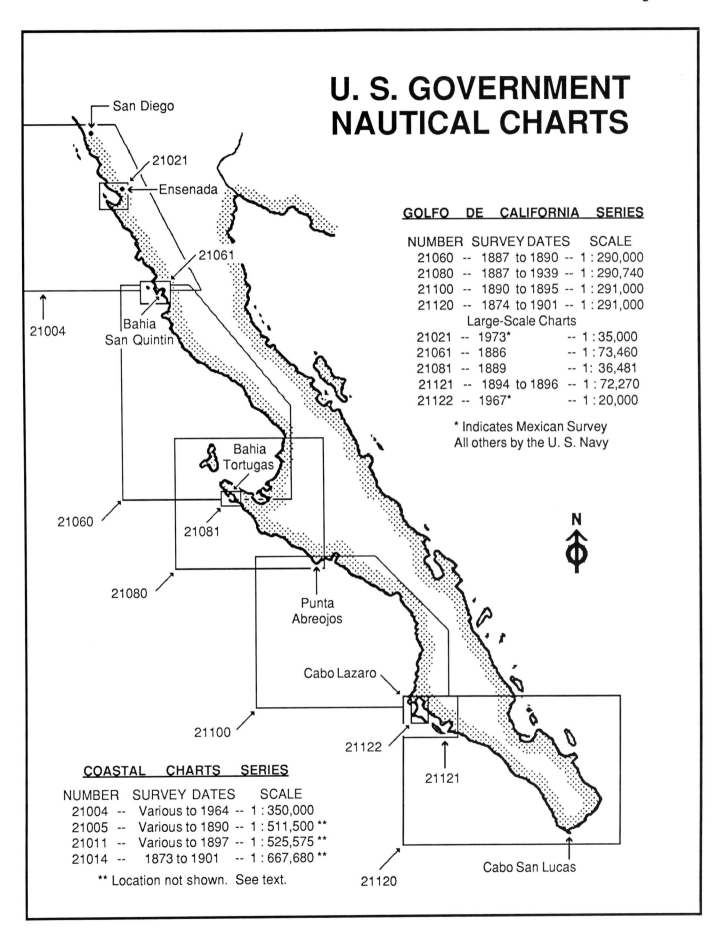

U. S. GOVERNMENT NAUTICAL CHARTS

San Diego

21021

Ensenada

21061

21004

Bahia
San Quintin

Bahia
Tortugas

21060

21081

21080

Punta
Abreojos

21100

Cabo Lazaro

21122

21121

21120

Cabo San Lucas

N

GOLFO DE CALIFORNIA SERIES

NUMBER	SURVEY DATES	SCALE
21060	1887 to 1890	1 : 290,000
21080	1887 to 1939	1 : 290,740
21100	1890 to 1895	1 : 291,000
21120	1874 to 1901	1 : 291,000
Large-Scale Charts		
21021	1973*	1 : 35,000
21061	1886	1 : 73,460
21081	1889	1 : 36,481
21121	1894 to 1896	1 : 72,270
21122	1967*	1 : 20,000

* Indicates Mexican Survey
All others by the U. S. Navy

COASTAL CHARTS SERIES

NUMBER	SURVEY DATES	SCALE
21004	Various to 1964	1 : 350,000
21005	Various to 1890	1 : 511,500 **
21011	Various to 1897	1 : 525,575 **
21014	1873 to 1901	1 : 667,680 **

** Location not shown. See text.

the Coastal Series is also needed. The remaining three Coastal Series charts are smaller scale duplications of the Golfo de California Series. Obtaining them is not fully necessary, particularly if cost is a factor. Their location is omitted on the illustration in this book to avoid unduly complicating the presentation.

What is shown are the dates of the surveys from which each chart was produced. Perusal of this information will show that most of their data was obtained by the U. S. Navy in the 1880s and 90s. Even though they have been updated in recent years, the cultural data (aids to navigation, towns, and other onshore features) is woefully out-of-date. Anyone making the passage along the Baja coast without them is, however, making a grave mistake.

Reproductions of the U. S. government charts are also available in a 14" by 20" publication entitled *Chart Guide - Mexico West*. It includes charts from San Diego to Guatemala including the Sea of Cortez. It provides a reasonably cost-effective way of obtaining the govern-

ment charting. Its principal advantage, however, is its inclusion of several of the large-scale, out-of-print charts for such places as Isla San Martin, Islas San Benitos, and Isla Cedros. The publication is available in most marine stores.

As noted in Chapter 1, the coastal outlines shown in the charts in this book were derived from Mexican government 1 : 50,000 scale topographic maps. These maps were made using stereoscopic, aerial photographic techniques. They are thus highly accurate. This accuracy, however, relates to the coastal outline and inland topographic and cultural features. Occasionally they show offshore islets, or islands, but there is no other maritime information. Nevertheless, these maps are extremely useful in determining one's position in relation to the land, although their usefulness is somewhat limited if the user is totally unfamiliar with the contour lines used on such maps.

It takes 134 of these maps to obtain complete coverage of both coasts of the Baja peninsula. Each map costs about $7.00 in the United States. (I obtained mine for $0.90 each in Mexico City.) The cost of obtaining a complete set is thus rather high. Some boaters, however, may be interested primarily in some relatively limited locale where one, or a small number of maps will provide the needed coverage.

There is one further alternative. The Mexican government also publishes 1 : 250,000 scale topographic maps. Each one covers the same area shown in 24 of the 1 : 50,000 maps. While this smaller scale produces less detail, these maps still show coastal conformations which are a considerable improvement over the U. S. nautical charts. It takes nine of these maps to cover Baja's Pacific coast. Seven more are needed for the Sea of Cortez.

If you can't make it to Mexico City, the above maps (both scales) are available from (1) Pacific Traveller's Supply, 529 State Street, Santa Barbara, CA 93101, or (2) The Map Center, 2611 University Avenue, San Diego, CA 92104. Both of these stores will mail you an index map upon request.

SAILING DIRECTIONS -- At one time the U. S. government's *Sailing Directions for the West Coasts of Mexico and Central America* contained 113 pages concerning Baja California. This material has now been revised and condensed into 36 pages. I carry the current *Sailing Directions* with me, but never use it. The original 113-page material was of considerable more value, and I quote from its 1937 edition on many occasions in this book.

NAVIGATION LIGHTS -- Only a few years ago there were very few navigation lights along the Baja coast, and these were of questionable reliability. Previous guide-

LATTICEWORK NAVIGATION LIGHT TOWER
This one has an apron-like device designed
to discourage climbing the tower.

book writers have traditionally called attention to this shortcoming, and my first voyage to Baja in 1976 found them to be correct.

My circumnavigation of the Baja peninsula in 1983-84 found this situation markedly changed in two respects. (1) Large numbers of additional navigation lights had been constructed along both Baja coasts. (2) Both the old and new lights are now powered by solar panels. The navigation lights along Baja's Pacific coast are of three types. These are:

1 -- Older, individually-styled lighthouse structures constructed many years ago. Some of these are four-sided, truncated-pyramidal structures approximately 25 feet in height. Others are various types of towers built atop sizeable caretaker residences. Some of these buildings contain six to eight rooms, showers, and flush toilets. (No water of course.) Some of these can be rightfully judged as lighthouses. They occupy high ground and the light can be seen a considerable distance. Examples are Cabo San Lazaro 21 miles, Cabo Falso 33 miles, and Punta Tosca 23 miles.

2 -- Aluminum latticework light towers (See Photo). The majority of the new lights are of this variety. Some of these structures mark a promontory of land and thus serve in the same manner as the above-noted lighthouses, except that they are usually located near sea level and their lights have a relatively short range. Some of them, however, are clearly designed to mark the location of a cove or landing used by local fishermen. These lights have thus often been constructed near the bight of a cove rather than on the promontory forming its headland and may be visible from only one direction (usually the south).

3 -- Concrete towers usually painted with broad, horizontal, red stripes (See Photo). These constitute the remainder of the newer lights noted above. The remarks made for the aluminum latticework lights also apply to this concrete variety.

The latest editions of the U. S. charts have included some but not all of these new lights. Sadly, in many cases, the locations are in error, sometimes by as much as three miles. The Sailing Directions in this book point out these errors. I have notified the Defense Mapping Agency of the problem and hope it can be rectified. In the meantime, if the Marines have to make a night landing along the Baja coast, they are in for some surprises.

I have found the navigation lights along the Pacific coast to be very reliable. On one occasion, I came on watch at 0200 so that I could see the 33 mile light at Cabo Falso at its outer range of visibility. The flashing light never materialized, but from my awakening until dawn I was confronted with an unusually bright, steady light

CONCRETE NAVIGATION LIGHT TOWER

coming from the desired direction. I went through a long series of speculations as to what ship, building, etc., was its source. In the end it proved to be Cabo Falso. Obviously, the lighthouse rotational device was inoperative, but the Mexicans did the best they could to provide a beacon.

RADIOS -- Most yachts traveling to Baja are equipped with VHF radios. This allows vessels to pick up the United States National Weather Service broadcasts as far south as about Isla San Martin. These reports come in clearly for short periods much farther south. They can be detected by keeping the weather channels programmed into the scanning features present in most modern VHF radios.

There is also a considerable exchange of chatter between yachts. Ten years ago there were few boats and most people simply used channel 16. Now there is considerable traffic, and proper radio etiquette is usually best, although this rule is followed in the breach by Mexican fishing boat skippers.

One can now rest quietly at anchor and listen to the powerboat skippers plowing down the coast and comparing notes with each other as to why their new $5,000 satellite navigation device seems to be telling them they are 20 miles from where they thought they were, and by the way, what time is it? If I had one of those, I would be lost constantly.

Some ocean-cruising vessels are equiped with HAM radios capable of communicating with stations in the United States and other countries. U. S. amateurs operate a "Baja Net" which transmits weather information on a regular basis.

THE MEXICAN NAVY -- Baja California is divided into two naval districts which correspond to the peninsula's two states. (Baja California north of the 28th parallel of latitude, and Baja California Sur to the south.) The northern district headquarters is in Ensenada. There is also a smaller base in Santa Rosalia on the Sea of Cortez. The southern district headquarters is in La Paz on the Sea of Cortez. This district also has a substantial base at Puerto Cortez in Bahia Magdalena.

The bases at Ensenada, Puerto Cortez, and La Paz operate sizeable 220-foot vessels which previously served as United States mine sweepers. There are also several more modern vintage patrol boats. These vessels will frequently be seen patrolling coastal waters. On occasion they will seek out visiting yachts and an officer will come aboard for an inspection of papers.

I am advised by the commandant at Puerto Cortez that the boarding officer is basically interested in seeking out firearms and drugs and not in searching for your wine cache. I have been boarded on two occasions by Mexican authorities and have been treated with the utmost courtesy. My record with the U. S. Coast Guard is four boardings, where all you rate is a 3rd class petty officer. His drug search goes under cover of a safety inspection. I once got a citation for an improper life ring, which after further investigation, proved to be acceptable for my class of vessel. The Mexican inspection is less painfull.

Mexican Navy 220' patrol vessel docked at the Puerto Cortez Naval Base in Bahia Magdalena.

BEFORE YOU GO

INSURANCE -- If one takes a motor vehicle, house trailer, or trailer boat to Mexico, they must be covered by an insurance policy issued by a Mexican insurance company. Such policies may easily be obtained through U. S. and Canadian agencies. These companies maintain offices in major cities and on the U. S. side, at all the ports-of-entry. Less expensive policies are usually available from automobile associations and travel clubs (See notice for the *Vagabundos del Mar* at the end of this book).

In contrast to the above, insurance coverage for a sea-going yacht is obtained through one's regular, north-of-the border, insurance agent. Unfortunately, the regular policies issued by these companies normally stipulate a specific area to which their coverage applies. Mexican waters are usually not included, although many policies issued in California permit travel south to Ensenada. Thus, a rider to the basic policy is usually required to travel to Mexico.

Mexican law requires that a yacht visiting their country must have basic liability coverage. If this is all you wish, some American and Canadian insurance companies will provide this coverage at minimal cost. If you want hull insurance, however, there may be considerable extra cost and complications.

I have had insurance coverage where I was granted the needed Mexican rider at no extra cost, provided only that travel was during the winter season. Most boat owners, however, will be required to have their vessel inspected by a marine surveyor, who in some cases will require that the boat be deposited on dry land for the occasion. The result may be a lengthy list of recommendations for new safety equipment, etc. that the insurance company will ask be complied with as a condition of policy issuance. All of the above can be quite expensive and time consumptive. The cost of the rider itself may also come high.

In summary, look into the insurance situation well in advance, and stand ready with your checkbook. As is often said, "if you have to ask the price of a yacht, you shouldn't own one." Most of us don't qualify but struggle along somehow, perhaps without insurance.

ENTRANCE PAPERS -- Whenever one enters Mexico, each person must have a Mexican tourist card (except in the border areas). These may be obtained at travel agencies, and Mexican tourist and cousul offices north of the border. Please consult my book, *The Magnificent Peninsula* , concerning details about tourist cards and other non-boat-related details.

ENTRANCE BY HIGHWAY -- If you are taking a boat into Baja by highway you need no special permit for the boat itself. You do, however, need fishing licenses for the boat and everyone using it. These fishing permits are widely referred to as boat permits, so in practice, you do need permits for such craft. See the Fishing Licenses Section below for details. Once you have your licenses, there is no further paperwork required for the boat or its users while visiting Baja. There are extra complications if you travel to the Mexican mainland.

ENTRANCE (ENTRADA) FOR THE YACHT -- To enter a yacht into Mexico by sea, one needs the above-noted tourist cards and fishing licenses plus special papers for the vessel and its crew. In addition, boat, crew, and papers must also be checked in, and out, at every port-of-call that has Mexican immigration and Port Captain officials.

The Spanish word for yacht is yate. And those who travel to Mexico in such vessels have come to be known as yates. The process of obtaining Mexican papers for one's yate begins at the office of the Mexican Consul General in San Diego. It is here that one may begin to hone one's skills in identifying genuine, gringo yates.

The species is usually adorned in blue jeans, cutoffs or shorts, together with a sweat or T-shirt containing some form of advertising. (My wife spent five hours trying to find sweat shirts for me that didn't say something.) A backpack, duffel bag, or clipboard is carried as an accessory. The yates usually arrive as mated pairs. The male frequently sports a beard, or is in the beginning stages of acquiring such an affliction. The female has accompanied him on the premise that if something dire is going to happen, "let's go together."

The yates stand in marked contrast to the Mexicans calling at the same office. The latter are usually as well dressed as their financial means permit, as their purpose is to obtain papers to stay in the United States, rather than to get out, as with the yates. The Mexican is also well composed, whereas the yates display a considerable degree of apprehension, knowing that if they are going to be maltreated, this is where it will all start.

I can fortunately report that I have never been treated with anything but courtesy at any Mexican office involved in the paperwork required for taking a yacht into Mexico, nor have I heard of anyone who has. Yet the process can be a bit of a pain in the aftward portion of the anatomy. Here are the details:

1 -- Obtain a supply of two forms devised by the Mexican government. Tablets of these may be purchased at many marine hardware and bookstores north of the border, or, you are welcome to photocopy those that are presented in the Appendix of this book. Instructions for filling in the blanks are also included. Complete four copies of each form. It saves time to do this in advance of your visit to the consulate.

2 -- Present the first form (Rol de Tripulantes) at the office of the Consul General. On my last visit this was at 1333 Front Street in downtown San Diego, but it has been at a different location on each of my visits; so check the phone book before your visit. Take along your vessel's registration papers or document. Completing the approval process can be a bit frustrating as the result of waiting your turn, and being shuffled from one person to the other, but bureaucracy must be served. You will leave with the forms appropriately

Mexican Navy party poses for a photo after checking our papers at the Puerto Cortez Naval Base.

stamped and signed, and your wallet relieved of a modest fee based on the size of your yate.

3 -- Check in at your first Mexican port-of-call that has a Port Captain and immigration officials. For practical purposes this is either Ensenada or Cabo San Lucas. In addition these officials are present along the Pacific coast at Isla Cedros, and San Carlos in Bahia Magdalena. The check-in process involves two steps:

(A) Report with all hands listed on the Rol de Tripulantes form to the Office of Immigration. If you leave some of the crew behind, it will not do. Tourist cards and the two forms will be stamped and signed, and you will be sent on your way to see the Port Captain. You can release the crew as the Port Captain is only concerned with the yate and its skipper.

(B) Report to the Port Captain. The forms will again be stamped and signed. Usually you will have to take one completed copy back to Immigration.

DEPARTURE (SALIDA) FOR THE YACHT -- If you are wise, you will tell the officials at any given port that you are leaving the day after you enter, and entering and leaving can be taken care of at one stop. Otherwise you need to check out with Immigration and the Port Captain when departing. (In both processes, always go to Immigration first, and the Port Captain second.) In leaving, you usually have to make out the second form over again, so have a supply on hand.

In summary, the process is never completely the same from one year to the next, or from one port to the other, so stand ready for some minor frustrations.

FISHING LICENSES -- Fishing licenses are needed for every boat taken into Mexico, whether by highway or by sea. Everyone (over 16) aboard a vessel used for fishing must also have a license whether they fish or not. Licenses may be obtained at the Mexico Department of Fisheries, 1010 Second Ave., San Diego, CA. 92101. There are also offices in Ensenada and La Paz.

A flat fee is charged for each boat based on its length. This includes not only one's yate, but its tender. Fees for individuals are by the week, month, or year. I have found that the amount of the fee varies widely from time to time depending on the U. S. -- Mexican exchange rate. On my last five-month trip for a 46-foot sailboat and three crew members, the fee was $61.00.

Full fishing regulations may be obtained from the above-noted address. However, here are two items that should be of concern to ocean cruisers:

(1) -- Underwater fishing may be practiced with scuba and a pole or speargun equipped with a rubber band.

(2) -- Fish can be captured by means of a fishing rod, reel, and hook, (no nets) except for totoaba and grouper, which are cooperative-reserved species as are lobster, abalone, and shrimp.

For the record, lobster are readily available from most panga fishermen along the Pacific coast when they are in season. In most places, the price is easily negotiated without sharp bargaining. Usually, these people wish to barter for beer, cigarettes, canned goods, and similar items. A bucketload of lobsters for a six-pack of beer has been my most common experience. I draw the line at trading for hard liquor or ammunition. Too many negatives can result.

Usually the fishermen will seek you out. They have a rather effective advertising approach. A lobster is grasped by one of its antennae and held high in the air for all to see as the panga draws near. There is little doubt what is proposed, and it cuts nicely through the language barrier.

OTHER ACTIVITIES -- Following is a very brief summary of recreational activities related to boating that may be enjoyed in Baja California. Sources for obtaining additional information are noted in each instance.

DIVING -- Baja's Pacific coast offers numerous excellent diving sites. A major attractions is diving in the numerous kelp beds that range southward to Punta San Hipolito. Divers should keep in mind that waters along the Pacific shore are cold and wetsuits are normally required.

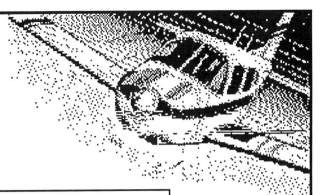
DIVE

The preeminent authorities on diving in Mexico are Michael and Lauren Farley. Their books, *Baja California Diver's Guide* and *Diver's Guide to Underwater Mexico* , are the definitive works on the subject. (See the BAJA BOOKSHELF and notice on page 24.) The dive sites shown on the charts in the *Baja Boater's Guide* are those for which detailed information is given in these books. Look for the **DIVE** symbol shown at the top of this paragraph.

KAYAKING -- The sport of sea kayaking has gained rapidly in popularity in recent years. I recall seeing no kayaks in Baja waters during my initial trips to the peninsula in the mid-1970s. By the late-1980s, there were clearly far more kayaks present in the Sea of Cortez than there were ocean cruisers. The most popular kayaking area along the Pacific shore is in Bahia Magdalena and the lagoon system to the north. Puerto Lopez Mateos is a popular launching site.

These small seaworthy vessels may be rented north of the border and easily transported over the Trans-peninsular Highway to scores of launching sites along both coasts. In addition, there are several outfitting organizations that market guided kayak tours complete with food, cook, and all equipment. Ocean kayaking enthusiasts can take advantage of small idyllic coves

and beaches that are too small for use by ocean cruisers. They can also become intimate spectators to the antics of the California gray whale during calving season in the Magdalena lagoon system. (See kayaking notice on page 26.)

PRIVATE FLYING IN BAJA -- Baja has long been a mecca for the owners of small private aircraft. In addition to several modern international airports, there are dozens of small, natural surface airstrips. Some of these are regularly maintained, others are not. The private flyers interface with Baja is through *The Baja Bush Pilots*, 1291 E. Vista Way, Suite 210W, Vista, CA 92084 - (619) 439-6865. In addition to other services, this organization publishes *Airports of Baja California & NW Mexico* (See the BAJA BOOK SHELF and notice on this page). This volume shows that there are some 28 airstrips along Baja's Pacific shore. Many of these can serve as supply points for boaters who have access to private aircraft.

THE BAJA BOOKSHELF -- A prolific number of books have been published about the Baja peninsula. Several of these that are currently in print are available by mail from the BAJA BOOKSHELF in the Appendix. Each of these represents my choice of the best title available on a particular subject.

CHAPTER 3
ANCHORING AND ANCHORAGES

In my view, proficiency in anchoring is the single most important skill needed by boaters along the coast of Baja California. This may not be true for the powerboat skipper making the nonstop run from San Diego to Cabo San Lucas, nor for racing enthusiasts who make similar lengthy ocean passages. The majority of boaters, however, will spend far more time at anchor than they will moving through the water.

Most of us enjoy taking our vessels to sea, but we do so to visit the land along the way. In Baja, most visits ashore will be made while the boat is at anchor. The boat may have to be left unattended while the crew is ashore. Much of our sleeping and eating will also be done while anchored. Thus, an anchored vessel is far more subject to being cast ashore or aground than while it is traveling at sea. Finally, an uncomfortable night spent poorly anchored will leave all hands exhausted after what was planned as a night of rest. For these reasons I direct your attention to the material in this chapter. I believe it is the most important in this book.

GROUND TACKLE

Entire books are available on the subject of anchors and anchoring techniques. Only a few brief comments are presented in this section on ground tackle.

ANCHORS -- A brief survey of marinas north of the border will show that most vessels are equipped with Danforth or CQR (plow) type anchors. A few have the newer Bruce model. These are the same anchors that are aboard most vessels taken south to Baja. There are a few other types. The great majority of anchorages on both sides of the peninsula have sand bottoms, so any anchor that will hold well in these conditions will prove satisfactory.

I recommend that vessels be fitted with a stern as well as a bow anchor. (I should note, however, that the majority of yachts traveling to Baja are not so equipped.) The stern anchor is often needed when anchoring in areas affected by refracted swells. This subject will be discussed in more detail under "Wave Refraction" later in this chapter.

It is interesting to note that scores of Mexican commercial fishing vessels are usually equipped with anchors fashioned by a welder from reinforcing rod so as to form a four-pronged grappling hook. They seem to get along quite well and the cost is minimal.

CHAIN VERSUS ROPE -- Owners of trailer boats and small ocean-cruising vessels may feel they are restricted to using rope for their anchor cables because of the excessive weight of chain. For the smallest boats this may be a necessity. I strongly recommend, however, that chain of the appropriate diameter be used wherever possible. For all but the lightest chain, this also mandates that the boat be equipped with a windlass.

Alain Gree's authoritative book on *Anchoring and Mooring* states, "There can be no doubt, whatever the size of the boat, the main cable should be wholly chain." The three reasons given are: (1) the heavy weight of the metal ensures that the anchor achieves its best penetration because the pull always comes horizontally; (2) resistance to abrasion; (3) the elasticity provided by the great length of chain prevents snubbing.

To these three, let me add the following additional justifications. In crowded or constricted anchorages it is important that all vessels react similarly to the effects of wind and currents. The great majority of ocean-cruising vessels used in Baja waters are equipped with chain. Such boats swing in relatively small circles in comparison to those utilizing rope. This is due to the characteristics of rope compared with chain, and the fact that providing the needed holding characteristics requires a much longer length of rope than is needed with chain. In addition, boats using rope tend to wander aimlessly about in calm waters while their neighbors are held almost stationary by their heavy chain. In summary, the line-anchored boat will be looked on with disfavor as a hazardous, floating battering-ram, and it will use up a disproportionate share of space in restricted locations.

Winds in the 20-25-knot range are common in the winter months on both Baja coasts. If you have ever watched a barehanded crew struggling under such conditions to retrieve their anchor without some type of mechanical assistance, you will need no further explanation concerning the advantages of a windlass.

ANCHORING CONDITIONS

BAJA'S TWO COASTS -- Sea and weather conditions prevailing along Baja's Pacific coast differ considerably from those encountered in the Sea of Cortez. Here is a brief comparison.

WINDS -- (1) In the Pacific, the prevailing wind is from the NW year-round. Storm-induced winds are normally from the SW. (2) The prevailing winter wind in the Sea of Cortez is from the north. In the southern portions it switches to the south during the summer. Storm-induced winds are normally from the south.

SWELLS -- (1) The Pacific coast is beset by swells coming from the NW except during SW-storm conditions. (2) The Sea of Cortez has no swells except those that refract from the Pacific into the southern portion as far north as about Cabo Los Frailes.

NW-winds and NW-swells are the principal weather-related factors that determine the quality of an anchorage along the Pacific coast, year-round, during prevailing weather conditions. SW-storm conditions are discussed later in this chapter. The situation in the Sea of Cortez is described in Volume II.

WHAT MAKES A GOOD ANCHORAGE -- Skippers seeking safe anchorage for their vessels along the Pacific coast of the Baja peninsula will be concerned with three basic criteria. Listed in priority order these are: (1) holding ground, (2) swell protection, and (3) wind and wind-wave protection. The following is a discussion of these subjects.

HOLDING GROUND -- This is the one indispensable item. There is simply no anchorage if one's ground tackle will not hold on a bottom that is within a few fathoms of the surface of the sea. Along Baja's Pacific coast there are hundreds of miles of shoreline with good holding ground. Much of this is located offshore from the extensive beaches found in the Middle Bight and Sections A and B of the Southern Bight.

In these places the offshore gradient is shallow and sandy . Good holding ground is usually present in 5 to 10 fathoms and outside the breaker line. These open roadstead anchorages, however, are all on lee shores swept by the prevailing NW swells. They are thus uncomfortable and dangerous for nearly all yachts and small vessels. Such vessels should use these areas only in emergencies. The early explorers were often forced to anchor in such exposed locations and even today, one will occasionally find heavy-displacement commercial fishing vessels resting in such places in calm weather.

Good holding ground is also readily found in 3 to 10 fathoms of water in all of the bights, coves, and bays discussed in this book. I cannot think of a single case where this is not so. The bottom is usually sand with finer silt in a few places. It is unusual to encounter rocky bottom conditions in these areas.

SWELL PROTECTION -- Since good holding ground is almost universally present, other factors are the key to judging anchorage quality. The most important of these is ocean swell.

Swells are wind-generated waves that have traveled away from the area in which they were generated. Swells along the Baja coast increase and decrease in height depending on the intensity of the wind in the area of origin, but they are never totally absent. During prevailing NW weather conditions, anchorages providing swell protection must be sought in enclosed coves or harbors, or on the SE sides of islands or headlands.

WIND AND WIND-WAVE PROTECTION -- When the wind picks up to over about 10 knots it generates local wind-waves which manifest themselves as white caps.

The prevailing NW wind on Baja's Pacific coast causes wind-waves coming from the same direction as the swells. Thus, anchorages that provide prevailing weather swell protection also provide wind-wave protection. In many cases, however, these anchorages give only modest relief from the wind itself. This condition prevails even at places considered to be good anchorages such as San Quintin, Punta Baja, Asuncion, and Abreojos. At these locations the headlands rise only a few feet above sea level, and the wind passes over them with little decrease in velocity.

There are a few anchorages that provide significant protection from the prevailing wind. Examples are Cabo San Agustin on Isla Cedros and Punta Rompientes. Here, high mountains form a barrier to the wind, and velocities are substantially reduced. Keep in mind that there are few such places along Baja's Pacific coast.

Two final points should be mentioned. At some anchorages, the offshore gradient is so shallow that vessels must anchor a considerable distance from the protecting headland. The prevailing wind thus has the opportunity to generate wind waves between the headland and the anchored boat. These are not as severe as those present outside the anchorage, but they can prove uncomfortable for small vessels. Also, these anchorages may be swept by local onshore or offshore winds, the directions of which will be different from the prevailing wind. This condition needs to be kept in mind in determining how close one anchors to the shore or to other boats.

SUMMARY -- The purpose of this discussion is to advise you that (1) the principal attribute needed from a good anchorage along the Pacific coast is protection from swells and wind-waves, (2) good holding ground is almost universally present in places that meet this objective, and (3) obtaining protection from the wind itself will be an unavailable luxury in most places.

SWELL REFRACTION -- So there you are at your anchorage, neatly tucked up in a bight under the SE side of a headland that will obviously block the path of the prevailing NW swells. Only it doesn't. The damn things bend around and follow you right into your hoped-for paradise. The Pacific Ocean has introduced you to the all-important subject of swell refraction.

Swell refraction is defined as "the change in direction which occurs when one portion of a swell reaches shallow water and is slowed down while the other portion is in deep water and moving relatively fast." The result is that swells arriving at the Baja coast from the NW bend around headlands as shown in the chart labled ANCHORING IN REFRACTED SWELLS.

Swells also refract around islands, even such large ones as Isla Cedros (See chart in Chapter 9). In anchoring off Cedros village, one's vessel will be impacted by swells which have bent around the island's northern tip and have traveled down the eastern shore in a generally north-south direction. At Morro Redondo, at the island's SE end, refracted swells coming around both shores will be encountered.

So what's a poor skipper to do about these refracted swells? As usual, there is good news and bad news. The good news is that swells lose much of their energy in the bending process. In the better protected anchorages, swell height is substantially reduced from that present in the open sea. Thus, these locations do in fact provide significant protection from Pacific swells.

The bad news is indicated in the ANCHORING IN REFRACTED SWELLS Chart. As shown, the swells change direction and sweep the bight heading more or less NE. A bow anchored vessel, subjected to the prevailing NW-wind, will lie parallel to the trough of the swells. Such a vessel will be rocked back and forth making life very uncomfortable for all hands. This then brings us to the subject of bow-stern anchoring.

BOW-STERN ANCHORING -- In anchoring in the bights along Baja's Pacific shore, the skipper must decide whether to swing from a bow anchor only, or to utilize both bow and stern anchors if the vessel is so equipped. Here is how I make my decision.

If the refracted swells are slight they will cause only minor rocking under such conditions. I will use a <u>bow anchor only</u>. If the swells are sufficiently great to be of concern, I will still use only a bow anchor if there is significant prevailing NW wind (10 knots or more). My vessel tends to tack back and forth in the wind like a

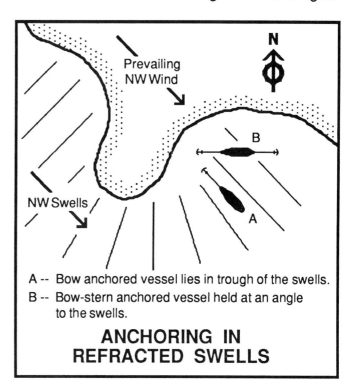

A -- Bow anchored vessel lies in trough of the swells.
B -- Bow-stern anchored vessel held at an angle to the swells.

ANCHORING IN REFRACTED SWELLS

horse discontented with its tether. This motion, and the effect of wind waves generated within the anchorage, keeps her from being captured by the rocking motion of the swells for any length of time. The resulting ride is acceptable, and I only have to deal with one anchor. In this situation, I consider the wind and its effects to be dominant over the swells.

In the absence of significant wind the swells will take over. The rocking motion will increase as the wind decreases and will be worst in dead calm. Small displacement boats will roll worse than heavier ones. This roll can be considerably dampened by anchoring the vessel at an angle to the swells using both bow and stern anchors (See chart). The negative feature of this method is that the broadside of the boat must be angled into the force of any prevailing wind which arises. This will place considerable strain on the anchoring gear and one or both anchors may drag.

I have recommended that all vessels cruising to Baja California carry both bow and stern anchors. (See discussion of ground tackle earlier in this chapter.) The need to dampen swell-induced roll is one of the reasons for this suggestion. Bow-stern anchoring is also needed when anchoring in coves that are too small to permit the boat to swing safely on only one anchor. There are relatively few of these places on the Pacific coast. They are more numerous in the Sea of Cortez. Two anchors are also a requirement if one chooses to locate where boats are so closely packed that no one vessel can be afforded the space to swing only on a single anchor. This can be the situation at Cabo San Lucas.

A vessel may also be induced to point into incoming swells by utilizing a bridle technique with the bow anchor. A stout line is attached to the anchor chain after the normal scope has been laid down. Additional chain approximating the length of the boat is then released and the line secured near the stern of the vessel. This method works well as long as there is a reasonably constant wind. If the wind stops, however, the bridle line becomes ineffective just when you need it most. If there is too much slack, it can become wrapped around the prop or rudder.

WATER DEPTH -- In reviewing my survey notes with my former associate, Leland Lewis, I was chided for not recording the water depths in many Pacific coast anchorages. I replied that this was not necessary because I always anchor in 4 fathoms. He angrily shot back, "You do not, they should have been recorded". I let the matter drop.

I do, in fact, always anchor in approximately 4 fathoms of water in all Pacific coast bights that are subject to swell action. I developed this rule during a stay in the lee of Morro Santo Domingo in Bahia Vizcaino. I originally set down in about 18 feet in calm water and went below to work. In coming on deck an hour later I discovered the boat was only a short distance outside a newly-formed swell line that was clearly feeling the bottom and about to break. The vessel was promptly moved to four fathoms.

I have seen other examples of breaking swells appearing where they had not formerly been. I assume that this situation was the result of changing tides or an increase in the intensity of the swells themselves. In any event, being caught in such a situation could be tantamount to losing one's vessel; thus my 4 fathom rule. I will cheat on it a little in the better protected bights such as those in Bahia Santa Maria. I will also accept 15 feet, and occasionally less, in enclosed harbors and bays such as Bahia Magdalena. In the Sea of Cortez, 3 fathoms rather than 4 is my standard.

I do not present 4 fathoms as being proper for every boat, or for every anchorage along the Pacific coast. My message is that skippers should establish a minimum water depth and should not anchor in shallower waters, even if the current sea is calm. Beach parties should not be attended by one's vessel.

It is a simple matter of observation to conclude that the smaller the boat, the closer the skipper anchors her to shore. This is partly justified by the fact that smaller boats have less draft than larger vessels. But draft is not significantly greater amongst most yachts, and I submit that many small-boat skippers put themselves in unnecessary jeopardy by dropping their tackle too close to shore along the Pacific coast. They leave no margin for error or storm conditions.

The *U.S. Sailing Directions* makes reference to various anchorages along the Baja coast. Anchor symbols are also shown on the U.S. nautical charts. The water depths and locations of these symbols make it clear that these anchorage locations are intended for vessels considerably larger than those normally used for recreational boating. For this reason, the anchorage information provided in this *Baja Boater's Guide* will indicate shallower water depths and locations closer to shore than those mentioned in these government publications.

DISTANCE TO SHORE -- There are a few locations where the 3-4 fathom anchorages used by skippers of most yachts and small boats will be within 100 yards of the shore. Santo Tomas and Punta Rompiente are such places. In most other Pacific coast anchorages water depths are shallow, close to shore, and 3 - 4 fathoms will be from 1/4 to 1/2 mile out. It is this considerable distance to shore that motivates some skippers to anchor in shallower water than is prudent. Because of the lengthy distance to shore it is very helpful for cruising yachts to have outboard-powered tenders.

BOTTOM CHARACTERISTICS -- Except in two cases, all of the anchorages shown on the chart in this chapter have sand bottoms. The two exceptions are the enclosed harbor at Ensenada and the shallow depth anchorage off the village at Bahia Tortugas. In these two locations fine-grained silt or mud prevails. I have rarely encountered the chain-rattling rasp of a rock bottom in Baja.

ENTERING AN ANCHORAGE -- I have established the custom of making several passes through any area where anchorage is planned. This is done with continual reference to the depth sounder and the condition of the swell. When the wind is calm, the boat is allowed to come to a stop parallel to the trough of the swells so that their roll-producing effect can be judged.

The anchor crew stands ready upon entering the anchorage area, but they have learned to rest easy until the dull-witted skipper makes up his mind concerning where to settle. We also have standard hand signals to indicate when to drop, and the amount of chain required. There is nothing more frustrating than having one's anchor drill accompanied by a yelling match that can be heard only by the beer-drinking bunch on the yacht downwind.

ANCHORING COURTESY -- Finally, I offer a few thoughts on anchoring courtesy. (1) If the vessels present in an anchorage are swinging on bow anchor only, you should do likewise unless you can settle far enough away so that these vessels will not impact your position should they swing 360 degrees from their location.

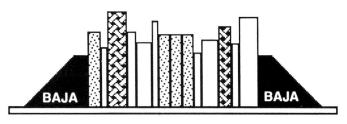

(2) Do not anchor so that your vessel will drift down on another boat in the event your anchor slips. There is nothing more aggravating than having to worry all night because someone has anchored directly upwind from your location in 25 knots.

(3) In confined anchorages try not to settle in the exact middle. Your courtesy in attempting to leave room for the next boat will be repaid, because it is going to stay, one way or the other, and you will both be better off to make the best use of the available space.

(4) Most Baja anchorages have space for many yachts, but there seems to be a magical attraction for the arriving skipper to want to position the vessel uncomfortably close to those already present. Most skippers will be visiting for the first time, and they will reason that the first vessel has found the best spot. Naturally, that must be the only place to settle. In reality, one location is often as good as another, so I suggest you always leave a comfortable margin of distance between you and your neighbors. If you are looking for company, make it a practice to pass close by the vessels already present and say hello. They may well give you a clue as to whether you would be welcome close by or whether they prefer the solitude you are interrupting.

EVALUATION OF PACIFIC COAST ANCHORAGES

NOTE -- **The anchorages indicated on the charts in** *VOLUME I* **of the** *BAJA BOATER'S GUIDE* **are for prevailing** <u>NW weather and sea conditions</u> **unless otherwise indicated.**

The authors of the *U.S. Sailing Directions* use various adjectives (very good, good, fair, and indifferent) in their descriptions of anchorages. These terms are allowed to stand on their own and are not further defined. One needs to be aware that these judgements of quality almost certainly were derived from the experiences of mariners sailing in vessels much larger than today's recreation boats. They therefore apply to locations farther offshore and in deeper water than areas used by most yachts and small craft. One should also be aware that the *Sailing Directions* describes only a small percentage of the anchorages available for small craft along the Baja coast.

In most cases I do not use a qualitative adjective in the text when denoting an anchorage. Instead, Baja's Pacific coast anchorages have been grouped into six broad classes. The first four of these are shown on the PRINCIPAL ANCHORAGES Chart. Assignments to these classes reflect my own judgements and I am certain that further experience would result in modifications.

CLASS 1 -- MAN-MADE HARBORS (5) -- There are eight locations in Baja California where the Mexican government has constructed harbor facilities. Three of these are along the Pacific coast, with a fourth at Cabo San Lucas where the Pacific and the Sea of Cortez are considered to merge. The U.S. port of San Diego is also largely man-made. There are thus five protected man-made harbors available to the mariner making the passage from San Diego to Cabo San Lucas.

Two of these harbors (El Sauzal and Cedros Village) are relatively small, breakwater-lined enclosures designed for commercial fishing vessels, with no facilities intended for visiting yachts. The remaining three (San Diego, Ensenada, and Cabo San Lucas) all have some type of marina development.

CLASS 2 -- ENCLOSED NATURAL HARBORS (2) -- Bahia Tortugas and Bahia Magdalena are nearly enclosed bodies of water with relatively narrow entrances. The former is the principal stopover and fueling point on Baja's Pacific coast. The more sizeable Bahia Magdalena is also frequently visited. Both places are sufficiently large to allow the creation of wind-waves within the harbors. This results in the need to move about within their confines under differing weather conditions.

CLASS 3 -- BEST NW-WIND ANCHORAGES (11) -- In addition to the seven harbors mentioned above, I have chosen 25 locations which provide reasonable protection from the Pacific's prevailing NW weather conditions. They are the places where I would choose to anchor my own 46-foot sailing vessel. Eleven of these are honored as being the best, and are included as Class 3; the other fourteen are Class 4.

CLASS 4 -- ACCEPTABLE NW-WIND ANCHORAGES (14) -- These are the lesser of the 25 locations noted above under Class 3.

The break point between Class 3 and Class 4 is obviously arbitrary and reflects my personal judgments. The criteria used in making these decisions are presented in the final section in this chapter entitled Judging an Anchorage.

CLASS 5 -- OTHER NW-WIND ANCHORAGES There are other places where one may anchor along Baja's Pacific coast. Some offer reasonable protection but are close to another haven that has superior quality. Others offer good protection but only for shoal-draft vessels that are smaller than most yachts. Still others are essentially roadstead anchorages that are usable only in the calmest of weather. Some of these anchorages are discussed where encountered in the text in PART II of this book. They are excluded from the PRINCIPAL ANCHORAGES Chart so as not to give the impression that acceptable anchorages are more prevalent than they really are.

CLASS 6 -- COASTAL LAGOONS -- There are many coastal lagoons along Baja's Pacific coast whose entrances permit the passage of various boats in calm weather. Three of these are regularly entered by various sizeable ocean-going vessels whose skippers have intimate knowledge of the entrance channels. Scammon's Lagoon is home to a fleet of ocean-going tugs that tow salt barges to Isla Cedros. San Ignacio Lagoon is entered by tour boat operators who take people to watch the calving activities of the California gray whale. Boca de Soledad provides a channel for

commercial fishing vessels headed for the cannery at Puerto Lopez Mateos.

Other shallower lagoon entrances are regularly navigated by shoal-draft Mexican fishing pangas. In some cases these lagoon mouths are completely fronted by breaking swells. The well-powered panga is maneuvered in directly behind an incoming swell and rides it into the lagoon.

My firm counsel to all cruising skippers is to avoid entering any of these lagoons. In particular, they are no place for a sailboat. You may ask, "How did Captain Scammon sail into the famous Lagoon named in his honor?" The answer is, "with great difficulty." The account of his first entry in his *The Marine Mammals of the Northwestern Coast of North America* is a *hairy* one.

I am aware that well-powered, shoal-draft recreational vessels do enter some of these Pacific lagoons. Obviously, if a Mexican panga can make such a passage, a similarly-powered recreation boat should also be able to do so. This book presents aerial photos of all of the principal lagoon entrances for the benefit of those who are so inclined. However, I hope that the major impact of these pictures will be to keep most coastal mariners safely out at sea.

In taking these photos I endeavored to capture the full picture of the breaker situation off each entrance. In some instances, however, it was difficult to get all the breakers into one exposure, and in other cases photos from different angles seemed to show different entrance channels. In addition, it is well known that these channels change rapidly after storm conditions. Thus, these lagoon entrance photos should be used only as a rough guide to what one may actually find during a given visit.

NW-ANCHORAGE SUMMARY -- The PRINCIPAL ANCHORAGES Chart tells the basic story. It shows 32 locations that provide fair to very good protection under NW-wind and swell conditions. This is really not a lot of anchorages for an 800-mile-long area of coastline. Fortunately, these havens are reasonably well dispersed except south of Punta Abreojos.

North of Punta Abreojos most cruising sailboats can reach a protected anchorage every evening with no night running, although auxiliary power may have to be used. Obviously, faster powerboats can achieve the same objective. South of this point some vessels will require a night's running to reach the next anchorage. The longest segment of coast with no anchorages (NW or SW) is from Punta Tosca to Cabo San Lucas, a distance of 135 miles.

SW-STORM ANCHORAGES -- Along the west coast of North America, storms resulting from frontal

PRINCIPAL ANCHORAGES

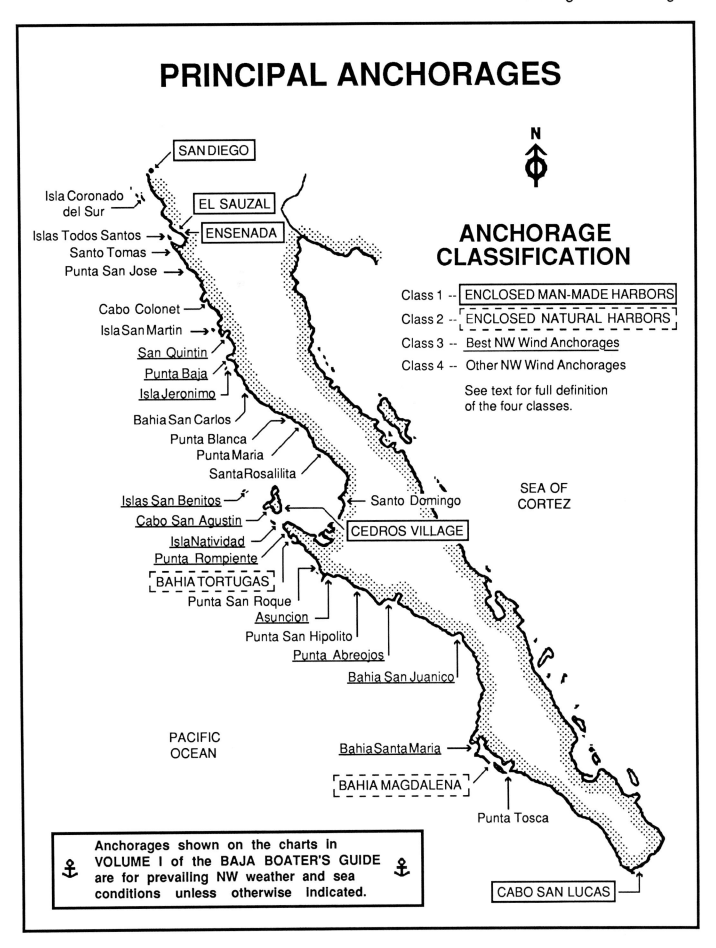

N

ANCHORAGE CLASSIFICATION

Class 1 -- ENCLOSED MAN-MADE HARBORS

Class 2 -- ENCLOSED NATURAL HARBORS

Class 3 -- Best NW Wind Anchorages

Class 4 -- Other NW Wind Anchorages

See text for full definition of the four classes.

SAN DIEGO

Isla Coronado del Sur

EL SAUZAL

Islas Todos Santos →   ENSENADA
Santo Tomas →
Punta San Jose →

Cabo Colonet →

Isla San Martin →

San Quintin

Punta Baja

Isla Jeronimo

Bahia San Carlos

Punta Blanca

Punta Maria

Santa Rosalilita

Islas San Benitos

Cabo San Agustin

Isla Natividad

Punta Rompiente

BAHIA TORTUGAS

Punta San Roque

Asuncion

Punta San Hipolito

Punta Abreojos

Bahia San Juanico

Santo Domingo

CEDROS VILLAGE

SEA OF CORTEZ

PACIFIC OCEAN

Bahia Santa Maria

BAHIA MAGDALENA

Punta Tosca

CABO SAN LUCAS

⚓ Anchorages shown on the charts in VOLUME I of the BAJA BOATER'S GUIDE are for prevailing NW weather and sea conditions unless otherwise indicated. ⚓

passages invariably cause SW winds prior to the passage of the front. NW winds return after this event. Thus it is in Baja. All of the seven harbors indicated as Class 1 and 2 offer protection in both SW and NW weather. All of the anchorages noted in Classes 3 and 4, however, are wide open to southerly weather. There are few other locations that offer protection from SW winds.

The best course of action is to avoid SW-storm conditions by traversing Baja's Pacific coast when it is not normally beset by such storms. I have been on the Baja coast in only two SW storms. By good fortune my vessel was safely anchored within the harbors at Ensenada and Bahia Tortugas on these occasions. Both provided good protection.

Outside of the Class 1 and 2 harbors, protection from SW winds should be be sought on the N or NE side of the relatively few islands along the Pacific coast. Beyond this, inspection of Baja coastal charts shows only two prominent points of land that should provide shelter from SW weather. These are Punta Banda (south of Ensenada), with good holding ground off La Jolla, and Punta Eugenia (near the center of the peninsula), with holding ground at Malarrimo and several other places.

In doing the field investigations for this book, I have taken my vessel to these various locations where logic indicates that protection would be afforded in the event of SW winds. In all cases soundings were taken to evaluate the gradient and depth of the bottom. These observations are presented as each location is encountered in the text. In addition, they are shown in the SW-WIND ANCHORAGES Chart.

As a competent airplane pilot is always alert to the location of the nearest landing field in the event an emergency arises, I suggest that skippers plying the waters of Baja's Pacific coast always have the nearest SW-wind anchorage in mind. In some cases utilizing such a haven could mean retreating many scores of miles. For example, there is no protection from SW-winds anywhere between Bahia Magdalena on the Pacific coast and the north side of Cabo Los Frailes in the Sea of Cortez.

JUDGING AN ANCHORAGE -- I have personally visited every one of the anchorages described in this book. In many cases I have spent one or more nights at these locations. In the others, I have motored through the cove or bight, observing the water depths and swell conditions. My descriptions and judgments are based in part on these visits.

While all of this sounds impressive, it has its limitations. My vessel is a 15-ton, 46-foot sailboat. What I found to be comfortable may not apply for smaller boats. My visits were of short duration and obviously did not test the full variety of weather and sea conditions that each harbor has to offer. I have not spent a lifetime on the Baja coast, nor do I intend to. Also, it is sobering when I find that authors of previous guidebooks sometimes arrive at recommendations differing considerably from my own.

On the positive side, I have visited most of the better anchorages on more than one occasion, and at different times of the year. In many cases, these stopovers have been during periods of 15-25 knot winds that are common along the Pacific coast during the winter season. Thus, I believe my judgments tend to be conservative and do not overrate anchorage quality. Time, and letters from outraged readers, may change my views.

Hopefully my judgments will prove of value. It is the intent of this section, however, to assist skippers in making their own determinations by referring to the charts and photos in this book and by considering such factors as northerly indent, water depth, and the alignment of the land west of the anchorage.

NORTHERLY INDENT -- Using the charts in this book, draw an E-W line projecting easterly from the point of land which provides the protective barrier for any of the Class 3 and 4 NW-wind anchorages. (See the NORTHERLY INDENT Chart.) The farther one can anchor north of the E-W line, the greater will be the protection provided by the anchorage. It thus follows that a major factor which may be used to judge the quality of an anchorage is the amount of distance between this E-W line and the head of the cove or bay. I have termed this distance the northerly indent.

NORTHERLY INDENT

A -- Most desirable anchoring position.

B -- Anchoring position often mandated because of shallow depths at position A.

C -- Anchoring position south of the E - W line offers little protection.

SOUTHWEST WIND ANCHORAGES

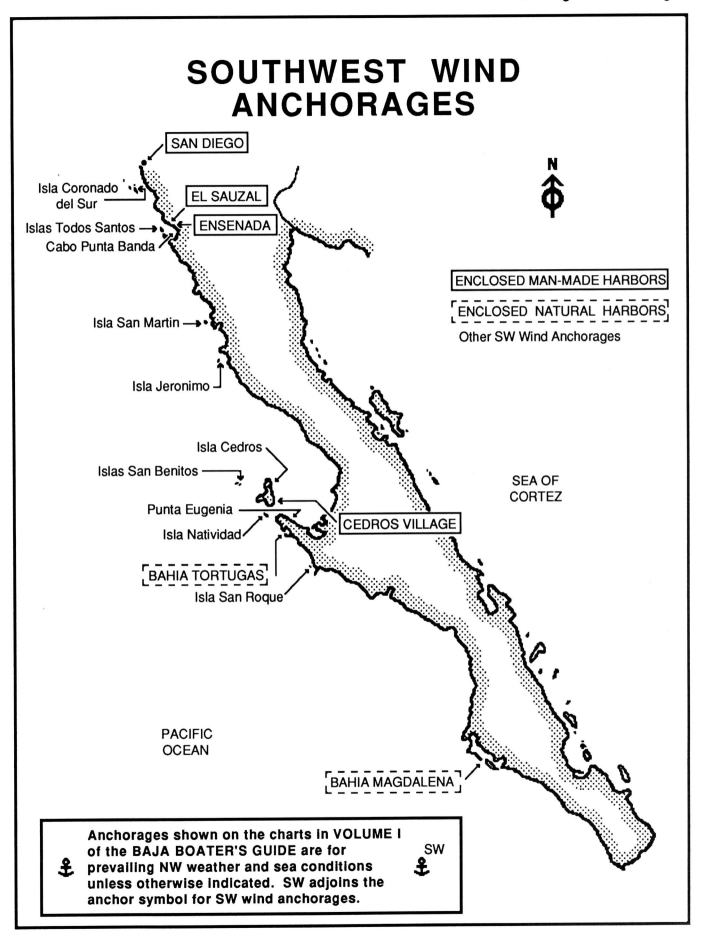

SAN DIEGO

Isla Coronado del Sur

EL SAUZAL

ENSENADA

Islas Todos Santos →
Cabo Punta Banda

N

Isla San Martin →

ENCLOSED MAN-MADE HARBORS

ENCLOSED NATURAL HARBORS

Other SW Wind Anchorages

Isla Jeronimo

Isla Cedros

Islas San Benitos

SEA OF CORTEZ

Punta Eugenia

Isla Natividad

CEDROS VILLAGE

BAHIA TORTUGAS

Isla San Roque

PACIFIC OCEAN

BAHIA MAGDALENA

Anchorages shown on the charts in VOLUME I of the BAJA BOATER'S GUIDE are for prevailing NW weather and sea conditions unless otherwise indicated. SW adjoins the anchor symbol for SW wind anchorages.

SW

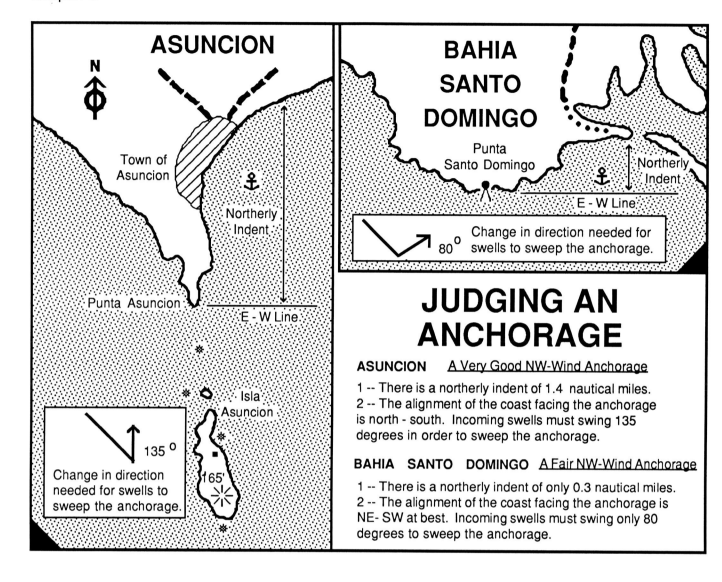

JUDGING AN ANCHORAGE

ASUNCION *A Very Good NW-Wind Anchorage*

1 -- There is a northerly indent of 1.4 nautical miles.
2 -- The alignment of the coast facing the anchorage is north - south. Incoming swells must swing 135 degrees in order to sweep the anchorage.

BAHIA SANTO DOMINGO *A Fair NW-Wind Anchorage*

1 -- There is a northerly indent of only 0.3 nautical miles.
2 -- The alignment of the coast facing the anchorage is NE- SW at best. Incoming swells must swing only 80 degrees to sweep the anchorage.

It has been my experience that if one's vessel is anchored along the E-W line (i.e., the protecting point lies due W) the vessel will receive marginal protection. South of this line an anchorage will be unsatisfactory and protection should be sought elsewhere.

The JUDGING AN ANCHORAGE Chart provides an example of this northerly indent concept. It shows that there is a northerly indent of 1.4 miles at the good anchorage of Asuncion, and the off-lying islands and rocks provide some additional protection. In contrast, there is only 0.3 mile at the much poorer quality anchorage at Bahia Santo Domingo. Clearly, the greater the northerly indent, the better the anchorage, other things being equal. Unfortunately, one of the factors which is not always equal is water depth.

WATER DEPTH -- The potential quality of some anchorages is significantly reduced because water depths are too shallow for safe anchoring in their inner portions. This is the result of sand deposited by coastal currents in the calm waters that prevail in such locations.

Thus, some bays with substantial northerly indents are not as good as they appear on the charts. In these places one is forced to anchor farther south, and east, than in the most desirable location. This situation is illustrated in the NORTHERLY INDENT Chart.

A good example of the siltation problem is present at Punta Tosca. (See SOUTH HALF Chart in Chapter 12.) Here the coastal alignment is good, and the northerly indent is a substantial 2.5 miles, but siltation is so heavy that the best available anchorage is barely north of the E - W line drawn from the point.

The soundings given on the U. S. navigation charts will help you make judgements concerning the siltation situation. In addition, on the charts in this book, I have attempted to place the anchor symbol in the place I have judged to be the best available anchorage. If this is other than the potentially best location, it is because that spot is unusable due to shallow water depths. In most cases, the estimated distance from shore to the anchoring position is also provided.

ALIGNMENT OF THE LAND WEST OF THE ANCHORAGE -- Another factor which may be used to judge the quality of an anchorage is the alignment of the land lying west of the anchored vessel. At Asuncion this coast lies in a general north-south direction (See JUDGING AN ANCHORAGE Chart). As a result, swells proceeding SW down the peninsular coast must refract 135 degrees to swing into the anchorage. Such a major change in direction will dissipate a great deal of their energy. At Bahia Santo Domingo the swells must bend much less. They thus arrive with far more of their energy still intact.

JUDGING SUMMARY -- It is my contention that skippers may judge the quality of the NW-wind anchorages along Baja's Pacific coast by observing (1) northerly indent, (2) water depth information provided by the U. S. charts and this book, and (3) the alignment of the land west of the anchorage.

Each of the these factors has its limitation as an aid to making advance judgments about anchorage quality. Nevertheless, I strongly believe that use of these aids will increase one's batting average and will allow skippers to better plan their activities along Baja's Pacific coast. Certainly they are superior to placing sole reliance on simple adjective ratings or author's recommendations given to various anchorages in this and other references.

Some final and important words. In the final analysis the most important factor in deciding where to anchor one's vessel is not my recommendations, or any of the guidelines suggested above; the critical element is common sense. On one occasion I approached the very good north-wind anchorage at Bahia de los Muertos in the Sea of Cortez. We were sailing into the anchorage with a following, southerly wind, which is not common during the winter. The anchorage itself was beset with strong, 20-knot westerly winds gusting through low mountain passes inland. This also was not normal; yet, six yachts were anchored dangerously on a lee shore in the traditional north-wind location recommended by all the guidebooks, and as each new vessel arrived they joined the pack. Not one of these skippers chose to join us in a well-protected west-wind anchorage only 1/2 mile away. These people were slaves to their guidebooks and were not using common sense.

Use all the guides available, but then look around and anchor in the place that your judgment tells you is best. On occasion I do this but then find that as the wind increases my first choice was wrong. The crew needs exercise. Move.

Los Nuevos Vagabundos del Mar
(The New Vagabonds of the Sea)

We sail in the wakes of Cortez,
    Of de Ulloa, Cabrillo, ... those daring men,
Exploring your bays and your islands,
    Very little has changed since then.
Some small settlements now are along your coasts.
    Asuncion....Abreojos.... San Carlos....the Cape,
But we new Vagabundos who cruise Baja's seas
    Do not come to ravish and rape.
Our goals are not inspired by greed,
    It's the serenity of your land that we seek,
The peace and tranquility that we find there
    Are the precious treasures we desire to share.

We come not with covetous quests
    but to explore your shores as grateful guests.

KEN REIMER

Poet Ken Reimer was kind enough to contribute several fine poems to my first book *The Magnificent Peninsula*. And now he is back again in this volume. ------ The original Vagabundos del Mar were poor Mexican fishermen who sailed the Sea of Cortez in small open boats, unaided by mechanical propulsion. I have placed Ken's poem in this book about the Pacific Ocean believing that those adventurous sailors who ply the waters of Baja's western shore best fit what he has in mind as *Los Nuevos Vagabundos del Mar*.

"It is as ugly and sterile and of as wretched aspect as the lands south of it."

Thus did Francisco de Ulloa describe Isla Cedros and the Pacific coast of the Baja peninsula after his epic voyage of exploration in 1539-40. Today we modern *explorers* view these same lands as possessing majestic beauty and splendid isolation. Gazing upon them from the decks of our modern vessels, their very *wretchedness* offers us release from the tensions of the hectic cosmopolitan world only a few hundred miles to the north.

By some quirk of our emotional makeup, our recreational travels are considerably enhanced by having knowledge of the historical background of the sites we visit. As a result, most travel literature is laced with historical tidbits. Even in touring a large city, we gain some degree of inspiration on being told that someone did something, somewhere in the vicinity, sometime in the past. But in such places, the ambiguities of where that something actually took place, and the massive changes in environment between then and now, make it difficult to fully savor the event.

In contrast, the great majority of the Baja coastline is little changed from the time when it was first viewed by the seamen of the sixteenth century. I have had the privilege of lying at anchor in numerous coves along this shore observing the antics of sea gulls on the beach, viewing the effortless flights of long lines of pelicans skimming the sea, and marveling as the evening shadows continuously transform the landscape. But, I was missing one of the most important elements. I knew little of the historic background of these places that provided me with sanctuary.

In preparing this volume, I have been able to relive these exploratory events through the pages of several well-researched historical accounts. I pass them on here in as much detail as space allows. Much of what is presented has been gleaned from Henry R. Wagner's outstanding *Spanish Voyages to the Northwest Coast of America in the Sixteenth Century* published in 1929. With the help of these accounts you will be able to share your anchorages with visions of Ulloa, Cabrillo, Vizcaino, their ships, and crews.

In some instances, there are questions as to just where these explorers visited. I will point these out and offer my own views on what may have occurred; and you, too, may participate in unraveling the mysteries. Where would you have anchored? Where were the watering holes and where did the skirmishes take place with the primitive people they encountered?

A more complete resume of Baja's overall history is unveiled in my land-oriented book *The Magnificent Peninsula* and relatively little of this is repeated here. What is related below is a more comprehensive presentation of the voyages of the earlier explorers than was possible in this prior book.

BACKGROUND REMARKS

LATITUDE ERRORS -- Historians point out that there were consistent errors in the latitude observations reported by all the early explorers. The readings showed that the ships were farther north than they actually were. This was apparently common in the sixteenth century, and was due chiefly to errors in the tables of sun declination then in use. The latitudes reported for Cabo San Lucas were fairly accurate, but observations became increasingly erroneous as they progressed northward.

These inaccuracies are one of the chief reasons why it is difficult to always be sure of the locations of certain landfalls. This is particularly true when there are several possible protected anchorages in the same vicinity.

ANCHORING -- Equipped with modern charts and motor-propelled vessels, today's sailors invariably drop their ground tackle as far as possible within the protection of a cove or headland. In contrast, it is apparent that the early skippers were frequently forced to stay anyplace where they could reach bottom with their anchors, often with little or no protection from the seas. Along the Northern Bight NE of Isla Cedros there are few places where today's cruisers would chose to anchor, even in fair weather. Yet the report of Cabrillo's voyage described this same coast as "clean and suitable for anchoring". In these open roadstead anchorages they often suffered considerable displeasure and lost anchors due to the parting of their cables.

We also need to keep in mind that the early captains had to give major consideration to leaving an anchorage under sail alone. Thus, the small deeply protected cove which today we would rate as excellent, may have provided an extremely uninviting haven for a square rigger. The open roadstead off San Jose del Cabo provides considerable wind and wave protection and maximum maneuvering room. It was thus a frequently used stopping point for early seamen. Today's sailors rarely use it. The same situation exists in the roadstead off Loreto in the Sea of Cortez. This site was chosen as the first permanent settlement on the peninsula, and ships anchored here for decades. There is good holding ground but absolutely no protection from the prevailing winds which will blow a ship ashore if the anchor should fail to hold. Today's vessels are anchored in the fully protected cove at Puerto Escondido only a few miles to the south.

This situation needs to be kept in mind when evaluating the accounts that the early captains give us of the places they stayed. What was good for them is clearly not the same for us today.

INDIANS -- The native Aztec and Mayan Indians encountered on the Mexican mainland had developed highly advanced civilizations. In marked contrast, the peninsular peoples were among the most primitive found in the Americas. They wore little or no clothing and had only the crudest of shelters.

Estimates of their original population range from 40,000 to 50,000 people. It is clear however, that these people were widely dispersed throughout the peninsula, as the early explorers encountered them in many locations. They frequently reported seeing fires by night and smokes by day as they traversed the coast. They also encountered Indians fishing from rafts made of canes.

ACTS OF POSSESSION -- The Spanish word *Acta* is defined today as "minutes (of a meeting)" or "document". When the Spanish explorers landed on previously-undiscovered terrain, they performed a ceremony wherein they took possession for the King. These events were recorded by a notary public in a written document, "an acta", which was then entered into the official records when the expedition returned home.

The ceremony performed by the expedition leader consisted of "actually and in reality taking possession, and placing his hand upon his sword and saying that if any person disputed it, he was ready to defend such possession, cutting trees with his sword, moving stones from one place to another, and taking water out of the sea and throwing it upon the land, all which was done in token of said possession." So, if you crave to settle down for a while the next time you go ashore on a deserted Baja beach, you will now know how to go about it properly.

COLUMBUS TO CORTEZ

Columbus's four voyages to the new world took place from 1492 to 1502. Spanish colonization of the Caribbean islands that he discovered was soon to follow. One of the first of the settlers was 19 year old Hernan Cortez. By 1519, the energetic Cortez lead a military force to the mainland, and by 1522 he had captured the Aztec capital of Tenochtitlan (now Mexico City). Cortez became the conqueror of New Spain (Mexico), and one of the most famous, rich, and powerful of the Spanish conquistadors.

In the decade that followed, Spanish adventurers spread out in all directions. One result was the generation of stories of seven golden cities to the north and other tales that inflamed the spirits of men like Cortez. Included in these legends was a report of an island lying to the west that was populated only by women and which was rich in pearls. These inhabitants had wea-

On October 15, 1542, Hernan Cortez wrote the King of Spain. The conqueror of New Spain reported on a legendary island that was populated only by women. It was also said to be rich in pearls and gold. These reports no doubt inspired Cortez to dispatch expeditions in search of this romantic land. They also provide the background for Ken Reimer's poem.

BAJA CALIFORNIA

Baja California...legendary land
  Of the warrior women,
Of precious pearls...;
  Stepchild appendix
Of a great continent...,
  Where the sands of time
Mark the ages languidly,
  as she dreams on and on
In her siesta 'neath the sun.

Ken Reimer

pons made of gold. This legend was popularized by a Spanish novel of the day where the island in question bore the name California. The allurement of these stories was enhanced by the desire to discover a sea passage (the Northwest Passage) above the North American continent that would provide an easy route from Europe to the Orient.

Cortez was prevented from mounting land expeditions north along the Mexican Pacific coast by the presence of a rival conquistador, Nuno de Guzman. Cortez, thus, turned to the sea. Under his direction a shipyard was constructed on the west coast of New Spain about 100 miles NW of present day Acapulco. In the years to follow he dispatched four expeditions into Pacific waters.

The first of these debarked in 1532 under the command of Diego Hurtado de Mendoza. It penetrated into the Sea of Cortez but was never to return. It met its end at the hands of Indians, Guzman, or both. A year later (1533) a second group of two ships departed from the site of present day Manzanillo. One vessel returned after discovering the Revilla Gigedo Islands which lie some 400 miles off the Mexican coast.

CALIFORNIA DISCOVERED -- The second ship, the *Concepcion*, was commanded by Diego de Becerra. This Captain's tyrannical nature was such as to engender a mutiny led by his Basque pilot Fortun Jimenez. Becerra was killed and others aboard were put ashore on the mainland coast. Jimenez sailed west and was the leader of the first known Europeans to set foot on what is now Baja California. The magnificent peninsula was thus discovered through accident by a group of mutineers.

Circumstantial evidence in the historical record indicates that Jimenez reached Bahia de La Paz at the same site which was to serve as Cortez's camp in the next expedition. Here he and most of the crew were killed by Indians. The few survivors sailed to the mainland where all but one were captured by Guzman. The lone escapee reached Cortez with the news of California along with the inevitable reports of gold and pearls.

THE CORTEZ EXPEDITION -- Cortez chose to lead the third voyage himself. But it was to be more than an exploratory expedition, for he clearly knew where he was headed as the result of the Jimenez discovery. This third venture was to be a serious effort to establish a settlement in California. It took place in the vicinity of La Paz on the Sea of Cortez. The settlement was named Santa Cruz. This event preceded the Pilgrim's landing at Plymouth Rock in Massachusetts by 85 years, and was 235 years prior to Junipero Serra's founding of the Franciscan mission at San Diego in Alta California. But Cortez's colonizing effort was to last only a year. (It is discussed in more detail in Volume II of this book which deals with the Sea of Cortez.)

Exploratory trips were apparently made inland, but no chronicles exist. When Ulloa later arrived at Cabo San Lucas by sea in 1539, however, his log entries lead one to believe that the Cape had been previously discovered and that the northwesterly trend of the peninsula's Pacific coast was already known. A map which is believed to have been made prior to this voyage confirms this conclusion. It clearly shows the Bahia de La Paz area with a narrow peninsula extending to the south.

THE VOYAGE OF FRANCISCO DE ULLOA

When Cortez returned to the mainland he encountered Antonio de Mendoza, the first Viceroy of New Spain. From then on, the conquistadors were to have far less of a free hand, but, without the Viceroy's approval, Cortez dispatched one final expedition under the command of Francisco de Ulloa. Ulloa had accompanied Cortez on his previous colonization effort at Santa Cruz.

Ulloa left Acapulco on July 8, 1539. The smallest of his three vessels was abandoned shortly after the trip started. The two remaining ships were the *Santa Agueda* (120 tons), and the *Trinidad* (35 tons). California was still believed to be an island so they proceeded north along the mainland coast, no doubt in search of the fabled seven cities which were thought to lie north of New Spain. The result was that Ulloa spent some two thirds of his voyage in the Sea of Cortez. The principal result was the discovery that California was a peninsula and not an island.

The Sea of Cortez portion of Ulloa's expedition is discussed in Volume II of this book. It took place only 47 years after Columbus's first voyage to the new world. It was accomplished without serious difficulty and took only slightly over two months. But ahead lay a five-month battle to sail only halfway up the peninsula's Pacific shore.

THE PACIFIC COAST -- Ulloa arrived at Cabo San Lucas on November 6, 1539. After staying here only one day he ventured north into the Pacific. The small fleet encountered severe weather. They were forced to anchor several nights along a stretch of coast where we know today there is no shelter. The two ships became separated but independently proceeded north to an agreed upon latitude which by good fortune was in the protection of Punta Tosca. Here, on November 27, Ulloa and the *Santa Agueda* were reunited with the lost *Trinidad*. The headland was named Punta de la Trinidad in her honor.

PUNTA DE LA TRINIDAD -- Ulloa describes the coastal indentation formed east of Punta Tosca as a "great bay", adjoining which is a "very large lagoon", the entrance to which "is so wide and deep that ships of any size can

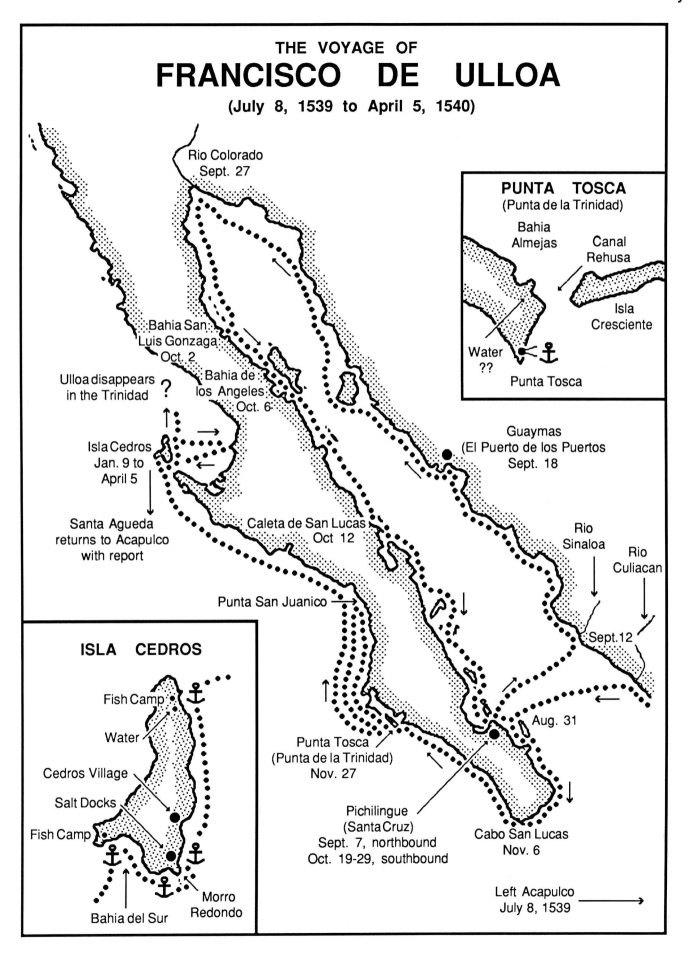

THE VOYAGE OF
FRANCISCO DE ULLOA
(July 8, 1539 to April 5, 1540)

Rio Colorado
Sept. 27

PUNTA TOSCA
(Punta de la Trinidad)

Bahia
Almejas

Canal
Rehusa

Isla
Cresciente

Water
??

Punta Tosca

Bahia San
Luis Gonzaga
Oct. 2

Ulloa disappears
in the Trinidad

Bahia de
los Angeles
Oct. 6

Isla Cedros
Jan. 9 to
April 5

Guaymas
(El Puerto de los Puertos
Sept. 18

Santa Agueda
returns to Acapulco
with report

Caleta de San Lucas
Oct 12

Rio
Sinaloa

Rio
Culiacan

Punta San Juanico

Sept. 12

ISLA CEDROS

Fish Camp

Water

Cedros Village

Salt Docks

Fish Camp

Bahia del Sur

Morro
Redondo

Punta Tosca
(Punta de la Trinidad)
Nov. 27

Aug. 31

Pichilingue
(Santa Cruz)
Sept. 7, northbound
Oct. 19-29, southbound

Cabo San Lucas
Nov. 6

Left Acapulco
July 8, 1539

The author's ketch *La Patricia.*

enter". The very large lagoon is of course Bahia Almejas, but the description of the bay and the lagoon's mouth do not fully fit today's observations. The entrance to the lagoon (Rehusa Channel) is today very shallow and fronted by breakers. It is admittedly wide, but certainly not deep. It is unsafe to anchor in the ocean bay farther inland than due east of the present-day lighthouse.

Yet Ulloa's account seems to say he entered the lagoon with his ships to access a second nearby channel to a watering place. The resolution of this dilemma is provided by the logs of Vizcaino written 57 years later. One of his ships entered Bahia Almejas through this channel, and the accompanying maps clearly depict the appropriate topography. It appears certain, then, that the entrance channel, and the bay east of Punta Tosca have silted in since the days of the explorers. It is thus probable that Ulloa's watering place was the excellent spring near a small ranch located on the shores of a small cove just inside the entrance channel (as reported by Leland Lewis's *Baja Sea Guide*).

On December 1st the ships were brought to the watering place and the men landed to fill. While thus engaged, they were attacked by some 20 naked Indians who rained arrows, javelins, and stones upon them. In this close combat, several of Ulloa's men were injured.

Following this battle, the ships sailed north and passed the mouth of Bahia Magdalena but declined to enter. They felt "there was nothing more to see here than at the last place". With this faulty rationale, Ulloa missed the opportunity to explore one of the finest natural harbors on the west coast of North America. Instead, he continued north and encountered fierce storms in the vicinity of Punta San Juanico. Here he lost several anchors while seeking protection in this uninviting section of coast. He was forced to retreat back to Punta de la Trinidad.

The *Trinidad* was maneuvered close to the previously-used watering place and here they stayed from December 15 to December 21st. Ulloa's log then provides us with a fascinating account of their interaction with the natives. The Indians wished to exchange gifts but would not approach close enough to do this directly. Instead, they thrust an arrow into a crevice in a rock lying in the bay near the watering place. Here they hung the various ornaments they offered. The ship's crew retrieved these and left their own gifts in return.

As the above event unfolded, more and more naked Indians appeared, many painted from the knee up in black and white. On shore they engaged in various ceremonies and pageantry all in full sight of the ships. Near the end hostilities again erupted and the natives were dispersed with cannon fire from the *Trinidad*. What would we not have paid to view these events? The best we can do is to pause off Punta Tosca and let our imaginations attempt to recreate the scenes.

ISLA CEDROS -- The two ships continued north where substantial adverse weather was encountered. After nineteen days of battling the elements, they finally took refuge January 9th along the SW shore of Isla Cedros. The passage here was not direct. They had been to the mainland shore to the east, and around and about the island. At times they were out of sight of land, fighting strong winds from the north. The Cedros anchorage was sought somewhat in desperation. The log reports that it provided good protection from the continuing, severe, northerly weather. The exact spot is a matter of speculation, but almost certainly it was in the western portion of Bahia del Sur, perhaps in the well-protected spot near the present-day fish camps.

After seven days in this shelter, they stood away east and clearly describe the rocks that lie off Morro Redondo. Here they found five or six rafts containing Indians fishing along the reef. The two vessels anchored here before rounding the point. Imagine the amazement of these Stone Age peoples on a Pacific Island in seeing Ulloa's fleet paying them a visit. They seemed, however, relatively unconcerned as they approached the ships on their rafts and continued fishing in the vicinity.

The following day the ships rounded Morro Redondo and anchored again. This spot was no doubt directly offshore from the present-day salt loading facilities. As the adventurers attempted to land at this point the docile behaviors of the Indians changed to defiance. They met the small boats on the beach and in the water with stones and clubs. Man-to-man combat followed. Some of the natives were shot with crossbows, one left dying on the beach. Numerous others on both sides suffered a variety of wounds. In the end, the Spaniards carried the day and the Indians retreated inland.

Ulloa's men found an Indian camp nearby. It consisted of crude enclosures where they found sealskin clothing, cactus-thorn fishing hooks, and seal bladders which they used to carry their water. On the beach were the rafts made from the trunks of trees that grow in the higher elevations of this island. As no water source was found in the vicinity, the ships sailed for the mainland but were unable to make significant progress north. Instead, they were driven back to Isla Cedros where they took anchorage below the NE end of the island, where a sand point makes a little harbor. Could there be any clearer description of the present-day fish camp at Punta Norte? Here they found another Indian camp.

After a minor skirmish with these Indians, they sailed south and located a good source of water in a gully some three miles south of the island's northern point. Here they filled their casks, although with some difficulty as the water was some distance from the sea.

This taking on of water was accomplished on January 23, 1540. Thus, the two ships were prepared to continue their journey north. During the next 65 days they battled their way back and forth between Isla Cedros and the adjoining mainland. They faced either strong northerly winds or no wind at all. After this extended period, the ships found themselves back in the protection of the south end of the island.

Here, Ulloa made a historic decision. Much of the remaining supplies were loaded into the smaller *Trinidad*, and many days were spent in repairing both vessels. On April 5, 1540, the *Santa Agueda* was dispatched south with the records of the voyage. From here she successfully sailed to Acapulco, and into the pages of history.

Ulloa stayed behind in the *Trinidad* with the intention of continuing to press farther north. Did he ever return? There are no firm records of what transpired. Wagner sites considerable indirect and circumstantial evidence that he did in fact survive. No one knows for sure. But certainly, we modern sailors will still discover his presence as we lie at anchor in the places that he discovered some 450 years ago.

THE VOYAGE OF JUAN RODRIGUEZ CABRILLO

The most important of the early Spanish explorers in relation to the history of Baja California were Francisco de Ulloa (1539-40) and Sebastian Vizcaino (1602). To residents of western United States, however, it is the name of Juan Rodriguez Cabrillo that is most famous. It was this adventurer that first penetrated into this country's Pacific waters . His expedition reached latitude 44 off the Oregon coast.

As noted in the previous section, much of the time and energy of the Ulloa expedition was expended within the

Sea of Cortez. Leaving Acapulco in July, Ulloa enjoyed following southerly winds on the journey north to the Rio Colorado. As the winds shift to northerlies in the late fall, he again often had the wind at his back in sailing south along the east coast of the Baja peninsula. But it was mid-November as he again turned north after rounding Cabo San Lucas. He thus faced the often-strong NW winds prevailing along the Pacific coast in the winter. As we have seen, the expedition was able to proceed only as far north as Isla Cedros.

Cabrillo also departed New Spain in summer (June 27, 1542), but Ulloa's legacy allowed him to proceed directly to the peninsula's tip. He no doubt had the summer southerlies behind him at the start, and he did not encounter the strong winter northerlies until he had reached a much higher latitude.

The account of the Ulloa voyage presented above is taken directly from the explorer's log which is heavily footnoted by historian Wagner who had access to an even more detailed first hand account. Unfortunately, the full log of Cabrillo's voyage has not survived, and Wagner's rendition is based only on summaries which omit most of the interesting details. What follows is extracted from such a hand-written summary.

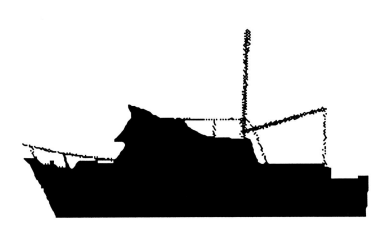

Cabrillo, a native of Portugal, left Navidad harbor on June 27, 1542 with two ships, the *San Salvador* and the *Capitana*. They sailed north along the mainland and crossed to the peninsular coast to a point that Wagner feels was in the vicinity of Cabo Plumo. Here they arrived on July 3 and anchored for two days. The narrative then relates that they arrived at "Puerto de San Lucas" on July 6, took on water and departed the same day.

PUERTO DE SAN LUCAS -- Wagner states without equivocation that this port was the cove lying under Cabo San Lucas. Historian Pablo Martinez notes matter-of-factly that the anchorage was at San Jose del Cabo. Certainly the latter location had the superior water

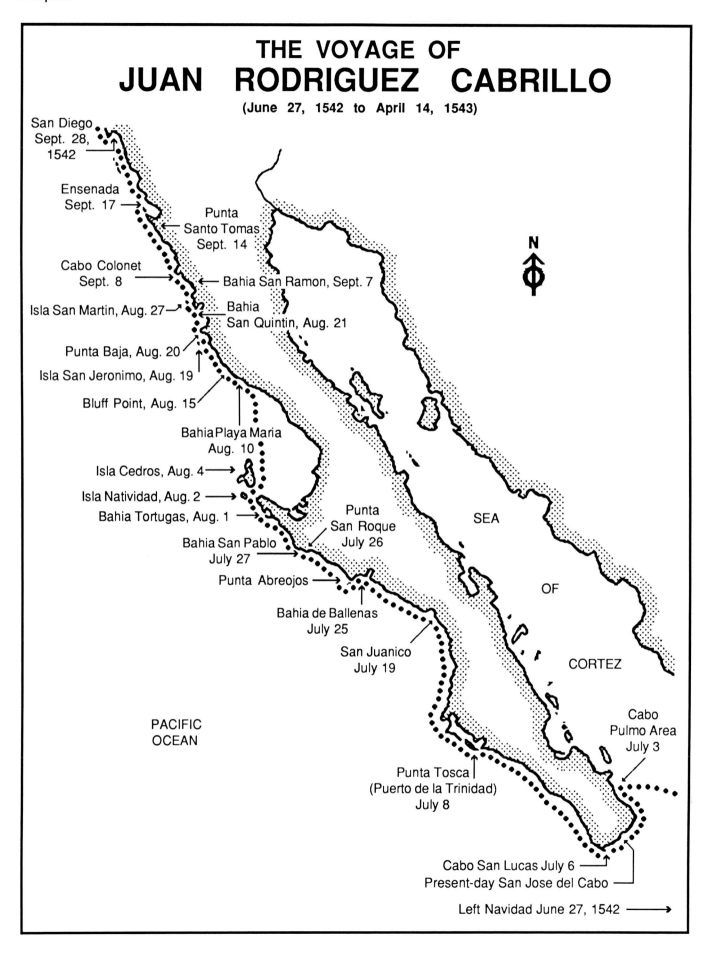

THE VOYAGE OF
JUAN RODRIGUEZ CABRILLO
(June 27, 1542 to April 14, 1543)

San Diego
Sept. 28,
1542

Ensenada
Sept. 17

Punta
Santo Tomas
Sept. 14

Cabo Colonet
Sept. 8

Bahia San Ramon, Sept. 7

Isla San Martin, Aug. 27

Bahia
San Quintin, Aug. 21

Punta Baja, Aug. 20

Isla San Jeronimo, Aug. 19

Bluff Point, Aug. 15

Bahia Playa Maria
Aug. 10

Isla Cedros, Aug. 4

Isla Natividad, Aug. 2

Bahia Tortugas, Aug. 1

Punta
San Roque
July 26

SEA

Bahia San Pablo
July 27

Punta Abreojos

Bahia de Ballenas
July 25

San Juanico
July 19

OF

CORTEZ

PACIFIC
OCEAN

Cabo
Pulmo Area
July 3

Punta Tosca
(Puerto de la Trinidad)
July 8

Cabo San Lucas July 6

Present-day San Jose del Cabo

Left Navidad June 27, 1542

N

supply, but maps and records surviving from Vizcaino's voyage 60 years later indicate there was also fresh water at Cabo San Lucas. Which place was the site actually visited by Cabrillo? I do not know. Martinez's book, however, also notes that early records refer to the entire area of the peninsula's tip as Cabo San Lucas, but that in most cases the actual locale in question was what we today call San Jose del Cabo.

After only two day's sail the ships arrived on July 8 in the protection of Punta Tosca (Punta de la Trinidad). It is described as a good port, thus providing further evidence that this anchorage's present marginal quality has resulted from recent siltation. After four days here the small fleet continued sailing past Bahia Magdalena, as did Ulloa before. A short stop was made at Punta San Juanico on July 19.

The account notes that south of Punta San Juanico the coast "makes a great *ensenada*" --"It is low sand dunes and the coast is white and clean". Today's Spanish dictionaries define the word *ensenada* as a "small bay or cove". Wagner points out that in the sixteenth century the word meant "a body of water of greater length than width, without protection from storms". This is a perfect description of the broad, 150-mile long coastal indentation (The Middle Bight) found in this area.

The journey continued rapidly in marked contrast to the pounding that the weather had bestowed on Ulloa. On July 25, Cabrillo anchored deep in the bight of Bahia de Ballenas. The record indicates that this anchorage was a considerable distance east of the rocks off Punta Abreojos. These they describe as "very dangerous reefs of rocks called Abreojo" Both the name and the description still apply today. North of here the ships spent one night at Punta San Roque (July 26) where they reported "a small island about a league from the land". On July 27 they arrived at Bahia San Pablo where they stay four nights because of contrary winds.

ISLA NATIVIDAD -- The next anchorage was in Bahia San Bartolome (Bahia Tortugas) on August 1. Here is located the most commonly used layover and fueling point for today's coastal cruisers. Cabrillo, however, was in no mood to linger, and the following night found him anchored off the SE end of Isla Natividad. The person who prepared the summary being used here was a master of apt descriptions. He states, "This island bears east-west with the end of the point of the mainland from which it is about a league distant; the coast runs NW-SE. From this point the mainland turns toward the east and NE, making a great ensenada in which land cannot be seen. Between the island and the mainland there is a good passage". Should you be so fortunate as to sail in these waters, you would be hard pressed to paint a better verbal picture.

Contrary winds forced Cabrillo to linger at Isla Natividad for three days where, the report notes, many fish could

be caught with a hook. The short journey to Isla Cedros followed. They stayed here from August 4 to August 10 taking on water and wood. There are no details, however, of specifically where they anchored.

It is also interesting to note that they found no Indians on Isla Cedros. The record also specifically states that they had not seen any natives the entire trip along the peninsular coast. Here again, Cabrillo's voyage is in significant contrast with that of Ulloa's which was only three years prior. As previously noted, Ulloa had frequent direct contact with the Indians and often saw their fires during the night. Because Cabrillo's voyage was undertaken during the heat of the summer, the natives may have retreated inland to higher ground, or perhaps the California Indians had already learned that the men in the tall ships should be avoided.

Rapid progress to the north was again achieved, although the record states that the ships were anchored each night. Specific stops seem probable at Bahia Playa Maria (August 10), Bluff Point (August 15), Isla San Jeronimo (August 19), Punta Baja (August 20), and finally, Bahia San Quintin. The historians may be in error about some of these specific anchorages, but the references to Isla San Jeronimo and Bahia San Quintin are unmistakable.

BAHIA SAN QUINTIN -- The record notes a brief sighting of four Indians at Bahia Playa Maria, but the first real encounter occurred at Bahia San Quintin where they anchored until August 27. Here they met about 30 native fishermen with whom they exchanged gifts. They made signs indicating that they had seen other men who had beards and who had with them dogs, crossbows, and swords. These men were five days journey inland. Could this have been Ulloa and his crew? It is well known that they were accompanied by dogs. Unfortunately, the historical record poses the question but does not provide the answer.

At Bahia San Quintin possession was taken in the name of the King of Spain. This is the first reference to this ceremony being performed by Cabrillo. He apparently was well aware that this responsibility had been met by Ulloa along the coast to the south.

After taking on wood and water they proceeded onward, and on August 27 found "an uninhabited island two leagues from the mainland, with a good harbor in it". This could only have been Caleta Hassler on Isla San Martin. While here, they noted seeing a great quantity of driftwood including the trunks of trees more than 60 feet in length "and of a thickness so great that two men together could not reach around them." Historian Wagner notes that this accumulation of wood was also noted by later visitors.

North of Isla San Martin it is possible to call anchorages at Bahia San Ramon (Sept. 7), Cabo Colonet (Sept. 8), and Punta Santo Tomas (Sept. 14). On September 17 the record notes arrival at a "good closed port, having passed a small island before reaching it". Historian Wagner believes this was at the present site of Ensenada. The island was no doubt Islas de Todos Santos, but Ensenada could hardly have been described as a closed port prior to construction of the present breakwater. Perhaps Cabrillo was anchored off the mouth of Estero de Punta Banda a few miles south of the city of Ensenada.

In any case, the expedition spent seven days at this location, encountered some forty Indians, obtained water, and took possession for the crown. Starting at about Bahia San Ramon, the record's description of the land begins to be more complimentary than it had been to the south. At Ensenada it describes "great savannas and grass like that of Spain" and substantial herds of animals which were probably antelope. Sailing north, beautiful valleys and groves of trees were reported. All of this would readily conform with the moister environmental conditions which are still readily apparent today.

North of this Ensenada anchorage the record clearly describes the Islas los Coronados. Further on they discovered a "very good closed port". They had reached the harbor at San Diego. Thus, on September 28, 1542, Cabrillo and his men became the first known Europeans to set foot on the Pacific coast of what was to become the United States of America. While here, they weathered a considerable storm with winds from the SW. (Such winds accompany the frontal passage of northern weather systems which start about this time of year, although this one was uncommonly early.) This event supports the contention that Cabrillo was in fact anchored within a protected inlet, rather than simply behind a point of land that would have provided shelter from only the prevailing NW winds.

NORTH FROM SAN DIEGO -- Cabrillo's voyage along the Baja coast was relatively uneventful. It took place during the summer months. The trip from Navidad to San Diego took almost exactly three months. The events that took place to the north were to be far more stressful. They are briefly summarized below.

Continued reasonable weather was encountered between San Diego and Point Conception. Large numbers of Indians and numerous towns were encountered in this region, which is described in glowing terms. (If you have visited the area in more recent times, you will note that substantial modifications have occurred, which, as viewed by a resident of San Francisco, had best go undescribed.) The natives were friendly and clearly possessed a higher standard of living than that of the natives encountered to the south.

The fleet encountered bad weather at Point Conception (so what's new?) and beyond. They penetrated north to the vicinity of Fort Ross in Alta California, but were forced to return south and took shelter for many weeks in Cuyler Cove, on the east side of San Miguel Island (the most westerly of the U.S. Channel Islands). Here Cabrillo met his death, the aftermath of breaking a bone in a fall. He was no doubt buried on the island but no trace of the site has survived.

Command of the fleet passed to Bartolome Ferrelo. In continued bad weather the ships fought their way north to a reported latitude of 44 degrees (more likely 42 degrees, considering the known latitude errors) off the coast of Oregon. From there they retreated south, and again sought refuge in Cuyler Cove. The return trip rates only a few lines in the record. The ships left Cuyler for the last time on March 23 and arrived eight days later on March 31 at Isla Cedros where they stayed for two days. The point of original departure at Puerto de Navidad was reached on April 14, 1543. The entire return voyage from Cuyler to Navidad was accomplished in only twenty one days.

ROUTE OF THE MANILIA GALLEONS

The results of Cabrillo's voyage were considered of little importance by Spanish officials. No further formal efforts at exploring the peninsula were undertaken for more than fifty years. The findings of the expedition were, however, to contribute to the next event of importance in the maritime history of the Baja coast.

THE EAST INDIES -- While the voyages of Ulloa and Cabrillo were unfolding, events of far greater importance had been taking place which were to have a bearing on the history of the California peninsula. Magellan left Spain in 1519, and passed through the Strait named for him at the southern tip of the South American continent. He sailed west to the islands of the East Indies. But these *spice islands* were also being ac-cessed more easily by Portuguese sailors from the east after passing south of Africa. The years to follow were to witness an intense rivalry between Spain and Portugal over settlement and possession of these territories and the resultant trade with the countries of Asia.

DEMARCATION LINE -- The famous *bull* of Pope Alexander VI of 1493 divided the new world between Spain and Portugal. The resulting line of demarcation split the globe into two segments, but the exact location of the division was the subject of considerable debate in the area of the East Indies. The situation seemed, however, to favor the Portuguese. The Spanish position was further compromised by a 1529 financial agreement between the two countries that debarred Spanish ships from sailing to the Indies from Europe around Africa's Cape of Good Hope.

In spite of these legal complications, the Spanish felt that some of the islands were subject to their exploration. They particularly coveted the Philippines. A sea route from Spain to this region through the Strait of Magellan was deemed to be entirely too long. Developing a trade and supply route from the west coast of New Spain (Mexico) to the Philippines thus became a high priority for the Spanish crown.

CONTRARY WINDS -- Explorers of this sea passage were soon confronted with another complication. By 1564, two expeditions from Spain, and three from the west coast of America, were able to sail west to the islands, but none could negotiate the return voyage to New Spain. Vessels sailing east from the islands were met by strong NE winds. Those that did attempt to sail a more northerly route were ill-prepared for the rigors of the northern latitudes.

The stage was thus set for a major expedition of five ships which was ordered to take possession of the Philippines and, at all cost, to discover a return route to the coast of New Spain. This fleet set sail from Navidad on November 21, 1564 under the command of Miguel Lopez de Legaspi. The Philippines were easily reached on February 13, 1565.

It is the view of historian Wagner that all of Legaspi's officers and pilots had surmised the proper northerly course for the return passage. The wind patterns in the Atlantic ocean at similar latitudes would certainly have given them a clue as to what to expect in the Pacific. They also were aware that Cabrillo had encountered strong NW winds at these higher latitudes in his voyage along the California coast. These were what were needed. This probable pre-knowledge of the proper return course was soon to lead to an interesting quirk of history.

THE VOYAGE OF ARELLANO -- Alonso de Arellano was in command of the small forty-ton vessel, *San Lucas,* that accompanied the fleet as a tender. Within a few days of departure, Arellano deserted the fleet and arrived at the Philippines on his own. It seems that his intent was to make the return voyage before Legaspi could dispatch one of the larger and slower ships, thus, gaining credit of the discovery for himself. While his motives were thus tainted, the decision to make this difficult and untested passage in a small vessel, without adequate supplies and equipment, must be considered one of the most daring feats in the annals of the sea.

Arellano and the *San Lucas* left the islands on April 22, 1565. He sailed north and NE taking advantage of the prevailing westerly winds. He reached as far north as Latitude 43, and the log notes that it snowed in the middle of June. Land was sighted on July 17 at about the midpoint of the Baja coast, perhaps near Punta San

La Patricia under sail with Alan Lamb and Frank Gieber in the cockpit.

San Hipolito. By July 28, the *San Lucas* cleared the "Punta de la California" (Cabo San Lucas). Three days later severe southerly weather drove them into the Sea of Cortez, but they were able to reach Navidad on August 9. The trip from the islands had taken a modest 110 days, but all the crew suffered from scurvy and could scarcely manage the sails at the end.

VOYAGE OF THE *SAN PEDRO* -- In the Philippines, Legaspi took possession of, and then dispatched his largest ship for the return trip. This vessel, the *San Pedro*, was commanded by Felipe de Salcedo. It left the islands on June 1, 1565. Following the same northerly route as Arellano, it arrived off San Miguel Island on September 18. It proceeded south along the Baja coast, apparently without landing. One of the surviving logs notes that a chart was being carried that noted some of the landmarks that were observed. Certainly this chart can be attributed to the voyage of Cabrillo made some twenty two years prior.

The San Pedro arrived off Navidad on October 1 and proceeded to Acapulco, landing there on October 8, 1565. The voyage from the islands to Navidad had consumed 122 days. The log notes that the master died on September 27 and was buried at sea off Cabo San Lucas. The chief pilot followed his captain in death the following day. The vessel arrived at Acapulco "with only some ten to eighteen men able to work. Sixteen had died on the voyage and all the rest were sick."

THE PHILIPPINE TRADE -- Within a few years, one or more heavily laden Spanish ships was making the circuit from Acapulco to the Philippine Islands and back each year. This trade route was to last an incredible 250

years (1565 to 1815). While only a few ships sailed each year, they carried cargos of silver and other items of high value that were of considerable importance to the economy of New Spain and the mother country.

Historian Wagner believes that the returning vessels made their landfall in the general area of San Diego or lower down on the Baja coast. As with the two original exploring vessels, the crews of the returning galleons were in sorry condition when they reached the Baja coast. They needed fresh food and water to alleviate the ever-present scurvy, but the unsettled and inhospitable California coast had none to offer.

To worsen matters, Baja soon became the haven for pirates that lay in wait for the galleons. In 1578 Francis Drake and his *Golden Hind* preyed on Spanish ships off the South American coast and took on water at Cabo San Lucas before completing his famous voyage around the world. Nine years later, Thomas Cavendish lay in wait at Cabo San Lucas for the passage of the galleons. On November 4, 1787 he sacked and burned the 700-ton *Santa Ana*, which was so heavily laden that her guns had been left behind. In 1598, sizable fleets of Dutch pirates entered the Pacific waters off New Spain and joined in the plunder of the Spanish vessels. These latter adventures were known as the *Pichilinques*, and left their name behind at the harbor north of La Paz.

Baja California thus became of considerable importance to the authorities of New Spain. They (1) wished to prevent raiders from using her harbors as a base for piracy, and (2) needed to find a port on the peninsula's Pacific coast which could be used to supply ships returning from the Philippines. During the closing years of the sixteenth century, several attempts were made to explore this coast using the returning trade vessels. These ships, however, were heavily laden, and their crews were suffering from the very privations they were seeking to alleviate. They thus were little interested in exploring.

THE VOYAGE OF SEBASTIAN VIZCAINO

In 1592 Sebastian Vizcaino appeared on the scene in New Spain. He was a merchant who had made voyages to and from the Philippines. He was on board the *Santa Ana* when she was sacked by Cavendish in 1587. In subsequent years he obtained a license from the Viceroy to engage in pearling and fishing and to establish a colony in California.

On September 3, 1596 he arrived on the peninsula leading a force of 230 seamen and soldiers, several women, horses, arms, and supplies for eight months. A settlement was made at La Paz in the Sea of Cortez, but

it met with a series of misfortunes. It was abandoned on October 18 after only a few weeks in existence.

Vizcaino's first effort was clearly a failure. Yet, he was chosen to command a second venture which was to be eminently successful. It was composed of three ships and left Acapulco on May 5, 1602. To guard against the whims of any one man, even the commander, a variety of experts trusted by the Viceroy were sent along. All important decisions were decided by a vote of these councilors. Vizcaino was to have a vote only in the case of a tie. God save us from decision by committee, but in this instance it seemed to prosper. In particular, the expedition is survived by extensive written records and detailed maps. The account included in Wagner's history is over 90 pages in length. The associated maps and land form profiles provide unmistakable records of the areas which were visited.

The objectives of Ulloa and Cabrillo were to search out the unknown, and to determine the general lay of the land. In contrast, the Vizcaino expedition was to examine California's Pacific coast in detail. He was instructed to make soundings of the ports, determine their landmarks, examine them for pearls, and to make maps of the discoveries. A major objective was to locate a port which could be used by the east-bound galleons returning from the Philippines.

CABO SAN LUCAS -- On June 11, 1602, the fleet took haven in the harbor at Cabo San Lucas. Here they found a large number of Indians with whom they developed friendly relations. The expedition map shows a small lagoon of sweet water at or near where the dredged inner harbor is located today. They found extensive piles of mother-of-pearl shells on the beach and fishes of many species were easy to catch in the bay.

Many of today's sailors take frequent refuge in the Whale Bar at the Hotel Finisterra. What they often see from this vantage point is the Pacific ocean laced with whitecaps resulting from NW winds that prevail along Baja's western coast. At the same time the harbor on the other side of the hotel is well protected. This situation is exactly what Vizcaino encountered.

The fleet departed from the harbor five times before it was able to make any progress up the coast into the NW winds. To make matters worse, they knew that if they waited for southerly winds before leaving, they would find themselves pinned within the confines of the harbor on a lee shore. The fleet was finally able to extract itself on July 5 after a stay of almost a month.

BAHIA MAGDALENA -- After leaving Cabo San Lucas the three ships of the fleet became separated and did not come together again until reaching Isla Cedros. A fortunate byproduct of this situation was that each of the vessels searched out different segments of the coast. Vizcaino himself entered Bahia Magdalena. The smaller of the three ships, the *Tres Reyes*, followed Ulloa's path and penetrated the southern end of this waterway through the Rehusa Channel. Upon joining Vizcaino in the main bay, this vessel was assigned to search it out in more detail. The result was a chart which unmistakably outlines the principal features of the area.

One of the larger vessels anchored off the mouth of one of the entrances to the long coastal lagoon north of Bahia Magdalena. Large numbers of Indians beckoned to them from the beaches. Attempts to land were made in small boats but the way was blocked by shoal water and breakers. They also encountered large numbers of whales and feared of being capsized when these animals came up from below. The crew was assigned to keep up a continual noise with bells, basins, and other instruments to frighten the animals. These conditions would correspond exactly with those one would encounter today.

North of the lagoons the expedition's charts show unmistakable renditions of the anchorages at Abreojos, Asuncion, and Isla San Roque. The written record also provides vivid descriptions of the multi-colored bands of rock clearly visible to today's mariner along Morro Hermoso south of Bahia San Bartolome.

BAHIA SAN BARTOLOME -- Vizcaino's vessel entered Bahia San Bartolome (Bahia Tortugas) on August 23. Land parties were sent ashore to search for wood and water, but none were found for this is one of the driest portions of the Baja peninsula. Today, Bahia Tortugas is the principal stopover point for vessels plying Baja's Pacific coast, and it is the best natural harbor for such vessels. Its dry environment, however, caused it to be quickly rejected as a port of refuge in the 17th century.

ISLA CEDROS -- The first of the three vessels arrived at Isla Cedros on August 19. The others followed on August 31. Considerable rejoicing followed as the crews had not seen each other for hundreds of miles. The smaller vessel was dispatched to circumnavigate the island and a scouting party was sent inland. They noted the large pines and cedars on the high mountains. The most important discovery was a rivulet of water flowing into the sea near the north end of the island on the east side. Wagner believes it to be the same water source used by Ulloa some 62 years prior.

North of Isla Cedros the vessels again became separated. Their combined efforts resulted in a larger number of coastal points being visited than would have resulted from a single ship, but much time was dissipated in searching for one another. There is considerable confusion in the historical record, however, resulting from several different eyewitness reports and the differences in place names.

BAHIA SAN QUINTIN -- Two of the three vessels anchored in Bahia San Quintin. Soundings at the mouth of the bay indicated three fathoms of water and the smaller *Tres Reyes* entered the inner harbor. Inside they found large numbers of naked Indians who fished from reed canoes. The Indians showed them fresh water wells. Clearly the expedition was fulfilling its objective of searching out the principal anchorages in detail. The vessels left Bahia San Quintin on October 20 where they were again joined by the third ship.

BAHIA COLONET -- The fleet anchored in the bay under Cabo Colonet on October 28. Here the native Indians taunted the Spaniards and the soldiers fired upon them. One report indicates that several of the Indians were killed.

Continuing on they saw the large ensenada (Bahia Todos Santos) along which the city of Ensenada is now built. They noted that it was guarded on the west by two small islands (Islas Todos Santos). Because of the nature of the wind it was decided to bypass this area and visit it on the return trip. The record clearly describes the Islas Coronados to the north.

SAN DIEGO -- On November 10, 1602 the fleet anchored off a fine port which they named San Diego. Vizcaino ordered his men to ascend a small hill that protected the port from the NW wind. From atop this hill, Point Loma, they could view "a port very capacious, good, large, and safe, and it was protected from all winds". Here it was decided to clean and repair the ships, and to take on wood and water. Again they were met by many Indians.

The expedition reports note that the land was fertile, level and with very fine meadows, but they were most pleased with the "extensiveness, capacity, and security of the port, its good depth and its many fishes". Here they remained until November 20.

NORTH FROM SAN DIEGO -- The fleet sailed north to the harbor at Monterey. They stopped at Santa Catalina Island and passed through the Santa Barbara Channel en route. From Monterey, one of the vessels was dispatched back to Acapulco with a full report of what had been learned. Vizcaino continued north to the vicinity of Cape Mendocino. Here he also turned south, and reached Acapulco on March 21, 1603.

CONCLUSION -- The area surrounding Monterey was described in Vizcaino's reports in even more glowing tones than was San Diego. Vizcaino recommended that a colony be established here. A royal order was actually issued to undertake such a settlement but the Viceroys in New Spain argued against it. They noted that the Philippine galleons were only 25-30 days from Acapulco when touching the North American coast and that a supply point here would not materially affect the outcome of their voyages. Also, most of these vessels made their landfall considerably south of Monterey.

Whatever the reasons, the potential of San Diego and Monterey soon faded from memory. They were not to be settled by the Spanish for more than 160 years. When this did occur, it was too late to implant Spanish influence with sufficient strength to stem the tide of English-speaking peoples who moved west across what is now the United States. The result was the eventual annexation of these lands into this country. Certainly the delay in settlement altered the course of North American history in a major way. The inhospitable barrier imposed by the Baja peninsula had to have been a major reason for lack of action by the Spanish.

SCURVY

As noted, one of Vizcaino's ships was dispatched home to Acapulco from Monterey. A principal reason for this action was that the great majority of the crew was suffering from advanced symptoms of scurvy and many had already died. The returning vessel was little more than a hospital ship. Most of the sick died before reaching Acapulco. Only three able-bodied men were aboard when the ship made port. These and six others were the only survivors.

Vizcaino and the two remaining ships turned south a few weeks later. When they reached the vicinity of Cabo San Lucas a decision was made to sail due east to seek shelter behind the small islands that adjoin the present city of Mazatlan. It was felt that the men could not survive the few remaining days required to make it south to Acapulco.

Upon reaching the desired anchorage, only Vizcaino and three soldiers were able to perform any duty. This group rowed ashore and wandered about aimlessly for several days in search of a road to an inland town. They were eventually found by the operator of a mule train who transported them to the town and the needed supplies. Upon returning to his ships, Vizcaino found that his crew had rapidly regained their health as the result of eating an agave-like fruit found growing on the islands. The supplies Vizcaino brought added to the recovery process. Today we know that scurvy is the result of a serious deficiency of the vitamins contained in fresh fruits and vegetables.

A total of nineteen days was spent at anchor at Mazatlan. When the two ships did return to Acapulco the men were in a reasonable state of health.

The account of Vizcaino's voyage made by Father Antonio de la Ascension provides us with a vivid first hand description of the symptoms of scurvy. It is not a pleasant thing to digest, but I present it below. Having read it, we modern sailors can become more appreciative of the sacrifices made by the early explorers.

It was to be eighty years after the Vizcaino expedition until a serious attempt was made to establish a colony on the Baja peninsula. This effort occurred in 1683 and ultimately led to the founding of the first permanent settlement at Loreto on the Sea of Cortez. The history of these events is presented in Volume II of this book.

SCURVY

WHAT FOLLOWS IS A FIRST-HAND ACCOUNT OF THE SYMPTOMS OF SCURVY AS RECOUNTED BY FATHER ANTONIO DE LA ASCENSION IN HIS LOG OF THE 1602-03 VOYAGE OF SEBASTIAN VIZCAINO.

"The first symptom is a pain in the whole body which makes it so sensitive that whatever touches it causes so much vexation and peevishness that there is no relief except with cries and groans. After this, all the body, especially from the waist down, becomes covered with purple spots larger than great mustard seeds. Then from this bad humor some stripes or bands come behind the knee joints, two fingers and more wide of the same blue or purple color, which extend through the thigh to the calves of the legs. These become as hard as stones, and the thighs become so straight and stiff that they cannot be extended or drawn up a degree more than the state in which they were when attacked. Then all the leg and thigh becomes purple, and after this it extends and spreads over the whole body, attacking mostly the shoulders. With this the whole body becomes stiff, and sore as a boil. It attacks the back and kidneys so

that one cannot move or turn from one side to the other, being just as in shackles.

The sensitiveness of the bodies of these sick people is so great that the very clothing put on them is felt like sharp darts or cruel lances. The upper and lower gums of the mouth become swollen to such a size that neither the teeth nor the molars can be brought together. The teeth become so loose and without support that they move while moving the head. There have been persons who have in expectorating spat out unexpectedly a couple teeth at a time. With this they cannot eat anything but food in liquid form. Those who are attacked by this disease come to be so weakened that their natural vigor fails them, and they die all of a sudden. Some died while talking, others while sleeping and were found dead in the morning, and others while sitting up in their beds and eating."

CHAPTER 5
NATURAL HISTORY

Whole books can be devoted to the subjects discussed in this chapter. What is presented here is but a brief summary of material of particular interest to the boater. Only a relative few species of plants and animals are included, but these are among the more common and interesting ones encountered near the Pacific shore. Many boaters will find their voyage to Baja waters considerably enhanced by taking along books specializing on the subjects in question. Several of these are available through the BAJA BOOKSHELF in the Appendix.

PLANTS

BAJA'S PLANT REGIONS -- There are three vegetative regions in the Baja peninsula. (These are shown on a map in my book *The Magnificent Peninsula*.) Briefly they are:

1 CALIFORNIA REGION -- This region is a continuation of the vegetational communities found to the north in the United States. The principal plants are a number of densely growing shrubs commonly referred to as chaparral. Along the Pacific coast, this region extends southward to the mouth of the Rio del Rosario near the southern end of the Northern Reach.

2 SONORAN DESERT REGION -- The Sonoran Desert Region is a true desert, as rainfall averages less than 10 inches per year. Most of this precipitation comes in the winter months which is when the desert plants bloom and put out their foliage. The region extends southward from the Rio del Rosario to the vicinity of Todos Santos near the middle of the Southern Bight.

3 THE CAPE REGION -- South of Todos Santos, rainfall occurs mostly in the summer as the result of high intensity tropical storms. Total precipitation is above the level associated with a true desert. Many of the plants common to the Sonoran Desert are still present but the overall vegetational density is much higher. Desert plants are also joined by a variety of low-spreading trees.

DESERT VEGETATION -- The desert, or near-desert vegetation, of the Sonoran Desert and Cape Region covers some 80 percent of the Baja peninsula. Eminent botanists have described these areas as con-

taining the most varied and interesting arid-land vegetation in the world. Certainly I have seen nothing to match them anywhere in North America. Many of the most outstanding plants are in view from the peninsula's main highways. *The Magnificent Peninsula* contains a full chapter on the desert and its vegetation. But for the serious amateur plant lover, Norman Robert's *A Field Guide to the Plants of Baja California* is a must (See the BAJA BOOKSHELF and the notice on page51).

Unfortunately, most of the larger and more interesting plants grow at elevations considerably above sea level. Thus, relatively few are in view along Baja's Pacific coast. Where interesting plants are visible, this fact is pointed out at the appropriate place in PART II. Often binoculars will aid in identification. For close-up inspection, may I recommend the shore excursions presented in PART II for Isla San Martin, Isla Cedros (Punta Norte Area), and Isla Santa Magdalena at Bahia Santa Maria.

GIANT KELP -- Anyone familiar with the coastal waters of western United States and Canada will have seen abundant beds of giant kelp growing in the ocean. There are several genera and species of these plants in temperate ocean waters world-wide. The species present along Baja's Pacific shore is *Macrocystis Pyrifera*.

DESCRIPTION -- Amazingly, giant kelp is an algae. It is thus related to thousands of other species of green, fresh, and salt water species, many of which are composed of only a single cell. In contrast, giant kelp will grow to heights of 130 feet. It is one of a group of plants called brown algae, where the green chlorophyll is masked by a golden-brown pigment called *fuco-xanthin*.

Giant kelp has four basic structural parts. These are: (1) A root-like <u>holdfast</u> which fastens the plant to the ocean bottom. (2) A stem-like <u>stipe</u>. (3) Round gas-filled <u>bladders or floats</u> which give the plant buoyancy. (4) Leaf-like <u>blades</u>. The float lies between the stipe and the blades.

When kelp has been dislodged from the bottom, all of these parts will be seen floating on the ocean surface, sometimes in sizeable, dense masses up to 50 feet across. The floating, upturned holdfast appears much like the antlers of a deer. These accumulations can be a hazard to the propellers and rudders of most ocean cruising vessels and the helmsperson needs to be alert to their presence, even at a considerable distance from the shore.

RANGE AND LIMITS -- *Macrocystis pyrifera* flourishes between Oceanside, CA. (50 miles north of the U. S. / Mexican border) , and Punta San Hipolito near the lower extremity of the Middle Reach. There is no other species of kelp in this area, and there is no kelp of any kind along the peninsular shore south of Punta San

Hipolito, or in the Sea of Cortez. Kelp does poorly in water temperatures above 20 degrees centigrade. The ocean south of Punta Hipolito is consistently warmer than this limit and is thus an unsuitable habitat.

Giant kelp grows only in relatively shallow water. The inner limit is controlled by wave action. Plants will grow in waters only 6 to 9 feet in depth in the lee of a protecting point, but 15 to 30 feet is more common along the open coast. The outer limit is controlled by light intensity as new plants need a certain level of illumination to become established on the bottom. In turbid coastal waters the most common outer depth is 45 to 60 feet. Depths of 75 to 90 feet may be observed in the clearer waters often present around islands. The outer edge of a kelp bed is usually sharply defined, while the inner limit is more diffuse.

PERIODIC FLUCTUATIONS -- The U. S. nautical charts indicate the presence of extensive kelp beds at many locations along the Pacific coast and its offshore islands. During my first circumnavigation of the peninsula, I observed little or no kelp in these areas. Many more plants were seen during the second voyage. This periodic variation is well recorded in the scientific literature which reports that "kelp beds undergo periods of luxuriance, followed by thinning or perhaps complete disappearance, returning again at a later time." This fluctuation is the result of several factors, the most common of which is the destruction of the plant's hold-

fasts by grazing sea urchins. Also, severe storms may generate surf conditions that have a devistating effect on kelp beds.

Coastal cruising vessels can be readily navigated through kelp bed areas when few plants are present. However, propellers and rudders can be quickly fouled in these same places during luxuriant periods. Vegetative parts can also be sucked into a vessel's salt water cooling system.

KELP HARVESTING -- The upper portions of kelp plants are regularly gathered by selfpropelled, square-ended vessels supporting cutting and gathering devices on their bows. Cruisers will often see the Mexican kelp barge *El Sargacero* in the Ensenada harbor, or at work along the coast. The harvest is delivered to processing plants in San Diego. The principal products obtained are potassium, and kelp meal for nutritional supplements used in human and animal foods. Dried kelp is also used as fertilizer.

Studies in U. S. waters indicate that heavy harvesting does not appear to affect the long-term productivity of kelp beds. The inshore waters are always laden with reproductive bodies and the species reproduces readily.

ANIMALS

Baja's Pacific coast offers the mariner an outstanding opportunity to observe marine mammals and birds. Large birds will be your almost constant companions, and I cannot recall a day spent cruising this shore when one or more marine mammals has not paid a visit. First the mammals, for after all, *we are one*.

MARINE MAMMALS -- Mammals are, of course, air breathing, the highest class of vertebrates and nourish their young with milk from the female's mammary glands. Several such animals are discussed below. I'm sure zoologists will be horrified at what is to follow, but for practical purposes, these creatures may be roughly classified as follows:

(1) Whales, Dolphins, and Porpoises -- Fish-like, except that the tail fluke is horizontal rather than vertical as with the true fishes. Never leave the water. Periodically break the water surface to breathe through a blowhole located on the top of the head.

(2) Seals and Sea Lions -- Streamlined bodies but clearly not fish-like in appearance. Front and hind limbs developed into flippers. Haul out on land to rest and give birth to young.

(3) Sea Otter -- A one-time land mammal with true legs, now adapted to living in the ocean. Closely related to such mammals as weasels, martens, wolverines, etc.

The massive back of a California gray whale in the lagoon inside Boca de Soledad in the Middle Reach.

CALIFORNIA GRAY WHALE -- In recent years, there has been wide public interest concerning whales in general and the California gray whale in particular. The Baja peninsula plays a prominent part in this gigantic animal's life history, as it is Baja's Pacific lagoons that are the destination of the whale's annual southern migration. The gray's basic characteristics are briefly described in an insert on this page.

It was recently estimated that there are some 17,000 gray whales. This population spends the summer months feeding in the Bering and Chukchi Seas off Alaska. Starting in October, they begin their annual southern migration to the subtropical waters of coastal

GRAY WHALE CHARACTERISTICS	
THE ANIMAL	A true mammal. Air breathing. Warm blooded. Nurse young on milk.
ADULTS	Length, 30 to 50 ft. Weight 20 to 40 tons. Avg. age 30 to 40 years, occasionaly 60.
CALVES	Length 15 ft., weight 1.5 tons at birth. Consume 50 gal. of milk, gain 60 to 70 lbs. daily.
MIGRATION	Travel 20 hours & 100 miles per day. Trip of 6,000 miles takes 6 to 8 weeks.
COLOR	Slate gray caused by natural pigments, barnacles, and barnacle scars.

lagoons from Laguna Guerrero Negro southward to Bahia Magdalena. Here the calves are born.

The whale migration route is close to shore as the gray is a bottom feeder. The best available evidence suggests that they follow the bottom contours at the depth they prefer. Ocean cruisers sailing in these same waters will frequently be in company with the migration. During my early voyages to Baja, many whale spouts were seen, but with the engine running, it was rarely possible to approach closely enough to see the actual animal. On my most recent trip this was easily done, and the course often had to be altered in the interest of safety. One can readily conclude that the whales are becoming accustomed to the approach of vessels and avoid sounding until the last minute. I have also observed whales swimming about my anchored boat on several occasions.

Reference to the ANNUAL MIGRATION CYCLE Chart will disclose that the several migration phases overlap each other. Some individuals are still arriving in Baja while others are already heading back north. Pregnant females, well into their 12-month gestation period, leave Alaska early with their mission clearly in mind. Others lag behind while males and in-season females court and mate on the way south.

By December, the whales begin arriving in the waters off northern Baja. By mid-January, most females have arrived at their destinations in the backwaters of the lagoons where most of the calving takes place. The return north occurs in somewhat reverse order. The newly pregnant females and other *single* whales begin north, starting in February, while the new mothers and their calves linger behind, occasionally as late as May and June. As a result, there are whales in Baja waters from December to June.

```
┌─────────────────────────────────────────────┐
│              APRIL   CALIFORNIA               │
│          A   MAY     GRAY  WHALE              │
│          L   JUNE                             │
│  ARCTIC  A   JULY    ANNUAL                   │
│  FEEDING S   AUG     MIGRATION CYCLE          │
│          K   SEPT                             │
│          A   OCT                              │
│              NOV                              │
│              DEC                              │
│          B   JAN     SOUTHERN                 │
│          A   FEB     MIGRATION                │
│  CALVING J   MARCH                            │
│  SEASON  A   APRIL   NORTHERN                 │
│              MAY     MIGRATION                │
│              JUNE                             │
│              JULY                             │
└─────────────────────────────────────────────┘
```

COMMON DOLPHIN -- By far the most frequent marine mammal to be encountered in Baja waters is the common dolphin. It is a rare day of sailing when at least one group of these animals does not pay a visit. I say "pay a visit", because dolphins frequently seek out vessels and frolic about on all sides. Many times they will take turns breaking the surface directly in front of the bow. Observing these antics from the pulpit is one of the great joys of ocean cruising. Most encounters are with groups of from 2 to 20 dolphins. On occasions, herds of several hundred will be seen hell-bent for someplace. In these instances, they seem to be too preoccupied to stop and visit.

On two occasions I have observed what I believe to have been a dall porpoise (black with a large white area across the belly and part way up the sides). The thousands of other visitors have been the common dolphin. In contrast to the porpoise, the dolphin has a pronounced beak. Near the middle of its back is a dorsal fin with a curvature toward the tail. This fin can initially mislead one into thinking they are viewing a shark. (I have never seen a shark fin in Baja waters. There is an occasional thresher shark where what appears to be the dorsal fin is actually the tip of the elongated tail moving back and forth as the animal swims.) The dolphin is 6 1/2 to 8 1/2 feet in length. The back and flippers are black, the flanks are yellowish, and the belly white. Around each eye is a white ring connected across the upper beak by two white lines.

CALIFORNIA SEA LION -- The California sea lion is also frequently encountered in Baja waters. The male has a high forehead. When the head is projecting above the water surveying your boat, it looks for all the world like the family dog lost at sea. A continual honking bark emanating from rookery areas is characteristic. The species is the most vocal of all the seals and sea lions. The male sea lion is about 8 feet in length, females 5 1/2 to 6 feet. When dry, the fur is various shades of yellow-brown, but wet animals are a much darker brown. When viewing a group of sea lions on shore, this color difference can lead one into thinking that two distinct species are present.

The California sea lion travels along much of the United States west coast, but most breeding occurs in the southern end of the U. S. Channel Islands, on Baja's Pacific coast, and in the Sea of Cortez. The southern extremity of the range is on the Mexican mainland about 100 miles south of the peninsula's tip, and in the Galapagos Islands.

Thousands of sea lions were killed for their oil and fur between 1860 and 1870. Charles Scammon's famous book on marine mammals predicted the animals would soon be exterminated along California shores. Fortunately this did not occur, and in 1979 scientists estimated the total population at 145,000. Of these, 46 percent populated Baja's Pacific coast, 18 percent the Sea of Cortez, and 36 percent southern California waters in the United States.

Boaters will see the sea lion in three situations. (1) By far the largest number of animals can be viewed in rookeries located on rocky islets and promontories. Many of these are pointed out in PART II. By far the largest and best viewing area on Baja's Pacific coast is on the shingle beaches lying south of the Punta Norte fish camp on Isla Cedros. (2) The male is known to migrate along the coast, and vessels at sea will often encounter individual animals many miles from shore. They normally dive when one's vessel comes closer than about 100 feet. (3) Occasionally mariners will see a small group of sea lions resting on the sea surface with their flippers projecting skyward. A cautious skipper can initially believe that this is some form of floating wreckage which needs to be avoided. Experience will tell that it is only some friendly *sea puppies* taking the sun.

Two elephant seals playing in a tide-pool on Isla San Jeronimo.

ELEPHANT SEAL -- Baja's Pacific shore supports two species of marine mammals classified as true seals. The lack of protruding external ears is one of their characteristics. They cannot stand raised on their fore-flippers as can the California sea lion. They thus hump themselves caterpillar-like along the beach. The elephant seal and harbor seal are both true seals.

The elephant seal is the largest marine mammal in the northern hemisphere. World-wide it is exceeded in size only by the southern elephant seal. The males reach 15 to 18 feet in length. At 8 to 9 feet, the females are much smaller, and this marked difference in size is readily apparent when viewing a group of seals on the beach. Old males have large, overhanging proboscis-

HUNTING THE GRAY WHALE

Aggressive hunting of the California gray whale by Yankee and European whalers began in 1845 and continued for 45 years until 1890. Populations were then so depressed that hunting was largely abandoned. The species was again subjected to slaughter starting 25 years later when steam and diesel powered boats became available. The gray was finally given complete legal protection in 1946 when it was declared a depleted and endangered species.

The gray whale was tracked down using three different techniques: (1) The females were taken in the shallow waters of the calving lagoons. (2) Whaling ships offshore sought animals in the open ocean, in kelp beds close to shore, and in the breakers off the calving lagoons. (3) Some eighteen shore stations were established at various locations. Three of these at Punta Banda, Punta Santo Tomas and Punta Eugenia were in Baja California. Shore whaling lasted from 1851 until 1901.

Pacific Ocean whaling vessels normally spent the spring and fall near the Hawaiian Islands, and the

summer in the north Pacific. This left them unoccupied during the winter months. When the migratory pattern and calving grounds of the gray whale were discovered, the whalers filled in this *between the seasons* period off the California coasts in pursuit of this species.

Most of the whaling captains and officers were Americans, but the crews were Hawaiian. In contrast, the shore stations were manned by Portuguese from the Azores and Cape Verde Islands. Most of these men had small farms in California and went whaling to fill in the winter season.

Hunting pressure reduced the gray whale population to a few thousand in 1946. Once protected however, the species made a remarkable recovery to what approximates the original population level. Much of this success may be attributed to the fact that mates are easily located because of the coastal migration pattern, and the concentration of the females in the calving lagoons. (Sort of a singles-bar arrangement for whales.)

like snouts which remind one of an elephant's trunk. My experience is that they are far less vocal than the California sea lion, but when the male is defending his turf, his snorts and clap-like sound are quite distinctive.

This large species was hunted almost to extinction from about 1818 to 1896. The population was reduced to less than 100 animals, all living on Isla Guadalupe which is located 160 miles off the Baja coast west of Punta Baja. It then staged a remarkable comeback. In Baja, Islas San Benitos were repopulated in 1918, Islas los Coronados in 1948, and Isla Cedros in 1965. There are also colonies at seven locations along the U. S. shore-line. (I personally observed elephant seals on Isla San Jeronimo in 1987.) In 1976, the total number of animals was estimated at almost 48,000 individuals. By 1988 the population was near 100,000. The Islas San Benitos population is by far the largest on the islands discussed in this book.

The species is migratory to the extent of an annual movement from unknown feeding grounds at sea, to the specific rookery site where each animal was born. The males arrive late in November. They may enter the water but are not believed to feed. The females arrive a few weeks later, give birth, nurse their pups, come into season again, copulate, and depart. They rarely enter the water while at the rookeries.

Islas San Benitos is the best place to observe the elephant seal. Groups will be seen resting in small coves and beaches at many places. Their obvious sedentary behavior is explained by the annual cycle noted above. It is in marked contrast to the hustle and bustle evident at California sea lion rookeries. The elephant seal may be observed by approaching the resting areas in small boats. These areas may also be approached by land on Isla San Benitos Oeste. Considerable care should be taken not to disturb the animals. Usually the large males seem to be sound asleep, but the smaller animals obviously become aware of human presence. If the seals head for the water, you are probably the cause.

HARBOR SEAL -- The other seal found along Baja's Pacific coast is the harbor seal. At only 5 feet in length, they are also the smallest. There is no appreciable size difference between the sexes. This is the spotted seal. Their color is yellowish with brown spots, or brown with yellowish spots. This animal frequents protected bodies of water such as lagoons and river mouths. They are probably the least vocal of all marine mammals.

The largest colony of harbor seals on Baja shores is in the small lagoon near Caleta Hassler on Isla de San Martin. There is also a lesser number of animals on Isla Asuncion. This latter group is at the southernmost extremity of the animal's range.

The literature also notes that harbor seals are easily frightened into the water . This characteristic is readily observable. I have approached the Isla de San Martin lagoon on two occasions, once by land and once by sea. In both instances the seals were off the beach and into the water before I was aware of their presence. Most of the herd promptly moved into the open ocean, popped their heads above water, and watched me intently. The area obviously needs to be approached slowly and low to the ground, or not at all.

SEA OTTER -- This presentation of marine mammals comes to a close with the discussion of an animal that is unfortunately no longer present in Baja. At one time there were extensive colonies of this animal in the U. S. Channel Islands and along Baja's Pacific shore south to

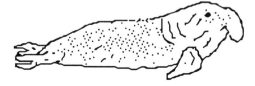

Morro Hermoso along the Middle Reach. This southern terminus of the original range corresponded closely with the southern limit of the kelp beds. Kelp appears to be an important element in the animal's environment.

As with many marine mammals, the sea otter was hunted almost to extinction. Early hunting occurred during the period 1784 to 1790. Spanish authorities needed products to take to the orient on their Acapulco-to-Manila galleons. The otter was seized upon to fill this need. Indians were enticed into capturing the animals, and the pelts were then taken to the missions for transportation to San Diego. From there they were shipped to San Blas on Mexico's mainland shore. Pelts were then moved overland to Mexico City where they were dressed. The next legs of the journey saw the finished furs being carried to Acapulco, and thence by sea to the Philippine Islands. Here they were traded for quick silver needed in the gold and silver mines in the Mexican Highlands.

Here a group of brown pelicans await the arrival of fishing boats at the marina in Cabo San Lucas. Frequently, as here, they are accompanied by sea gulls ever hopeful that one of the pelicans will drop a portion of its meal.

The sea otter was thought to be extinct in the Californias until they were rediscovered south of Monterey in 1938. The population is now recovering rapidly along the central California coast, and it is not inconceivable to conclude that sea otters might again find their way south of the border. However, the odds seem heavily against this occurring.

The sea otter is purely and simply, a glutton. Because the animals lack subcutaneous fat, they must eat 20 to 25 percent of their body weight each day to maintain themselves. Much of this nourishment comes from several species of shellfish eagerly sought by both amateur and commercial fishermen. In the United States, the conflict between these people and the otters is won by the otters, under the watchful eye of environmentalists and the long arm of the law. Mexican fishermen are wonderful, friendly people, but I am confident that any otters they encounter would promptly find themselves in the stew pot.

In any case, mariners might keep alert for otters in Baja and report any sightings to the California Department of Fish and Game. If one sees a four-legged, furry animal swimming on its back, and eating its meal from atop its belly, it has to be a sea otter.

BIRDS

Many people have an interest in birds, but find that they do not have the time or inclination to trudge out to the forest, field, or marsh in search of these often elusive creatures. And if one does make this effort, it often proves unrewarding, as our feathered friends were out

to lunch that day. In total contrast, bird life in Baja's coastal areas is prolific. And, one does not have to seek them out, for if you are boating, you are already there. The birds will find you. Of equal importance, these are not of the titmouse and chickadee variety, but large, easy-to-spot species with wingspans up to 8 feet. And they are in plain sight, in the air or on the ocean surface, without vegetative hiding places. They may dive for a while, but what goes down must come up. So why not go bird watching in Baja?

Binoculars are of course very helpful, but any vessel taken to sea should already have a pair . A good book on seabirds is also most helpful. My recommendation in this regard are contained in a notice on page 60. For those who do not avail themselves of this opportunity, here are brief discussions of four of the larger species found along Baja's Pacific coast.

BROWN PELICAN -- Here is a bird assembled by a committee from leftover parts (See Photo). While the overall conformation is unmistakable, the plumage has considerable variation, which could lead one to suspect there is more than one species in Baja. Not so. During the bird's first year it has a white belly and brown head, neck, back, and wings. The adult has a black belly with gray back and wings, while the head and neck change color seasonally from yellow to white, and then white to black. The wingspan is 6 1/2 to 7 1/2 feet.

The brown pelican was in danger of extinction in many locations because DDT contamination was making the egg shells so thin that reproduction was drastically reduced. Elimination of this chemical has allowed the species to make a major comeback. Breeding takes place in rookeries in the Sea of Cortez, but the bird is plentiful along both coasts of the Baja peninsula. The pelican will closely approach a cruising vessel to look things over, and will be driven into the water from the sea only if one's craft is on a near collision course. You will have no trouble finding pelicans.

MAGNIFICENT FRIGATEBIRD -- The magnificent thing about the magnificent frigatebird is its ability to fly. The species has the greatest wing area in proportion to weight of any living bird, and is one of the most aerial of all sea birds. Its wingspan is from 7 to 8 feet. This aerial ability is sorely needed, as frigates can neither swim nor walk. They are helpless if they light on the water and cannot become airborne except from a tree, cliff or similar lofty position. For this reason they are frequently seen perched on the rigging of commercial fishing boats.

The male frigatebird is totally black. The female is black with a white breast, while immature birds display all white heads and underparts. The tail is deeply scissor-like and the wings have a swept back design. The normal range is limited to the southern portion of Baja's Pacific shore and in the Sea of Cortez. I have found them particularly prevalent near Punta Tosca south of Bahia Magdalena.

A trivia question is appropriate concerning the frigate-bird. "Why does a prudent sailboat skipper keep a hammer in the cockpit area in Mexican waters?" Answer, when over the open ocean the frigate can become fatigued because he cannot settle down to rest on the water. The top of one's mast presents an inviting pit stop. In addition to the obvious sewage disposal problems, I don't care to have Senor Frigate up there because on two occasions they have damaged my wind indicator. Banging on the base of the mast with a hammer helps discourage their settling, although they don't take no for an answer without repeated passes.

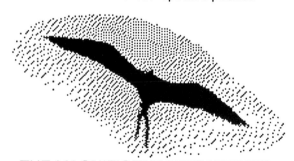

THE MAGNIFICENT FRIGATEBIRD

BROWN BOOBY -- Brown boobies are good flyers, but their outstanding feature is a spectacular dive. When the pelican dives, it looks like somebody pushed a mail sack out of an airplane, and the dive ends with a un-seemly splash on the water surface. In contrast, the booby's streamlined, spindle-shaped body drops from dizzing heights, enters the water with little or no effort,

and pursues its prey beneath the surface. Their favorite food is the flying fish. Boats passing through the water often disturb these fish, so boobies may follow your vessel ever watchful for a meal.

The booby has a wingspan of 4 to 5 feet. The body is uniformly brown except that the underparts behind the wings are white. The separation between the brown and white is very sharp so that the bird appears to be wearing a brown hood. The range is normally in the southern portion of Baja's Pacific coast and the Sea of Cortez.

Booby does not sound like a complementary name. It is not. It is derived from the Spanish word *bobo*, meaning stupid, or dunce. When the bird alights on the deck of a ship, or is approached on land, it can be easily caught by hand. Early-day sailors bestowed the bird with its name because of this behavior.

CORMORANT -- If you see a group of large black birds flying rapidly within a few feet of the water surface, they have to be cormorants. There are several species, but the distinctions are beyond the scope of this book. The cormorant will be seen all along both coasts of the Baja peninsula. The birds will often be seen roosting in a straight vertical position on ledges along rocky shores.

This brief listing is but an appetite wetter. Please consider taking a good bird identification book with you to Baja so as to add a frosting of enjoyment to your sea-borne adventure.

COASTAL GEOLOGY

What follows is a brief review of the geology of the Baja peninsula, with particular reference to features which will be encountered along the Pacific coast. A full chapter on geology is contained in my book *The Magnificent Peninsula*.

GEOLOGIC PROVINCES -- The Baja peninsula embraces three geologic provinces as shown on a chart in this chapter. Two of these are in view along the Pacific shore. Most of Baja's mountains are in the Peninsular Range Province, with the main backbone ridge rimming the Sea of Cortez shore. The upper half of the Pacific coast is formed by lower mountains on the western side of this province. This mountainous terrain is briefly interrupted by a section of the low-lying Continental Borderlands Province (Valle de Camalu and Valle de San Quintin).

The topography of the southern half of the Pacific coast is essentially the reverse of that found to the north, that is, level plains of the Continental Borderlands Province predominate, with only brief interruptions by isolated ranges of mountains (Sierra Vizcaino, Sierra Magdalena,

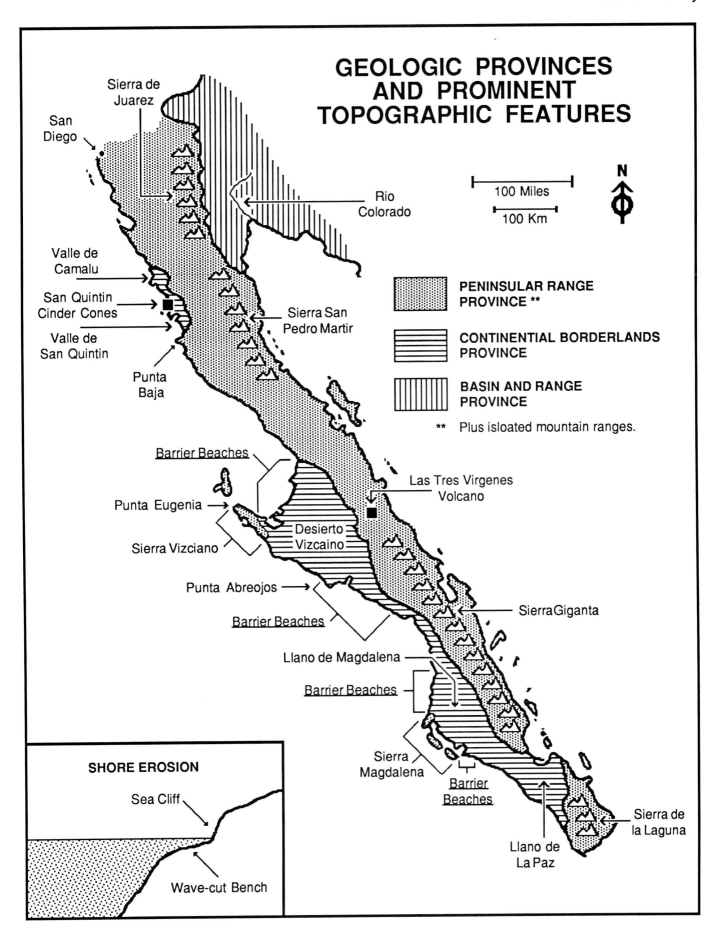

GEOLOGIC PROVINCES AND PROMINENT TOPOGRAPHIC FEATURES

Sierra de Juarez

San Diego

Rio Colorado

100 Miles
100 Km

N

Valle de Camalu

San Quintin Cinder Cones

Sierra San Pedro Martir

Valle de San Quintin

Punta Baja

	PENINSULAR RANGE PROVINCE **
	CONTINENTIAL BORDERLANDS PROVINCE
	BASIN AND RANGE PROVINCE

** Plus isloated mountain ranges.

Barrier Beaches

Las Tres Virgenes Volcano

Punta Eugenia

Desierto Vizcaino

Sierra Vizciano

Punta Abreojos

Barrier Beaches

Sierra Giganta

Llano de Magdalena

Barrier Beaches

Sierra Magdalena

Barrier Beaches

Sierra de la Laguna

Llano de La Paz

SHORE EROSION

Sea Cliff

Wave-cut Bench

and Sierra de la Laguna). Sizeable sections of these lowlands are fronted by linear lagoons and barrier beaches (see below). As can be seen from the chart, a far larger proportion of the Sea of Cortez coast contains mountainous topography than does the Pacific side.

SHORE CURRENTS AND DEPOSITION -- As stressed in Chapter 3, the prevailing wind and swell impacts Baja's Pacific coast at an angle from the NW. The result is a southward trending current close offshore. This current carries quantities of silt and sand. These materials are deposited in the bays SE of coastal promontories, as the waters in these areas are comparatively quiet and cannot support the sediment load. These are the same bays that are the principal anchorages along this coast. Consequently, their water depths are shallow. The 4 fathom anchoring position is frequently from 1/4 to 1/2 mile offshore. There are only a few exceptions to this situation such as at Puerto Santo Tomas and Punta Rompiente where deep water is found close to the rocky shore.

Shore currents also tend to deposit silt off the tips of promontories. It should also be stressed that most promontories are made up of ridges of relatively hard rock, and that these ridges invariably extend to sea below the surface. The combination of silt deposits and underwater rocks thus form underwater hazards off almost every promontory along the Baja shore. The U. S. Sailing Directions occasionally warns that a certain point should be given a wide berth. The wise skipper should make this advice a universal rule. In preparing this book I have frequently cruised far closer to shore than would normally be prudent, and constant attention to the depth sounder was required. I can thus assure you that an area of shallow water is almost universally present off the headlands along the Baja peninsula. Trust me on it, and stay clear. I have a picture of my vessel in dry-dock after one occasion where I failed to follow my own counsel.

BEACHES -- Beaches will be present along a wave-swept coast unless the waters immediately offshore are very deep. Deep water prevails along almost all of the mountainous terrain off Baja's Pacific shore. Thus, there are few extensive beaches in these areas. Most of those that are present are confined to the heads of bays. The materials making up these bay-head beaches are the same as those deposited in these same areas by the coastal currents noted above. Most of these beaches are composed of light colored, sand-sized particles. Beaches made up of small, rounded stones are referred to as shingle beaches.

Water depths off the low-lying Continental Borderlands Province are much shallower than in the mountainous areas. Thus, extensive beaches are present. Some of these stretch for scores of miles without interruption. In the lowest lying terrain these beaches are referred to as barrier beaches. They are build by wave action close to the coastline, from which they are separated by lagoons of shallow water. These barrier beaches are breached by shallow openings at various places. These openings allow passage of tidal currents, and are universally fronted by underwater bars upon which the sea breaks heavily. The chart in this chapter shows the four areas which are rimmed with this barrier beach topography.

SHORELINE EROSION -- Ocean waves are constantly wearing away the shore. Where the coastal slope is steep, waves erode sea cliffs. At the base of these cliffs, the waves also erode a surface sloping gently out to sea, called a wave-cut bench (See insert on the chart in this Chapter). Hundreds of miles of sea cliffs may be seen along the mountainous sections of Baja's Pacific coast. Where the seacoast has risen in elevation over geologic time, wave-cut benches may be seen traversing the mountain slopes above the present water line. A prominent example may be seen in the area north of Bahia Soledad in the Northern Reach.

Wave action tends to attack the ends of promontories more than other areas. Where some rock formations are softer than others, the less resistant areas give way first. This differential erosion often produces islands in these areas. Examples are found off Punta San Carlos, Punta Asuncion, Punta Rosalilita, and many other headlands. A preliminary stage in this erosional process may be the cutting of an arch at sea level. With the collapse of the roof a stack rock is separated from the shore. Examples of both of these phenomena are clearly in evidence at the tip of Cabo San Lucas.

CHAPTER 6
THE NORTHERN REACH (NORTH PORTION)
SAN DIEGO TO CABO PUNTA BANDA

CHAPTER SUMMARY

For two reasons, the coastal area described in this chapter is unique in all of Baja: (1) Recreational boating traffic consists largely of vessels being used in short duration excursions from metropolitan areas in the United States. It is in effect an extension of the United States boating world. Many stateside insurance policies indicate Ensenada as the southern terminus of their range of coverage. (2) Most of the coastal area is heavily urbanized, and in this regard it is little different from the U. S. shore to the north.

SECTION			DESCRIPTION
NO	FROM	TO	
A	San Diego Harbor		A fully enclosed harbor with urbanized shorelines and many boating facilities and anchorages.
B	San Diego	Bajamar	Gentle coastal topography backed by steeper mountains. Coast is heavily urbanized in most places.
C	Bajamar	Punta San Miguel	Steep coastal topography with little urbanization.
D	Punta San Miguel	Cabo Punta Banda	Most of this area is backed by a large, level, coastal plain. Much of it is heavily urbanized and includes the city of Ensenada.
E	Islas los Coronados		A group of four islands only a few miles south of the international border.
F	Islas de Todos Santos		Two islands guarding the western edge of Bahia Todos Santos. There is an anchorage on the east shore of the southerly island.

SECTION A
SAN DIEGO HARBOR

SAN DIEGO HARBOR APPROACH -- There are a variety of reasons why most ocean cruisers will choose to call at San Diego Harbor both going to and coming from the Baja peninsula. It is thus important to have some minimal knowledge of this port. Most features of interest to the Baja-bound mariner are located in the Shelter Island area.

San Diego is a busy port with a relatively narrow entrance. This channel can at times be shrouded in fog. At night there are such a myriad of lights ashore and on moving vessels that the unfamiliar skipper will have difficulty in locating the approach buoys and their lights.

To complicate matters, San Diego is the home of a sizeable portion of the United States Pacific Fleet and its associated air arms. As a result, you may find it necessary to share the approach channel and offshore area with sizeable naval ships and submarines, and at night you may encounter such vessels offshore illuminated by only minimal running lights; and be prepared to be buzzed by low flying helicopters and jet aircraft.

In spite of these complications, the San Diego channel can be easily entered. However, paying close attention to the various aids to navigation and the harbor charts is essential.

SHELTER ISLAND -- The destination of most visiting vessels bound for Baja will be the Shelter Island Municipal Yacht Harbor. When inbound, its entrance lies

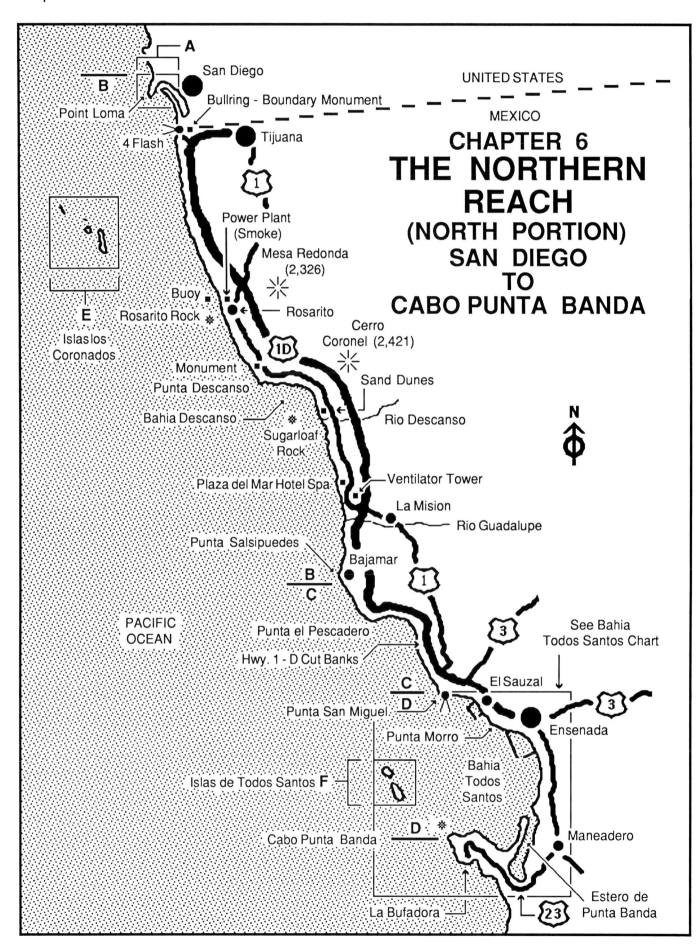

UNITED STATES

MEXICO

CHAPTER 6
THE NORTHERN REACH
(NORTH PORTION)
SAN DIEGO
TO
CABO PUNTA BANDA

San Diego

Bullring - Boundary Monument

Point Loma

4 Flash

Tijuana

1

Power Plant
(Smoke)

Mesa Redonda
(2,326)

Buoy

Rosarito Rock

Rosarito

Cerro
Coronel (2,421)

Islas los
Coronados

E

1D

Monument

Punta Descanso

Sand Dunes

Bahia Descanso

Rio Descanso

Sugarloaf
Rock

N

Plaza del Mar Hotel Spa

Ventilator Tower

La Mision

Rio Guadalupe

Punta Salsipuedes

Bajamar

B
C

1

3

PACIFIC
OCEAN

Punta el Pescadero

See Bahia
Todos Santos Chart

Hwy. 1 - D Cut Banks

El Sauzal

3

C
D

Punta San Miguel

Ensenada

Punta Morro

Islas de Todos Santos F

Bahia
Todos
Santos

Cabo Punta Banda

D

Maneadero

La Bufadora

23

Estero de
Punta Banda

on the left of the main harbor channel between buoy pairs 14-15 and 16-17, at a distance of about five miles from Point Loma.

On the southbound journey it is wise to top-off one's fuel tanks, to take care of last minute food, supply, and repair needs, and to obtain Mexican entrance papers and fishing licenses. Upon returning to the United States it is required that vessels clear with customs officers at the Harbor Police Dock. The location of the most important facilities are shown on the SHELTER ISLAND AREA Chart. Consider also the following additional items:

1 -- Vacant berths in San Diego's marinas are hard to find. Visiting vessels may stay at the guest docks adjoining, and administered by the harbor police on a first come-first served basis. A fee is charged and there is a maximum stay of 10 days. Space here is at a premium during the period October 15 to November 15 when many Baja bound boaters are laying over in San Diego.

2 -- Anchorage may be taken in 7 to 9 fathoms all along the SE face of Shelter Island. Holding ground is very good. I am advised that there is a problem in San Diego Harbor with vessels that are anchored on a long-term basis in this and other areas. Thus, some form of anchoring restrictions may be encountered by skippers visiting in the future.

3 -- City bus Number 29 may be boarded at the corner of Rosecrans and Shelter Island Drive. This bus proceeds directly to downtown San Diego, a trip of about six miles. The Mexican Consul and fishing license offices are in the downtown area. Lindbergh International Airport is located about halfway along this bus route.

4 -- Vessels inbound from Mexico should immediately tie up at the Harbor Police Dock and report to their office. The Harbor Police will arrange for customs officers to come to this location for the necessary inspection, or they may already be on hand.

If your vessel arrives after normal customs hours, you may pay for an after-hours inspection. (Normal working hours are 0800 to 1700 Monday through Saturday.) Should you care to wait for regular working hours, you may be permitted to spend the intervening time at the Harbor Police Dock, or you may be required to tie up at one of the nearby *quarantine* buoys.

The Harbor Police operation is courteous, but rather militaristic. When returning from Baja, the contrast in styles between this staff and most of the Mexicans you have met will be a stimulating reintroduction to the northern republic. You will be able to easily determine why the United States loses very few wars, and why the Mexicans rarely become involved in one.

BAJA'S MISSIONS

Most of the important seaborne explorations of Baja California occurred off the Pacific coast. In contrast, the early day efforts at colonizing the peninsula took place along the Sea of Cortez. But some 164 years were to elapse between the 1533 discovery of the peninsula and the first successful settlement. This was established at Loreto in 1697.

Jesuit missionaries were the agents of colonization. With Loreto as headquarters, 20 missions were founded during the next 71 years. Only one of these, at Todos Santos, was on the Pacific coast. The rest rimmed the Sea of Cortez or the mountains backing its shores.

In 1768, the Jesuits were expelled from Baja as part of a worldwide vendetta against their order. Franciscans and Dominicans vied to succeed them. The latter group were given Baja California, while Alta California was assigned to the Franciscans. As a result of this compromise, Franciscan padre Junipero Serra departed overland from Loreto and made one of the most momentous journeys ever to affect the American West Coast. After a strenuous 50-day journey north along the chain of former Jesuit missions, Serra arrived at San Diego Bay on May 14, 1769. Here he founded the first of many missions which were to follow in Alta California. Western civilization had been established on what is now the United States Pacific coast. It came from Baja.

The missionary trail from Loreto to San Diego involved crossing the Baja peninsula and accessing to the Pacific coast at the southern end of the Northern Reach at present day El Rosario. During the 65 years after Serra's journey, the Dominican order founded nine new missions between El Rosario and the present international boundary. Several of these served as stepping stones in the supply line between San Diego and Loreto. Today's sailors passing along Baja's Northern Reach may thus view the lands that gave sustenance to the last of the missionary era in Baja California.

SECTION B
SAN DIEGO TO BAJAMAR

It is approximately 41 miles from the San Diego harbor entrance at Point Loma to the recreational subdivision of Bajamar. Back of the coast lie mountains and mesas of moderate steepness, so that the lay-of-the-land is readily apparent from the sea. However, the immediate coast is of gentle topography and in most places it is fully occupied with residences and other urban developments. Baja's only freeway, Highway 1-D, lies only a short distance inland from the sea.

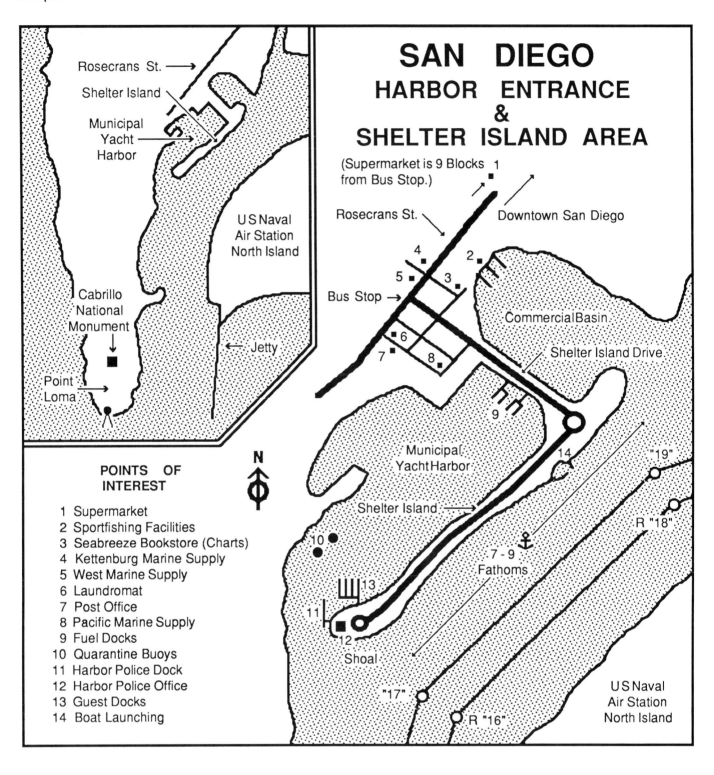

SAN DIEGO
HARBOR ENTRANCE
&
SHELTER ISLAND AREA

POINTS OF INTEREST

1 Supermarket
2 Sportfishing Facilities
3 Seabreeze Bookstore (Charts)
4 Kettenburg Marine Supply
5 West Marine Supply
6 Laundromat
7 Post Office
8 Pacific Marine Supply
9 Fuel Docks
10 Quarantine Buoys
11 Harbor Police Dock
12 Harbor Police Office
13 Guest Docks
14 Boat Launching

This mainland coast is without special interest to the boater although it provides pleasant scenery for the offshore cruiser. There are no protected anchorages, launching ramps, or other boating facilities. Vessels cruising south may stay close to shore to view this area, or may sail farther offshore and enjoy a close-in inspection of the Islas los Coronados. (See description in Section E of this chapter.) The latter course adds only a short distance to the journey from San Diego to Ensenada.

If you are beginning your first boating expedition south to Cabo San Lucas or into the Sea of Cortez, you are embarking on a never-to-be-forgotten adventure. Please except my well-wishes, and those of the others who have worked so diligently to bring you this volume.

POINT LOMA TO TIJUANA -- The coastal land between Point Loma and the international border at the north end of Tijuana is low-lying. In hazy weather this section of the coast will not be visible from the sea.

Under these conditions Point Loma will show as an island and the steep terrain directly inland from the Tijuana bullring will appear as a prominent point.

TIJUANA -- The international boundary is marked, regrettably, by a tall <u>chain-link fence</u> which can be seen proceeding inland up the face of a hill. About 100 yards from shore, a 12-foot-high <u>stone obelisk monument</u> is constructed in the fence line. Its inscription reads "Initial point of boundary between U. S. and Mexico established by the joint commission Oct. AD 1849 agreeable to the treaty dated at the City of Guadalupe Hidalgo the 2nd of Feb. 1848."

Seventy-five feet south of this monument is a 60-foot-high round masonry <u>lighthouse</u> (four flashes) with four sup-porting flukes at its base. Its light is clearly visible when entering the San Diego harbor to the north. Immediately inland is situated the <u>Bullring By the Sea</u>. The combination of these structures provide an <u>unmistakable landmark</u> for the international boundary.

ROSARITO POWER PLANT -- A large thermo-electric <u>power plant</u> lies on a coastal bench 11 miles south of the international boundary (See Photo). The plant is fronted by four stubby stacks which often emit <u>considerable smoke</u>. North of the plant are a large number of sizeable oil storage tanks. At the north end of the tanks is a tall latticework tower which is heavily

---

BOUNDARIES BETWEEN ALTA & BAJA CALIFORNIA

The original boundary between the areas assigned to the Franciscan (Alta California) and Dominican (Baja California) religious orders was established at what is now named Rio Guadalupe. It was later moved northward to Rio Descanso, and then again to the Arroyo del Rosario near the present town of Rosarito (See Chapter Chart). The present international boundary was the result of the 1848 Treaty of Hidalgo which added California and much other territory to the United States following the Mexican-American War.

United States military forces were stationed at La Paz and San Jose del Cabo during the Mexican-American War, and several battles were fought. The United States initially proposed that Baja California be included in the area to be ceded to it through the treaty of peace. Perhaps this was done to provide an item of trading stock, as the peninsula was permitted to remain part of Mexico when the the latter country objected to its loss.

---

illuminated and makes an <u>excellent landmark</u> at night. Directly to seaward from the plant is a rock breakwater with a crooked end opening to the south. It protects the entrance of the cooling water intake channel.

ROSARITO POWER PLANT (Looking NE) -- The tank farm and smoke from the power plant stacks create a prominent landmark. Note the tall tower in upper left of photo (See text).

One mile offshore from the water intake is stationed a red buoy equipped with an electronic horn which omits 3 blasts at 30-second intervals. Several mooring buoys are located closer in toward shore, and several hundred yards north of the the red buoy. You may observe oil tankers anchored farther offshore awaiting to offload fuel for the power plant.

ROSARITO -- The community of Rosarito (El Rosarito on Chart 21004) stretches for several miles along the coast southward from the power plant. Its most prominent landmark is the 8-story Quinta del Mar Resort, a condominium development. The building's long axis runs at right angles to the coast. Three-quarter miles farther south is the historic Rosarito Beach Hotel (See HISTORIC CASINOS Box). It is a low lying structure fronted by a glass wall that protects the swimming pool area. The hotel and adjoining three-storied structure immediately to the south have red tile roofs.

MESA REDONDA -- Seven miles inland from the Quinta del Mar Resort, at 90°, lies a prominent flat-topped mesa named Mesa Redonda (Shown as Punta Redonda on Chart 21004). A large, 15-foot-high rock lies 400 yards offshore 1/4 mile south from the resort. Rosarito is a major center of tourist-oriented shops, motels, and restaurants. Government statistics indicate that 11 percent of the tourists entering Baja have this area as their destination. Sail on.

MONUMENT -- A substantial concrete structure is constructed 1.3 highway miles north of Punta Des-

PUNTA DESCANSO (LOOKING 315 Degrees)

canso along the coastal highway. It is clearly visible from sea. It consists of a wall supported on each side by curved buttresses. It appears to be a significant monument. In reality, it is much smaller than it appears from sea and contains no markings or other indications of its purpose. That's how things sometimes are in Mexico. However, it serves as a point of reference for Punta Descanso, a promontory which you might otherwise overlook (at no great loss).

PUNTA DESCANSO -- Punta Descanso is a modest projection of land 17 miles south of the international boundary (See Profile Photo). Its outer end is relatively low and level and supports numerous buildings. A steep-faced ridge lies a short distance inland and to the NW. Its SW face shows several road scars one above the other. The change in coastal direction which occurs to the south forms a broad bay (Bahia Descanso) called an ensenada by the early explorers. This, and similar ensenadas, offer little or no relief from the prevailing winds and swells even though they look rather pronounced when viewed on a chart.

RIO DESCANSO AREA -- Rio Descanso is a modest drainage that empties into the Pacific some 7 miles SE of Punta Descanso. A short distance north of the river is an extensive area of sand dunes which form a prominent natural landmark. These dunes are extensively used by dune buggies and as a takeoff point for hang gliding.

Highway 1-D crosses the river on lengthy bridges built near its mouth. Inland from the bridges can be seen a large group of greenhouses. Still further behind and to the south is a church with a bell tower on its north side. This church occupies the site of the Descanso mission built here in 1814 by the Dominican order. It is one of nine missions established by this order in northern Baja after the founding of the San Diego mission by Junipero Serra in 1769.

CERRO CORONEL -- Cerro Coronel is a prominent 2,420-foot-high mountain situated about 5 miles easterly from Punta Descanso (See Profile Photo). This

---

HISTORIC CASINOS

Baja's border communities reaped substantial income during the late 1920s and early 1930s (the prohibition era in the United States) from the combined allurements of alcohol, prostitution, and gambling. The latter activity fostered development of three opulent gambling casinos in the coastal area. The first of these was some distance inland in Tijuana. The second was the building currently used as the Rosarito Beach Hotel in Rosarito (See main text for location). Finally came the sprawling Riviera del Pacifico in Ensenada (See Ensenada map).

The Rosarito Beach Hotel adjoins Highway 1 and may be readily visited by highway travelers. It is a currently operating hotel with all facilities. Visitors are welcomed to view the public rooms. The Riviera del Pacifico is within easy walking distance of the marina area adjoining Ensenada harbor. It has been restored to its former glory by the city's people and is used for a variety of civic events. Both buildings are worth a visit, but Riviera del Pacific is the more impressive.

promontory and Mesa Redonda (noted above) are the two most prominent topographic features in Section A. The pointed peak of Cerro Coronel stands in sharp contrast to flattopped Mesa Redonda.

SUGARLOAF ROCK -- A 13-foot-high, birdlimed rock is situated about 1 3/4 miles offshore, and 4 miles SE from Punta Descanso. This is Sugarloaf Rock (Pilon de Azucar) (See photo of Cerro Coronel).

PLAZA DEL MAR HOTEL -- Approximately 3 miles north of the mouth of the Rio Guadalupe lies the Plaza del Mar Hotel. It is constructed on a level bench several hundred feet above sea level. At the southern end of the hotel complex is a truncated pyramidal structure topped by a large room with an overhanging roof. This is a replica of one of Mexico's Mayan pyramids. It makes a good landmark for vessels coasting within a few miles of shore.

RIO GUADALUPE AREA -- A conspicuous stream channel makes its way to the coast 13 miles southward from Punta Descanso. This is the canyon of the Rio Guadalupe. The canyon dissects a broad tableland that lies to both the north and south. On the slope north of the canyon a tall cylindrical concrete tower is clearly visible from sea. This is a ventilator in the aqueduct which conveys water from the river north to Tijuana.

Old Highway 1 leaves Highway 1-D at this point and takes an inland route to Ensenada. About 1 mile up the river on the old highway lies the school for the community of La Mision. Within the school yard, a chain-link fence surrounds the ruins of the San Miguel de la Frontera mission founded in 1787 by the Dominican order.

BAJAMAR -- About 2 miles south from the Rio Guadalupe a cluster of white buildings with red tiled roofs may be seen at the seaward edge of a coastal bench about 200 feet above sea level. This is the recreational community of Bajamar. There is a nearby golf course. Bajamar is the southernmost of the almost continuous urban developments that line the coast from here north to the international boundary. The very modest point of land at Bajamar is labled Punta Salsipuedes on Chart 21004. (See below under Punta El Pescadero.)

SECTION C
BAJAMAR TO
PUNTA SAN MIGUEL

This relatively short 12-mile area is the only section of coast presented in this chapter which contains little urbanization. This is the consequence of its steep topography and the fact that it is not served by a developed water system. At Bajamar, Highway 1-D moves inland and does not rejoin the coast again until immediately east of Punta El Pescadero.

PUNTA EL PESCADERO -- Chart 21004 identifies Punta Salsipuedes as being at the site of the Bajamar community as noted above. The coastline at Bajamar makes only a slight change in direction and the place hardly seems worthy of being classified as a *punta*. Mexican topographic maps and the AAA road map show Punta Salsipuedes lying some 8 miles SE of the Rio Guadalupe where there is a considerably more pronounced point. The U. S. Chart refers to this latter projection as Punta El Pescadero, and it is so identified in this volume. Between this promontory and Punta San Miguel to the south there is a pronounced bay which has not been honored with a name on any chart.

Salsipuedes may be translated as "get out if you can," and is no doubt a reference to the difficulty encountered by early day sailors in keeping their vessels off from a lee shore. The name is also used for a small community north of Ensenada and in other places along both shores of the Baja peninsula.

HIGHWAY 1-D CUT BANKS -- Highway 1-D, which proceeded inland near Bajamar, reemerges on the coast about 1 mile east of Punta El Pescadero. From here south to Punta San Miguel, the highway has been constructed in the steep topography forming the shore of the above noted unnamed bay. The result is an almost continuous series of cut banks and denuded slopes. These light colored areas stand out clearly from the surrounding darker terrain and provide an unmistakable landmark to seaward (See Photo).

CERRO CORONEL (Looking NE) -- Sugarloaf Rock lies to the right of the mountain. The breaking swell adjoining the rock indicates the presence of a reef.

HIGHWAY 1-D CUT BANKS (Looking E) -- Photo shows the steep coastal topograhpy present in Section C of this chapter. The light colored areas adjoining the highway are an unmistakable landmark.

PUNTA SAN MIGUEL -- At Punta San Miguel the coast makes a 90° turn from north-south to east-west forming a significant point. However, this promontory affords little or no protection from the prevailing winds and swells. It may be identified by the presence of a 20-foot-high white navigation light. Punta San Miguel forms the northern headland of Bahia Todos Santos.

EL SAUZAL FISHING PORT (Looking NW) -- Here the author's ketch is moored along El Sauzal's steep concrete pier in company with numerous commercial fishing vessels.

SECTION D
PUNTA SAN MIGUEL TO
CABO PUNTA BANDA

This section describes the shores of the broad U-shaped Bahia Todos Santos (All Saints Bay). Most of its shores are heavily urbanized as has been true of most of the coast discussed in this chapter. The land at the base of the U differs from the area to the north in that it is level for several miles inland. This area is the sedimentary delta of three sizeable streams that converge and empty into the sea in this 8-mile stretch of coastline. It supports the city of Ensenada and a sizeable area of agriculture south of the city. The southern side of the bay is accessed by Highway 23.

BAHIA TODOS SANTOS -- From the air, it can be seen that Bahia Todos Santos is landlocked on three sides and looks like a bay ought to look. However, its large size, (8 miles between the main headlands) and the fact that its open side faces NW, results in its providing only modest protection from the prevailing wind and swells. Large commercial vessels do anchor in the open roadstead off Ensenada, but the skippers of small pleasure craft will find insufficient comfort in this area. Such vessels seek shelter in the man-made harbors at El Sauzal and Ensenada.

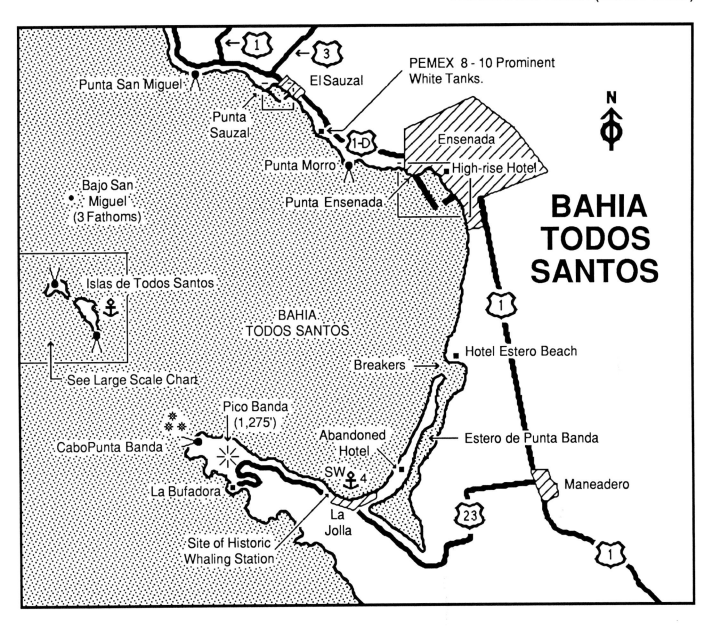

Reference to Charts 21004 and 21021 will show a <u>three fathom shoal</u> (Bajo San Miguel) and a lighted buoy 2 1/2 miles north of Islas Todos Santos. I have found the buoy to be absent on several occasions. The Port Captain at Ensenada reports that this is frequently the case at this exposed location.

EL SAUZAL -- By the grace of God, and perhaps the planning department, most of the Ensenada area's fish packing industry is located NW of the city at the smaller town of El Sauzal. A small breakwater-protected harbor was completed here in the mid-1980s. The main arm of the port projects southward from <u>Punta Sauzal</u> (See Photos). Large numbers of commercial fishing vessels tie up here. The harbor is lined with concrete walls which rise some five feet above high tide. Rubber tires and fenders hang from their sides.

Pleasure craft are not prohibited from seeking shelter at El Sauzal but the harbor is not designed for such ves-

sels. The port is thus only recommended for a quick visit or in case of emergency.

PUNTA MORRO -- A small low point projects from the coast 3 miles SE from El Sauzal. This is Punta Morro. Morro is the Spanish word for knob, or knoll. It is a strange name to apply to a point which is entirely flat, and thus not easily distinguished from sea. A white, concrete, navigation light tower is located at its outer end. Inland are numerous buildings.

PUNTA ENSENADA -- Look closely for Punta Ensenada. Find it? If so, your may have the wrong place, as much of what was Punta Ensenada has be quarried away to construct the breakwaters and dock in Ensenada Harbor. What remains is a massive light-colored scar which stands out from the surrounding terrain and makes an <u>excellent landmark</u> when viewed from the south. This quarry area is clearly visible in the left portion of the Ensenada Harbor photo immediately

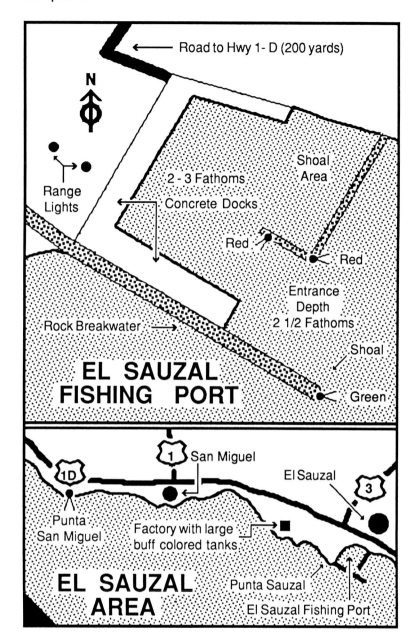

← Road to Hwy 1- D (200 yards)

N

Range Lights

2 - 3 Fathoms

Shoal Area

Concrete Docks

Red

Red

Entrance Depth 2 1/2 Fathoms

Rock Breakwater →

Shoal

EL SAUZAL FISHING PORT

Green

1 San Miguel

1D

El Sauzal

3

Punta San Miguel

Factory with large buff colored tanks

EL SAUZAL AREA

Punta Sauzal

El Sauzal Fishing Port

below the large flattopped building (See Photo). The main harbor breakwater projects from this point bearing 122°.

ENSENADA HARBOR -- The Ensenada rock breakwater and its navigation lights are difficult to distinguish when approaching from any distance, particularly at night. The problem of locating the harbor was made easier in 1986 with the construction of the high-rise Hotel Villa Marina. (See ENSENADA HARBOR Chart.) At this writing, it is the city's only high-rise building. Steering a short distance south of this structure will bring you nicely to a point where the harbor entrance is in view.

The city of Ensenada produces a considerable amount of air pollution. The principal culprits are a burnout dump located inland east of town, and a cement plant

and other industries at the community's southern edge. Smog thus often forms a blanketing landmark for the city. With offshore winds this layer drifts over Bahia Todos Santos obscuring the coastline.

Ensenada harbor has been undergoing expansion of the breakwaters and construction of a wharf area on its SE side for many years (See Photo). In the future, you may find things changed from how they are presented on the chart and photo in this chapter. A major drainage reaches the sea within the harbor and will almost certainly cause future siltation problems, particularly in the small craft anchoring area in the northern portion. I have anchored off this arroyo during a severe winter storm and upon leaving had difficulty in extracting the anchor which had become buried under considerable silt and assorted debris. The water within the breakwater is not of the highest quality, although it is considerably cleaner than in past years.

The harbor provides excellent protection from all directions, including the SW winds that accompany winter storms. In such storms, heavy swells crash nearly at right angles to the main breakwater throwing up towers of spray. The Capitan de Puerto reports that it is possible to enter the harbor under such conditions and that no breakers form at the entrance. (I have not made such an entrance, but can only speculate that it might provide a bit of a thrill for those in a small boat.)

Food stores, restaurants, hotels, tourist shopping, ship repair facilities, the Port Captain and Immigration offices are all within walking distance of the small craft anchoring area. Baja Naval is planned to be a modern marina with floating slips for about 50 vessels, gasoline and diesel fuel at dock-side pumps, a travel lift for vessels up to 70 tons, boatyard repair facilities, restaurant, bar, restrooms, and showers. These facilities were only partially completed at press time.

Immediately to the west of Baja Naval is the smaller Juanito's Landing Marina (See Photo). It has a floating dock with space for about 6-8 vessels up to 45 feet. Moorings and water taxi service are also available. The marina monitors channels 14 and 16. Also, visiting yachts will often be met at the harbor entrance by one of the marina's representatives. These particular Mexicans are never asleep under the traditional cactus and sombrero (as are very few of their fellow citizens).

ESTERO DE PUNTA BANDA -- Estero de Punta Banda is the northernmost of the many sandbar-protected lagoons that rim the low-lying sections of

EL SAUZAL FISHING PORT (Looking N) -- Note commercial fishing vessels end-tied to the dock in the upper left portion of the harbor. -- The large object in the right portion of the harbor is a dredge which has been broken down for several years. This section of the harbor is unfinished as a result, and its shoal area shows in the photo. A shoal area just inside the outer breakwater is also visible. Highway 1 - D can be seen running parallel to the coast.

ENSENADA HARBOR (Looking SE) -- Note the group of pleasure craft and other small boats anchored in the left portion of the harbor. The Baja Naval Marina noted in the text was not completed when the photo was taken. The dock area under construction noted in the text can be seen in the upper right portion of the harbor.

Chapter 6

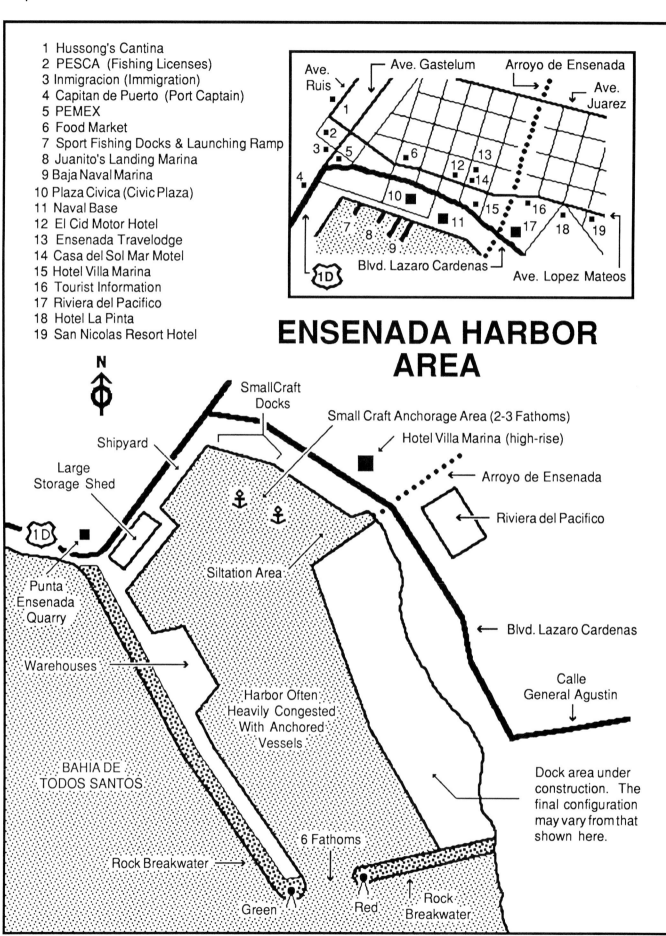

1 Hussong's Cantina
2 PESCA (Fishing Licenses)
3 Inmigracion (Immigration)
4 Capitan de Puerto (Port Captain)
5 PEMEX
6 Food Market
7 Sport Fishing Docks & Launching Ramp
8 Juanito's Landing Marina
9 Baja Naval Marina
10 Plaza Civica (Civic Plaza)
11 Naval Base
12 El Cid Motor Hotel
13 Ensenada Travelodge
14 Casa del Sol Mar Motel
15 Hotel Villa Marina
16 Tourist Information
17 Riviera del Pacifico
18 Hotel La Pinta
19 San Nicolas Resort Hotel

Ave. Ruis — Ave. Gastelum — Arroyo de Ensenada — Ave. Juarez

Blvd. Lazaro Cardenas — Ave. Lopez Mateos

ENSENADA HARBOR AREA

N

SmallCraft Docks

Small Craft Anchorage Area (2-3 Fathoms)

Hotel Villa Marina (high-rise)

Shipyard

Arroyo de Ensenada

Large Storage Shed

Riviera del Pacifico

Punta Ensenada Quarry

Siltation Area

Blvd. Lazaro Cardenas

Warehouses

Calle General Agustin

Harbor Often Heavily Congested With Anchored Vessels

BAHIA DE TODOS SANTOS

Dock area under construction. The final configuration may vary from that shown here.

6 Fathoms

Rock Breakwater

Green   Red   Rock Breakwater

72

Baja's Pacific coast. It is some 4 miles in length. It is of no interest to the ocean cruiser, but may be entered at its northern end by shallow draft vessels with current knowledge of the bar conditions (See Photo). Such craft may be launched at one of two ramps situated at the Estero Beach Hotel (See Photo). This, in my judgment, is the finest hotel in the Ensenada area. It, and its adjoining R.V. park, are located at the northern end of the estero.

Government officials in Ensenada have shown me plans to (1) close-off the present entrance to the estero, (2) dredge a new breakwater-protected entrance at the extreme southern end, and (3) turn much of the estero into a marina and tourist-oriented residential area. Time will tell. For the present, mariners can observe a massive, two-story, concrete building constructed about 2/3 of the way south down the sand bar from the present estero entrance. This is the abandoned shell of a hotel begun by the Mexican government in the mid-1960s. You Gringo capitalists might care to ponder the results of this government enterprise in comparison to the privately built Estero Beach Hotel. This latter facility took years to unfold, but it is a beautiful development which is in operation at a profit. (End political comment.)

LA JOLLA -- La Jolla is a community of tourist-oriented residences and trailer parks constructed near the point where the Estero de Punta Banda bar joins the mainland (See Photo). (The town is referred to as Punta Banda on Chart 21004.) It has numerous trees and is a pleasant appearing place from the water. There is a boat launching ramp facing the open Pacific.

This corner of Bahia Todos Santos is fully open to the NW, yet its location seems to provide a considerable degree of protection from prevailing NW weather. My visits here in light winds and swells indicate that one could anchor off the village with reasonable comfort. More importantly, this location provides one of the best natural anchorages along Baja's Pacific coast during SW storm conditions. These views are supported by the *1937 U. S. Sailing Directions* which notes "The prevailing NW wind in its usual force is not seriously felt here; during the southerly gales it is, with the exception of the harbors, the best anchorage along this coast."

CABO PUNTA BANDA -- Cabo Punta Banda is one of the most prominent points of land in Baja, lying as it does at the NW extremity of a narrow, 7-mile-long peninsula (See CABO PUNTA BANDA AREA Chart in Chapter 7). Clearly this peninsula continues underwater to the NW and emerges as the Islas de Todos Santos. In addition, there are a great cluster of rocks lying off the point on a line toward the

ENSENADA

Historian Pablo Martinez described Ensenada in the early 1880s as "no more than a miserable ranch." It then received a spurt of activity in 1887 as a result of one of the many concessions which were granted to foreign speculators in Baja California. A town was laid out which had 1,375 residents a year later. Most of this activity faded away when the land speculation schemes evolved into bankruptcy, and gold was discovered inland.

Rapid development and population increase occurred in northern Baja in the 1920s and 1930s, but most of this centered along the international border at Tijuana and Mexicali. The *U.S. Sailing Directions* described Ensenada in 1930 as a town of little commercial importance with a population of only 3,071. There were no sewage system or hospital facilities, with typhoid and intestinal fevers being common. Today it is Baja's third largest city and its most important commercial port. If it falls a little short of perfection, keep in mind that it is the product of only a few decades of development during an era of enormous social difficulties for Mexico.

islands (See Photo). Vessels approaching from the south may readily proceed to Ensenada by passing between Cabo Punta Baja and the islands where there is a mid-channel depth of 128 fathoms. The course should be laid well toward the islands so as to avoid the above-noted rocks.

JUANITO'S LANDING MARINA (Looking SW) -- A large tuna clipper may be seen in dry dock at the shipyard in the background.

ENTRANCE TO ESTERO DE PUNTA BANDA (Looking SW) -- Bahia Todos Santos is in the upper portion of the photo. Note the breakers guarding the shoal entrance to the estero. Portions of the Hotel Estero Beach and its breakwaters may be seen at the bottom. Compare these with the same breakwaters shown in the photo of the hotel launching ramp below.

HOTEL ESTERO BEACH LAUNCHING RAMP (Looking SE) -- Two side-by-side launching ramps are located immediately above the lower of the three breakwaters. The corner of the hotel shows in the extreme lower left corner. Most of the buildings in the photo are recreation residences.

The terrain immediately inland from Cabo Punta Banda is fairly gentle. It then rises sharply to over 1,250 feet at Pico Banda some 1 mile to the SE. The peak supports a prominent radio tower. The terrain then descends to 730 feet at a broad pass 1 mile farther down the peninsula. Through this saddle passes Hwy. 23 which runs from Hwy. 1 to La Bufadora on the peninsula's SE coast. Portions of Hwy. 23 show well to sea from both side's of the Cabo Punta Banda peninsula.

SECTION E
ISLAS LOS CORONADOS

It is possible to avoid all the urbanization along the main-land coast between San Diego to Punta Banda. This is easily done by setting one's course to visit the two groups of islands described in Sections E and F. Both groups of islands are basically undeveloped, and each offers a small craft anchorage.

LA JOLLA (Looking NW) -- A patch of sunlight illuminates a portion of the recreational subdivision of La Jolla on an otherwise cloudy day. The photo was taken during prevailing NW swell conditions. These can be seen impacting the coast parallel to the beach. -- Note the group of small fishing boats moored off the cove in the upper left portion of the photo.

SHORE WHALING AT PUNTA BANDA

The California gray whale was hunted using several strategies. One of these, shore whaling, involved establishing the trying works, crew quarters, etc., at fixed stations on land, thus eliminating the need for a whaling ship. Whales were pursued in the coastal waters using small boats. When captured they were towed to the shore station and flensed on the beach. The first California shore whaling station was established in 1851 at Monterey. The shore whaling industry lasted not much more than three decades.

Charles Scammon's classic account of the American whale fishery lists eleven such whaling stations from Half Moon Bay (20 miles south of the Golden Gate) on the north, to Punta Banda on the south. This latter station is noted on the early editions of U. S. nautical charts and *Sailing Directions*. The station was located at a point 4 miles east of Cabo Punta Banda where coastal cliffs give way to the sand beach fronting the present community of La Jolla (See BAHIA TODOS SANTOS Chart).

CABO PUNTA BANDA & OFF-LYING ROCKS --
(Looking SE) -- Here punta lies under a layer of low clouds. The point may often appear as an island when viewed from the north as the result of lower-lying terrain along the eastern shore of Bahia Todos Santos.

Islas los Coronados are a group of four islands lying some 7 miles from the Mexican mainland and 15 miles from the entrance to San Diego harbor. They are little more than the upper portions of several underwater mountain ridges. There is virtually no gentle terrain and the steep sides of the main islands drop into the sea at angles in excess of 45 degrees. Mexican fishermen cross from the mainland in pangas to tend lobster traps along the islands' wave-swept shores. Other boats contain air compressors used by divers going down over 100 feet in search of sea urchins.

The islands are composed of sedimentary rock with layers of conglomerate and sandstone visible throughout. The strike of the sedimentary layers rises from east to west and may be viewed at the north and south ends of the two main

islands. Vegetation is grass and low shrubs with abundant stands of prickly pear cactus.

The smaller of the four islands are Roca Medio and Coronado del Medio. An out-of-print chart shows a small cove on the eastern shore of the latter island, but my visit here indicated it is too open to swells to be of interest as an anchorage.

CORONADO DEL NORTE (NORTH) -- Coronado del Norte is the second largest of the Coronados group (See Profile Photo). There is a small cove 1/4 mile south of the the island's northern point on the eastern shore. Located here is an edifice known as the Lobster Shack. Its occupants moor their panga a short distance away by tying its bow and stern to projecting rocks. The area off from the shack is touted as an anchorage in previous guidebooks. However, I have recorded 12 fathoms only 150 feet from shore and a steep gradient leading to much

ISLA CORONADO DEL NORTE (Looking 195 Degrees)
The island resembles a body draped in a shroud. For this reason it has been referred to Isla Corpus Christi (Body of Christ Island).

ISLA CORONADO DEL SUR (Looking 240 Degrees).

deeper water further off. I believe this to be a very poor anchorage at best.

CORONADO DEL SUR (SOUTH) -- This is the largest of the islands (See Profile Photo). It is nearly 2 miles long with a high point of 672 feet. At the NE end is a small cove measuring approximately 100 yards across its entrance. This is Puerto Cueva (See Photo). Near waterline on its southern shore lies the remains of the once stately *Coronado Yacht Club*. The ridge SE of the cove is the island's only significant flat area. It supports several additional buildings including the structure that in the past was the island's northern lighthouse. It has been re-

PUERTO CUEVA ON ISLA CORONADO DEL SUR (Looking W) -- The cove shows indistinctly due to poor light conditions. The old Coronado Yacht Club building on the cove's left side is indistinguishable. The buildings on the ridge to the left of the cove are clearly visible from sea and serve as a good landmark. Note lighthouse on the ridge at the right of the photo.

placed by a new concrete navigation light located on the main ridge NE from Puerto Cueva. A second light is constructed on the extreme southern end of the island.

Puerto Cueva is roughly translated as Smugglers Cove. Its waters can be flat with little trace of swell. In contrast, I have seen it in a state of considerable agitation, and freely swept by the prevailing NW swells refracting around the island's north end following many days of stormless weather. In this state is it of little value as an anchorage for small vessels. Fishing pangas are often moored in 6 fathoms between the cove's headlands. Venturing into Puerto Cueva far enough to avoid these boats leaves little or no room for anchoring.

On the same day as the above noted agitated conditions were noted in Puerto Cueva, I traversed the shore of the island south of the cove. Here the sea was relatively flat, and suitable for anchoring. Depths of 6-8 fathoms were sounded 150-200 yards offshore all the way from Puerto Cueva to the island's southern tip. A mooring buoy is set in 8 fathoms 250 yards offshore, and 3/4 miles south from the southern headland of Puerto Cueva. Depths of 6-8 fathoms may be sounded between the buoy and shore. On another occasion I have anchored here in NW gusts up to 40 knots with reasonable comfort. It is possible to anchor up to 1/2 mile offshore in this same area in 10 fathoms.

It is also my view that this anchorage area would provide protection in SW weather (I have not

been here under such conditions). In support of this contention, the 1937 edition of the *U. S. Sailing Directions* notes "The *U. S. S. Ranger* found comfortable anchorage here in a moderate gale." What is good for the navy should be good for the cruisers.

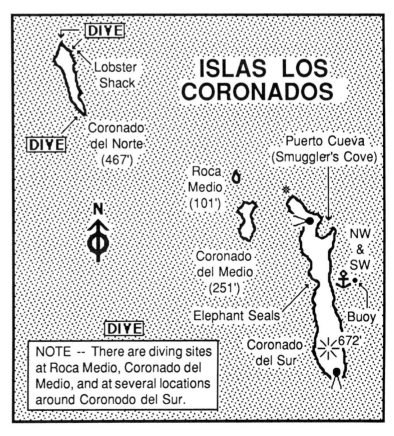

ISLAS LOS CORONADOS

NOTE -- There are diving sites at Roca Medio, Coronado del Medio, and at several locations around Coronodo del Sur.

ISLAS LOS CORONADOS

Juan Rodriguez Cabrillo noted the presence of the Coronados Islands during his voyage in 1542. He named them Las Islas Desiertas (The Desert Islands), a clear reflection of their scant vegetation. When Sebastian Vizcaino ventured by in 1602, they acquired the name Los Cuatro Coronados in honer of four brothers of that name who were put to death for their Christian faith in the time of Diocletian. Since that time they have witnessed a wide variety of historic events including rum running, the smuggling of Chinese immigrants into the United States, and even a pirate legend.

The islands' most prominent historic artifact is the *Coronado Yacht Club*. This rambling building constructed on the shore of Puerto Cueva at Isla Sur was used as a casino for a brief period early in the 1930s. Its quick demise was the result of the end of prohibition in the United States in 1933, and the abolishment of gambling in Mexico the following year. The casino building is now partially collapsed but it is still used as a residence by a detachment of Mexican naval infantry (marines). They enforce a rule which prohibits landing on the island. This regulation was made necessary many years ago in order to prevent molestation of the island's badly depleted bird and animal life.

SECTION F
ISLAS DE TODOS SANTOS

Terrain of the two Islas de Todos Santos (All Saints Islands) is reasonably gentle. They thus provide ocean cruisers with their first opportunity to prowl about on one of Baja's Pacific islands (See Photo).

ISLA NORTE -- The northern extremity of Isla Norte (north island) supports three structures: an old concrete lighthouse with a caretaker's residence at its base, a new taller concrete lighthouse, and a guyed radio tower. At the island's southern end is the northernmost of the many fish camps that will be encountered along the Baja coast and its adjacent islands. Fair weather anchorage may be taken directly off the camp.

Isla Norte's shores are mostly rocky bluffs less than 50 feet in elevation. Above these bluffs the island's profile is totally flat. In approaching the two islands from a distance, Isla Sur shows first due to its higher elevation and steeper topography.

ISLA SUR -- Isla Sur is the larger of the two islands. It reaches a high point of 313 feet near its southern end. It also supports a fish camp on the shore of a small cove south of this peak. A navigation light is located at the extreme southern tip (See Photo).

ISLAS DE TODOS SANTOS (Looking SE) -- Isla Norte with its two light towers is at the bottom of the photo. Isla Sur is at the top. Note that Isla Norte is quite level. Isla Sur has steeper, although moderate terrain. This difference in profile is readily apparent from sea level.

A series of small coves lie on this island's eastern shore (See Photo). The largest of these provides a snug harbor for small craft. The sea surface inside this cove in the presence of strong NW winds is considerably smoother than that found immediately outside, but there can be a substantial surge. It is quite calm at other times.

Previous guidebooks note that the customary procedure is to lie bow out with a stern line secured to the rocks ashore, and that the cove is often host to many craft using this procedure. My observations are that this is a poor practice when there are substantial swells. The impact of surging water on the rocks only a few feet from one's stern can make for an uneasy night. I have anchored with bow and stern anchors in the center of the cove and felt more secure.

The cove's shore is quite precipitous to a height of some 30 feet. The best landing is on a slight projection of land near its center. Climbing up the rocks from this point brings one to level terrain. Here are located several building foundations relating to a prior mining operation. The vegetation is low and scant so walking about can be done with ease.

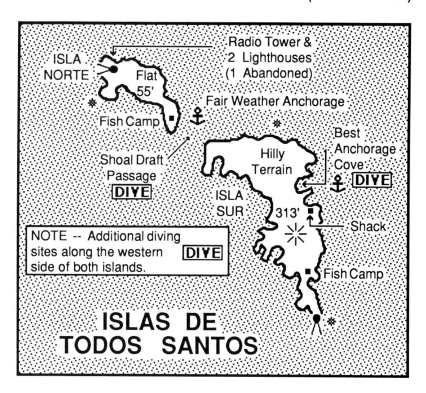

ISLAS DE TODOS SANTOS

Anchorage may also be taken immediately outside this cove in 12 fathoms, although the swell action is more pronounced in this location than inside the cove. NW swells refract around the north end of Isla Norte and run

COVES ON THE EAST SHORE OF ISLA SUR, ISLAS DE TODOS SANTOS (Looking W) -- There are three coves in this area. The most southerly of the three is only partly in view to the left. The largest and best cove is in the center of the three (See text). A 4-foot-high number 5 is painted on the face of the rock forming its southern headland. -- The cove to the right is filled with kelp and is connected with the center area by a narrow passage lying behind the white birdlimed islet.

SOUTHERN EXTREMITY OF ISLA SUR, ISLAS DE TODOS SANTOS (Looking NE) -- Note the navigation light near the center of the photo.

down the east side of both islands at right angles to the shore. There is holding ground here for only about two boats as water depths increase rapidly as one proceeds east from the cove.

Wesley A. Bush's 1954 book *Paradise to Windward* relates the author's experience anchoring in one of the Isla Sur coves during storm conditions (presumably with SW winds). The cove provided adequate protection under these conditions, although Wesley secured lines to the shore from both ends of his vessel. Hearing a commercial fishing vessel in distress he guided its skipper to the area immediately outside the cove where he was able to weather the storm.

SUMMARY COMMENT

Travelers on Baja's Transpeninsular Highway recognize that they must motor to a point south of the town of San Quintin before feeling that they have left most of civilization behind. This is a distance of over 190 highway miles from the international border. The coastal cruiser can achieve this same result much sooner. South of Cabo Punta Banda lies a largely deserted coastline, with occasional small towns, fish camps, and majestic desert topography. Prepare to enjoy it, but keep ever watchful for the antics of the sea.

CHAPTER 7
THE NORTHERN REACH
(SOUTH PORTION)
CABO PUNTA BANDA TO PUNTA BAJA

CHAPTER SUMMARY

This book refers to the combined areas described in Chapters 6 and 7 as the *Northern Reach*. This entire shore may be traversed close-in while deviating little from a straight-line course drawn from San Diego to Cabo San Lucas. The southern portion presented here in Chapter 7 differs from the north portion in that: (1) There is very little urbanization visible from the sea although there are several sizeable towns lying a few miles inland. (2) There are several good natural anchorages. The only mainland ports in the Chapter 6 area were in two man-made harbors. (3) Most of the short duration boating traffic from the United States has been left behind. You are now clearly south of the border. Enjoy.

SECTION			DESCRIPTION
NO.	FROM	TO	
A	Cabo Punta Banda	Punta San Jose	Coastline is mountanous with few flat areas.
B	Punta San Jose	North of Punta Colnett	Mountains move inland 1 to 3 miles with the intervening land being of relatively gentle terrain. Some agriculture.
C	North of Punta Colnett	Punta Baja	Mountains move many miles inland. Coastal area is a broad gentle plain with considerable agriculture.
D	Isla San Martin		A solitary volcanic island. Good anchorage at Caleta Hassler.

SECTION A
CABO PUNTA BANDA TO
PUNTA SAN JOSE

A bold and precipitous coast greets the mariner from Cabo Punta Banda south to Punta San Jose. It is backed by mountainous terrain dominated by Cerro Soledad. This 3,349-foot peak lies 3 miles inland from Bahia Soledad. Puerto Santo Tomas is the only notable anchorage in this section. There are large quantities of kelp in the coastal waters from Bahia Soledad to Punta San Jose.

CABO PUNTA BANDA (S. E. FACE) -- Numerous offshore rocks are strewn along the SW facing slope of Cabo Punta Banda. In this

CABO PUNTA BANDA (Looking 340 Degrees)

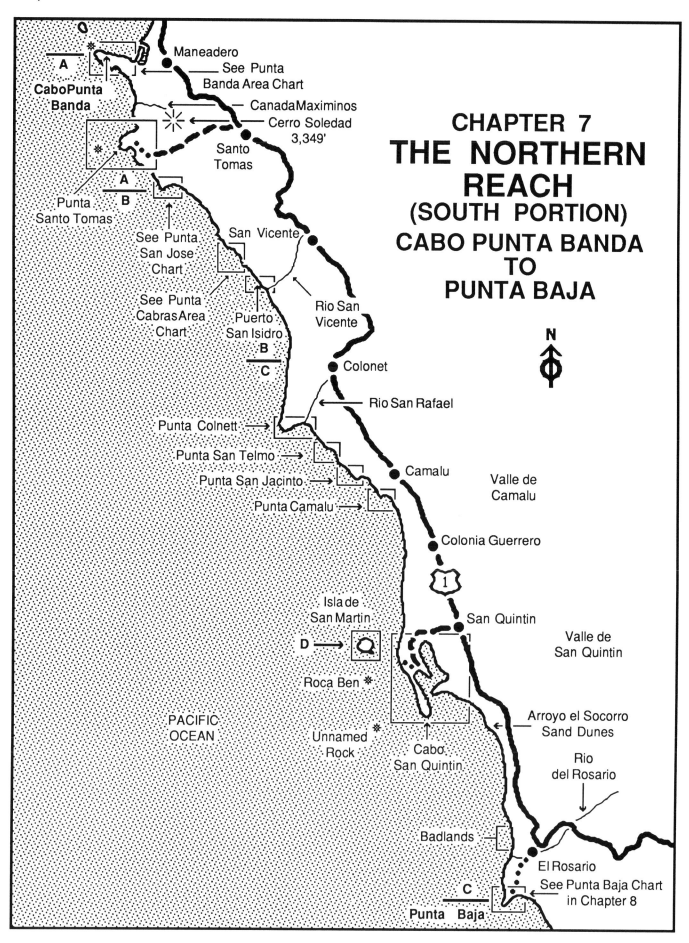

CHAPTER 7
THE NORTHERN REACH
(SOUTH PORTION)
CABO PUNTA BANDA TO PUNTA BAJA

N

Maneadero

See Punta Banda Area Chart

A

CaboPunta Banda

CanadaMaximinos

Cerro Soledad 3,349'

Santo Tomas

Punta Santo Tomas

A
B

See Punta San Jose Chart

San Vicente

See Punta Cabras Area Chart

Puerto San Isidro

Rio San Vicente

B
C

Colonet

Rio San Rafael

Punta Colnett →

Punta San Telmo →

Punta San Jacinto →

Punta Camalu →

Camalu

Valle de Camalu

Colonia Guerrero

1

Isla de San Martin

D →

San Quintin

Valle de San Quintin

Roca Ben ※

PACIFIC OCEAN

Unnamed Rock

Cabo San Quintin

Arroyo el Socorro Sand Dunes

Rio del Rosario

Badlands

El Rosario

See Punta Baja Chart in Chapter 8

C

Punta Baja

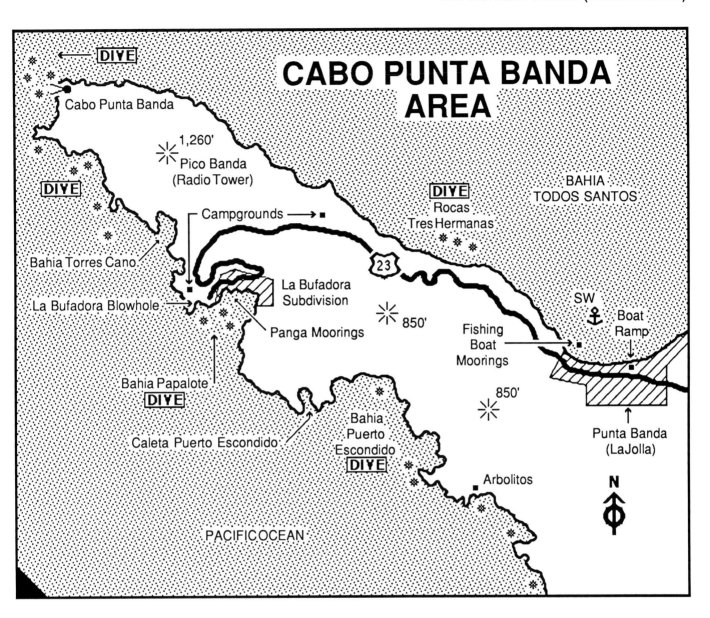

CABO PUNTA BANDA AREA

regard I believe it is the rockiest portion of shore-line in the entire Baja peninsula. There are also a series of small picturesque coves along this face (See CABO PUNTA BANDA AREA Chart), but the presence of rocks makes them uninviting as anchorages for any but the smallest boats. These rocky areas, and those lying off Cabo Punta Banda itself (See Photo in Chapter 6), make excellent areas for rock fishing and diving. When first seen from a distance Cabo Punta Banda may appear as an island.

The shore back of the second largest cove, Bahia Papalote, supports the settlement of La Bufadora. It contains recreation homes and tour-ist facilities that are frequented by people from Ensenada (See Photo). This is the last sig-nificant group of buildings along the coast until one reaches the Hotel La Pinta immediately south of Bahia San Quintin.

PUNTA SANTO TOMAS (Looking 120 Degrees) -- Note the rhinoceros horn inland from the point. The low-lying promintory in the far distance is Punta San Jose.

BAHIA PAPALOTE (Looking N) -- Highway 23 can be seen switchbacking toward the community of La Bufadora on the shores of Bahia Papalote. The farthest left light-colored building is the viewing structure which overlooks La Bufadora Blowhole. The blowhole shows as a small dark area immediately left of this building.

LA BUFADORA BLOWHOLE -- At the western most portion of Bahia Papalote is the unrivaled La Bufadora blowhole. Its antics may be viewed by vessels close to shore. There are occasional points along the Pacific coast where rock formations cause incoming swells to cast up a spout of water. However, La Bufadora is a substantial sea level cave. Water is taken in and then expelled by air compressed by the inrushing swells. Heavy seas cause a large vertical geyser.

I have entered Bahia Papalote to a point just inside the outer headlands. Soundings were rapidly changing in this area indicating a boulder-strewn bottom. Further penetration of the cove without local knowledge seemed imprudent.

WAVE-CUT TERRACES -- A substantial arroyo (Canada Maximinos) makes its way to the coast at a point 8 miles SE from Punta Banda. Starting about 1 mile north

BAHIA SOLEDAD (Looking E) -- The rocky coast on the right of the photo is the southern shore of the bay.

NOTE -- The U. S. Sailing Directions notes:
"A sunken rock, on which the sea breaks, lies 700 yards NNW of Punta Santa Tomas. This headland should be given a berth of at least 1/2 mile."

Bahia Soledad

PACIFIC
OCEAN

DIVE

Punta Rif
(Low & Flat)

High Point
(Elevation 1,375 Ft)

See NOTE

Santo Tomas
Fish Camp

El Islote

540'

Fancy
Residences

DIVE

Punta Santo Tomas

To Santo Tomas &
Hwy 1 --- 20 miles

Landing

5

DIVE

Puerto
Santo
Tomas

La Bocana

Campsite
& Meadow

Rio
Santo Tomas

**PUERTO
SANTO TOMAS
AREA**

Campsite

DIVE

Punta China
Limestone Mine

Mine Hq.

DIVE Punta China

5

Barge Mooring

LimestoneLoading Equipment

of the arroyo, and extending to Bahia Soledad, a narrow terrace is visible about 100 feet above sea level. It is the result of wave action in the geologic past when the sea was higher than at present. Smaller segments of such terraces are present at many other places along the steeper sections of the Baja coast.

BAHIA SOLEDAD -- (See PUNTA SANTO TOMAS AREA Chart.) About 3 miles north of Punta Santo Tomas is a sizeable cove named Bahia Soledad (See Photo). At its head is a broad sandy beach and a group of fish camp shacks. Unfortunately, this otherwise inviting inlet faces westerly and is swept by the prevailing NW swells. The *1937 U. S. Sailing Directions* also

notes that "a southerly gale would bring in a heavy sea." Logic supports this conclusion. Bahia Soledad is thus usable in only the calmest conditions.

EL ISLOTE -- El Islote is a compact group of several rocks some 20 feet high lying westerly and 1 mile off from Punta Santo Tomas (See Photo). Islote means "small island". It is mispelled on Chart 21004 as Isolote. The rocks are also referred to as Rocas la Soledad. Depths of 30 fathoms may be sounded within 150 yards on all sides. A colony of sea lions is usually present.

PUERTO SANTO TOMAS AREA -- Punta Santo Tomas projects from the coast 12 miles SE from Cabo

EL ISLOTE ROCKS (Looking 50 Degrees) -- Cerro Soledad is in view inland above the rocks.

Punta Banda. A small, sharp peak located several hundred yards inland from the point looks somewhat like a rhinoceros horn. The resultant distinctive profile is apparent when approaching from both north and south (See Photo). The presence of the El Islote rocks west of the point provide an additional landmark. The *1937 U. S. Sailing Directions* note that the channel between these rocks and Punta Santo Tomas may be used with

safety. I have found this to be true on several occasions.

A short distance easterly from Punta Santa Tomas the coast indents forming Puerto Santo Tomas, an anchorage partially protected from the prevailing swells. Small fishing vessels are normally moored in the cove taking up the best anchoring positions (See Photo). The adjoining area offers good holding ground in 5 fathoms, but receives less protection from refracted NW swells. I have spent a rather rocky night anchored here in company with 25-knot winds and moderate swell conditions.

A steep road extends to the water's edge near the moorage where land-based fishermen can launch small lightweight boats with some difficulty. Inflatable vessels are the best choice at this spot. The sea between Punta Rif and the mouth of Rio Santa Tomas contains many areas of kelp. The anchorage at Puerto Santo Tomas is particularly overgrown.

A small area of gentle terrain adjoining the moored vessels supports a fish camp and several buildings which at one time were a motel and cantina. On one of my visits these were inoperative. On a more recent trip

PUERTO SANTO TOMAS (Looking NE) -- Note numerous small fishing boats moored in the area best protected from the prevailing weather. The best anchoring position is as close as possible to the moored vessels. The small point of land near the center of the photo considerably reduces the intensity of NW swells refracting around Punta Santo Tomas. Punta Santo Tomas is out of sight to the left.

PUNTA CHINA (Looking NE) -- The farthest left buildings are the mine headquarters. The highest portions of the mining scar referred to in the text may be seen in the top center.

they were being remodeled. What will be found in the future is open to speculation. This settlement bears the name Puerto Santo Tomas. Some 1.5 miles to the SE near the mouth of the Rio Santo Tomas is situated the small village of La Bocana. It supports a modest grocery store and two minimum facility camping areas. One of these is situated in a meadow adjoining a lagoon behind the barrier beach at the mouth of the river. Trees near the meadow can be seen from the sea. My notes following a night camped in this spot read, "the place is frog heaven."

PUNTA CHINA -- Punta China is a small low point lying 3 miles SE of Punta Santo Tomas. Modern limestone crushing and loading facilities are constructed on the SE side of the point (See Photo). Rock is loaded into barges which are towed to Ensenada. A buoy in 5 fathoms is used to moor the cement barges. A wide dirt road leads south from these facilities down the coast for a distance of 1 mile. At this point the road turns inland and proceeds about 1/2 mile up an arroyo to the mine. The mining scar makes a good landmark when approaching by sea from the south, but goes out of sight when abeam of Punta China.

The bight east of Punta China is too small to provide a satisfactory anchorage except in fair weather. There is holding ground in 5 fathoms between the buoy and shore. In an emergency, vessels could tie to the buoy.

PUNTA SAN JOSE -- Seven and 1/2 miles SE from Punta Santo Tomas lies Punta San Jose (See Photo).

A broad bay lies eastward from the point providing a fair weather anchorage in 4 fathoms. A 35 foot tall, white, concrete navigation light tower is located on a terrace about 1/4 mile easterly from the point. This is the most

PUERTO SANTO TOMAS

Juan Rodriguez Cabrillo spent the night of September 14, 1542, anchored at Puerto Santo Tomas during his epic-making exploration of the Pacific coast. Almost 250 years later in 1791, the broad valley 20 miles inland up the Rio Santo Tomas became the site of one of the Dominican missions founded in the northern portion of the peninsula. This area was to become famous for wine making. Wine casks were transported to Puerto Santo Tomas for further shipment by sea. Most protected coves along Baja's Pacific coast have shallow water depths, and vessels must be anchored some distance seaward. In marked contrast, an anchoring position within a few yards of shore is available at Puerto Santo Tomas. It was thus possible to load cargo by overhead line from the cliffs rimming the cove. As a result, it became an important port during the peninsula's colonial period.

Today, Santo Tomas is one of the leading brands of wine sold throughout Mexico, although the winery itself has been located in Ensenada for many years. This famous old facility is open for tours Sunday through Friday. It is located about 1 mile from the Ensenada marina area. There are still vineyards at Santo Tomas and at several other coastal valleys a few miles inland along the Northern Reach.

PUNTA CHINA LIMESTONE LOADING AREA -- (Looking NE) -- Note mooring buoy in foreground.

the sea. The presence of this relatively narrow, level terrain is the characteristic that distinguishes Section B from the steep coast to the north, and the far broader plains lying to the south in Section C.

Some of the gentle lands along Section B are used for agriculture. Occasional buildings and farm equipment are in view.

PUNTA CABRAS AREA -- The segment of coast from 8 to 12 miles SE from Punta San Jose contains several minor points of land. Each of these forms a small south facing cove. (See PUNTA CABRAS AREA Chart.) El Destiladero is a community of some 50 buildings lying on the shore of the southern most of these coves. This village is the area's most prominent landmark as

northerly of many lights that are constructed near an anchorage or landing site rather than on a prominent point. They serve primarily as guides into an anchorage rather than as aids to offshore navigation. A fish camp is present nearby, north of the light.

SECTION B
PUNTA SAN JOSE TO NORTH OF CABO COLNETT

Punta San Jose is situated at the northern end of a relatively narrow belt of level terrain which stretchs for many miles to the south (See Photo). Within a few hundred yards to several miles inland this terrace blends into steeper mountains. These steeper lands are very evident from

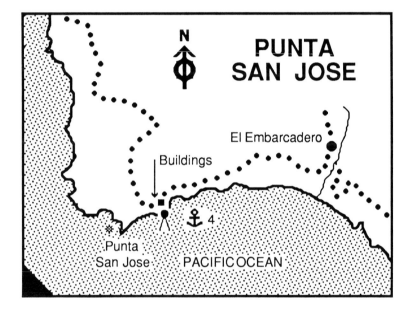

the points themselves do not stand out well from the sea.

Punta Cabras is the most important of the points in this area. It encompasses a small cove which provides an anchorage for one or two yachts whose skippers are comfortable in 3 fathoms (See Photo). Deeper waters here are swept by NW swells even in fair weather.

PUERTO SAN ISIDRO AREA -- Here is a port which barely merits the title Puerto. It lies 15 miles south from Punta San Jose, and 1 mile SE from Punta San Isidro. Its only protection from the sea is provided by a small, low point of land, and a reef of rock several hundred yards long which projects from the point in a SE direction (See Photos). Fishing pangas may be moored in the small area of protected water formed in the lee of the reef.

PUNTA SAN JOSE (Looking E) -- Note terrace lands above navigation light in the photo's center right.

A steep road running from the terrace land to the sea is used for boat launching and landing. On shore are several warehouses, two 30' diameter white tanks, a group of small rental cabins, and other buildings. This development is <u>Puerto San Isidro</u>. Rental boats are available for fishing.

The terrace lands south of Puerto San Isidro are cultivated with water from the <u>Rio San Vicente</u>. It reaches the coast at the southern edge of the substantial community of <u>Ejido Enrendira</u>. Rio San Vicente is a sizeable stream which runs inland at right angles to the shoreline. For this reason it stands out well when viewed from the sea. It makes a <u>good landmark</u>. It is 13.1 miles from Puerto San Isidro to Highway 1 on a road running along the river. The easterly 9 miles of this route is a paved highway.

SECTION C
NORTH OF
PUNTA COLNETT
TO PUNTA BAJA

Unfortunately, the Baja peninsula was not created to fit neatly into the system of sections developed for this book. Thus, the

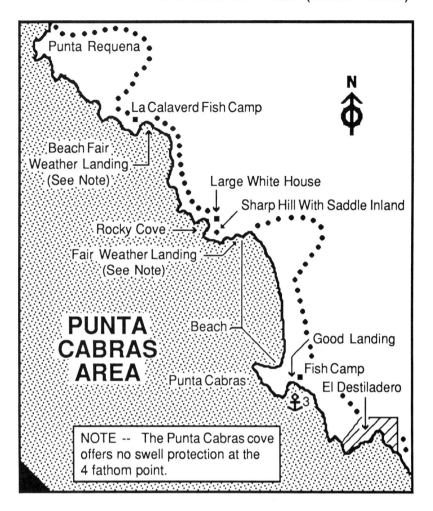

PUNTA CABRAS AREA

Punta Requena

La Calaverd Fish Camp

Beach Fair Weather Landing (See Note)

Large White House

Sharp Hill With Saddle Inland

Rocky Cove

Fair Weather Landing (See Note)

Beach

Good Landing

Fish Camp
El Destiladero

Punta Cabras

⚓3

NOTE -- The Punta Cabras cove offers no swell protection at the 4 fathom point.

PUNTA CABRAS (Looking SE) -- The cove above rounded Punta Cabras provides a shallow water anchorage.

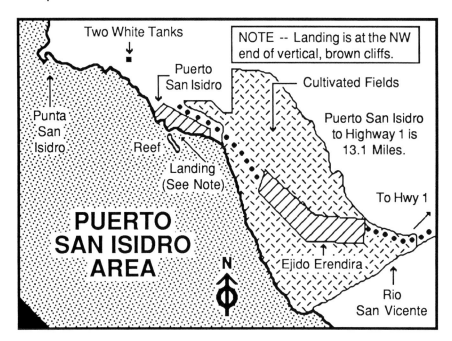

Two White Tanks

NOTE -- Landing is at the NW end of vertical, brown cliffs.

Puerto San Isidro

Cultivated Fields

Punta San Isidro

Reef

Puerto San Isidro to Highway 1 is 13.1 Miles.

Landing (See Note)

To Hwy 1

PUERTO SAN ISIDRO AREA

N

Ejido Erendira

Rio San Vicente

Because of the flat terrain, the coastline along section C is of low scenic quality. Ocean cruisers who have been traveling close inshore to *see-the-sights* to the north might now well consider proceeding directly toward Isla San Martin. Paying a visit to this island should prove more rewarding than laying a course which closely parallels the coast.

On clear days the north-south running ridge of the Sierra San Pedro Martir may be seen inland from the northern portion of Section C. The highest mountain in the Baja peninsula is 10,126-foot Picacho del Diablo. This peak bears approximately 70 degrees from Punta Colnett and 20 degrees from Cabo San Quintin.

PUNTA COLNETT -- While the coast north of Punta Colnett is without distinc-

dividing point between Section B and C falls some 9 miles north of Punta Colnett rather than directly at the cape. The coast in this vicinity is totally straight with no points or any other feature which can be used to identify the dividing line.

While it lacks a name, the change in topography is readily apparent. The steep mountains which have been only a short distance from the coast along Section B now recede inland. What is in view along Section C is a broad coastal plain. The northern segment is named Valle de Camalu, and the southern portion Valle de San Quintin. Much of this area is devoted to agriculture, and many sizeable cities lie inland along Highway 1. Their lights are visible from the sea at night.

PUERTO SAN ISIDRO (Looking E) --Shelter for a boat landing is created by a minor point and off-lying reef. Note cultivated fields on the level lands typical of Section B.

PUERTO SAN ISIDRO REEF (Looking NE) --Several boils of white water mark the reef.

tion, the point itself is unmistakable and is an excellent landmark. I believe it to be the peninsula's most easily recognized point of land. The current Mexican spelling and usage of Colnett is *Colonet*. I have deferred to the former version as it is used on Chart 21004, and this was no doubt the spelling used by the Englishman for whom the point was named. It should also be noted that the long-time usage of Cabo Colnett has been changed to Punta Colnett on the most recent edition of Chart 21004. Confusion reigns.

Most baja points are formed where a ridge of rock projects seaward. In contrast, Colnett is a massave flattopped segment of coastal plain. Where it meets the sea it is several hundred feet in height (See Photo). The upper portion is brown volcanic rock which forms vertical cliffs.

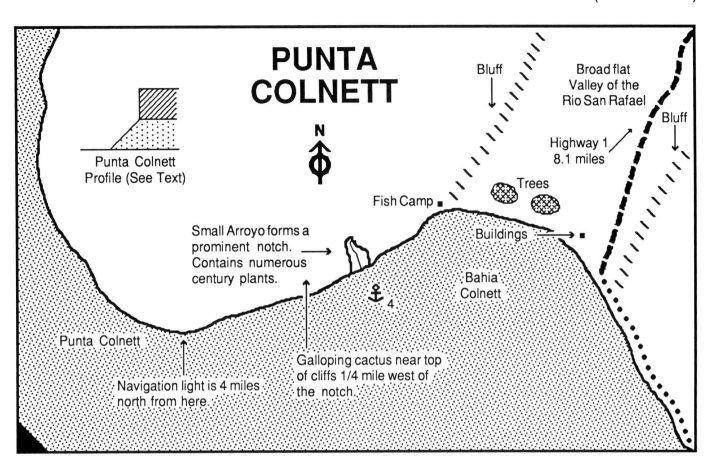

PUNTA COLNETT

N

Punta Colnett Profile (See Text)

Bluff

Broad flat Valley of the Rio San Rafael

Highway 1 8.1 miles

Bluff

Fish Camp

Trees

Small Arroyo forms a prominent notch. Contains numerous century plants.

Buildings

Bahia Colnett

Punta Colnett

Navigation light is 4 miles north from here.

Galloping cactus near top of cliffs 1/4 mile west of the notch.

Below is a lighter colored conglomerate deposit which has weathered at a 45 degree angle and is often overlain with segments of the darker rock fallen from above. The combination of these two layers creates a distinctive profile (See PUNTA COLNETT Chart). When first seen from a distance only the upper vertical portion may be in view.

As the point is rounded, there is no particular place that can be identified as *the point*. Thus, the profile is about

PUNTA COLNETT (Looking E) -- Note the points distinctive profile as discussed in the text.

THE NOTCH AT CABO COLNETT (Looking NW)

moderate and steady NW wind is blowing off-shore, and when even on top of the plateau there is no indication of a disturbance."

The cliffs promptly terminate NE from the anchorage where a fish camp is nestled at the base of the rocks. The head of the bay consists of low flat land which lies at the mouth of the broad valley of the Rio San Rafael. A good secondary road is constructed on the south side of this valley. In 8 miles it leads to Highway 1 at a point 3 miles south of the farming community of Colonet (Mexican spelling) where fuel and supplies are available.

the same as viewed from any angle. The point bears a latticework light tower which is neither on top of the cliffs or anywhere near what might be considered the center of the point. Rather, it is located 4 miles north of the center, near sea level, at the mouth of a small arroyo. This light would not be visible when approaching the point from a southerly direction from close inshore.

The bay south of the point provides a fair anchorage in 4 fathoms. The best anchoring site is adjacent to a notch formed by a short, but very apparent, arroyo which cuts through the south facing cliffs (See Photo). NW swells are considerably decreased by Punta Colnett but they refract into the anchorage at right angles to the shore. Thus, a bridle, or bow-stern anchors, are often required to assure a comfortable stay. *The 1937 U. S. Sailing Directions* notes "the anchorage .... is subject to heavy squalls which sweep down from the cliffs without warning; this may occur when a

PUNTA COLNETT

Colnett is a name that cries out as not being of Spanish origin. One author notes that this dominant cape draws its name from Captain James Colnett of the British Navy who commanded a charting expedition of the Baja coast in 1793. Another historical source references a different British Captain Colnett whose ship delivered the first Chinese to labor at fur trading posts in California, and speculates it was he for whom the promontory was named. In any case, the donor of the title would appear to be an Englishman.

MINOR POINTS -- Three minor points lie to the SE. Their names and distances from Punta Colnett are: Punta San Telmo 4 miles, Punta San Jacinto 10 miles, and Punta Camalu 14 miles (See Photos). These points are of little interest to either the ocean cruiser or land-based trailer boater and they do not stand out well from

PUNTA CAMALU (Looking NE) -- Steep cliffs provide the point with a degree of distinction.

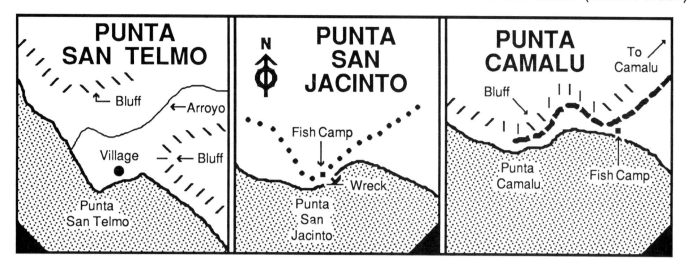

sea except from close in to shore. The most prominent landmark is the wreck of a three-masted freighter at Punta San Jacinto.

In all cases, landing in the bights south of the points would be difficult due to swell action, and there is insufficient northerly indent to provide good anchorages. Offshore water depths are shallow and in all three cases the 3 fathom point lies well off the points. The extensive kelp beds shown on chart 21004 between Punta San Telmo and Punta San Jacinto are present and should be avoided.

CINDER CONE LANDMARKS -- I have contended above that Punta Colnett is Baja's most distinguishable point of land. In similar fashion I will now anoint the San Quintin Cinder Cones as the most remarkable coastal landmark (See Photo). Having done so, I will no doubt have set in motion a debate aimed at proving me in error. If so, your nomination is welcome. Our mutual attention may also motivate the cones to be even more shy than they frequently are, as they are often obscured in the fog and low clouds that frequent this low-lying section of coast. However, in clear weather I have observed the taller peaks from a distance in excess of 40 miles.

The most northerly of these volcanic cinder cones is the 497-foot-high crest of Isla San Martin. The other seven are clustered along the western edge of Puerto San Quintin (See BAHIA SAN QUINTIN AREA Chart.) The remarkable feature is not the massiveness of the individual peaks but their cone-shaped profiles, and the presence of a sizeable number of cones in a relatively small area. They range in height from Cerro Kenton, 876 feet, to Monte Mazo, 160 feet.

In approaching from sea, the cones appear initially as islands. It is easy to mistake the first

PUNTA SAN TELMO (Looking E) -- Note the small village lying above the point.

PUNTA SAN JACINTO (Looking E) Note the prominent wreck lying above the rounded point.

93

CABO SAN QUINTIN (Looking NE) -- Note Punta Entrada and its 2 off-lying islets. Punta Entrada is also shown in the other photo on this page.

one to appear as being Isla San Martin. However, several of the mainland peaks are actually the first to emerge as they are taller than the island. If your helmsman proudly announces, "Land-ho, Isla San Martin" at each sight of a cone, he will prove to be correct about the fifth time. One can only hope that the course is not altered on each occasion. If all else fails, trust the compass.

BAHIA SAN QUINTIN AREA -- Puerto San Quintin is a large, shallow, two-armed body of water. It is the only one of Baja's Pacific lagoons whose entrance faces south, and is thus shielded from the prevailing NW winds by a protecting point of land. Even so, it is often fronted by breaking bars, even in calm weather. No directions are given for entering the bay. (See comments under Coastal Lagoons in Chapter 3.) If you simply must enter Puerto San Quintin with an ocean cruiser you might seek piloting assistance from the many fishing pangas that enter the bay during the afternoon. Fast shoal draft boats may simply follow the pangas through the entrance.

Land-based trailer boaters may approach the bay from inland over a good standard secondary road from Highway 1. Launching may be achieved with some difficulty over the beach near the oyster farm or at the motels near the old railroad causeway (See Photo).

Ocean-going vessels may take good anchorage in Bahia San Quintin east of Punta Entrada in 4 fathoms, or NE in 3 fathoms. Anchoring positions farther north or NW toward the lagoon entrance will put one's vessel over the breaking bars (See Photos).

The above noted anchorage is theoretically the best protected location. In addition, it offers ready access to a landing beach close NW of Punta Entrada. Its disadvantage is that skippers may stray too far toward the entrance to the lagoon and its breaking bars. In fair weather these breaks may be absent at high tide.

BAHIA SAN QUINTIN AREA (Looking N) -- The 2 dark islets lie off Punta Entrada. They consist of dark volcanic rock with no vegetation and serve as a landmark to the anchorage. The entrance from Bahia San Quintin into Puerto San Quintin is situated below the second cinder cone from the right.

To avoid the breaker problem, anchorage may be taken in 4 - 5 fathoms anywhere along a general line between Cabo San Quintin and the Hotel La Pinta San Quintin. Toward the east it is possible to penetrate considerably north of this line, and I have observed yachts comfortably anchored abreast the Cielito Lindo Trailer Court in 4 fathoms. (These observations were made in fair weather.)

The navigation light on Punta Azufre was observed to be very dim in contrast to the 15 miles visibility noted on the U. S. Charts. In contrast, there is a new light near Cabo San Quintin which appears to have 15-mile range. It is not shown on U. S. Charts.

The area's most prominent man-made landmark is the Hotel La Pinta San Quintin (See Photo). This large, two-story, white structure bears 30 degrees from Cabo San Quintin. This hotel and the nearby Cielito Lindo Motel and Trailer Court are frequented by tourists. Ocean cruisers in need of fuel, supplies, or assistance should best work their way to these facilities. Note that the

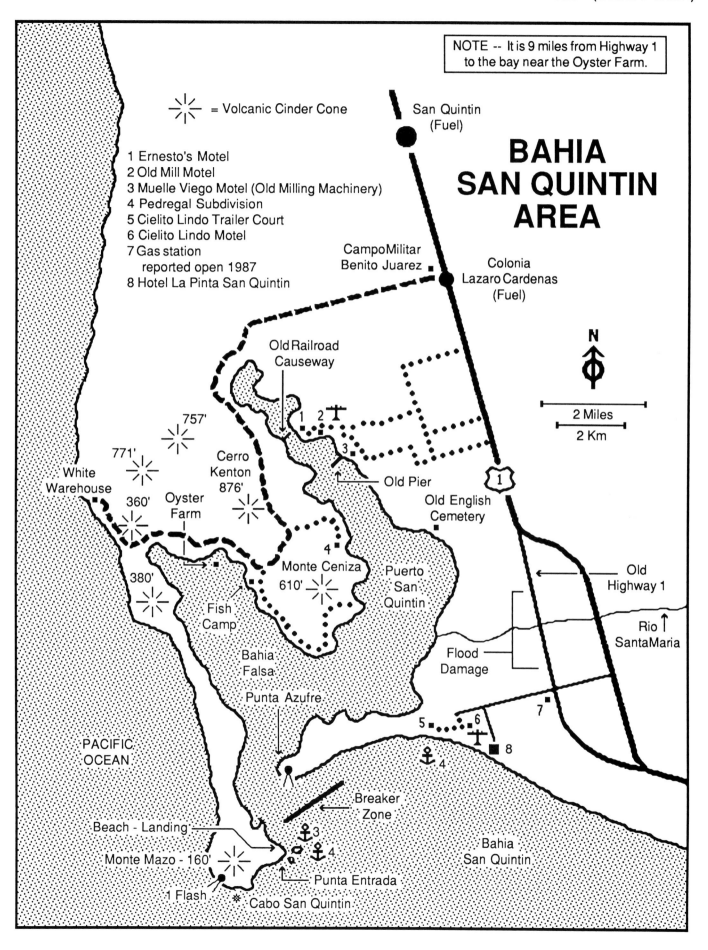

NOTE -- It is 9 miles from Highway 1
to the bay near the Oyster Farm.

San Quintin
(Fuel)

= Volcanic Cinder Cone

**BAHIA
SAN QUINTIN
AREA**

1 Ernesto's Motel
2 Old Mill Motel
3 Muelle Viego Motel (Old Milling Machinery)
4 Pedregal Subdivision
5 Cielito Lindo Trailer Court
6 Cielito Lindo Motel
7 Gas station
    reported open 1987
8 Hotel La Pinta San Quintin

CampoMilitar
Benito Juarez

Colonia
Lazaro Cardenas
(Fuel)

N

Old Railroad
Causeway

757'

2 Miles
2 Km

771'

Cerro
Kenton
876'

White
Warehouse

Old Pier

1

Old English
Cemetery

360'

Oyster
Farm

380'

4

Monte Ceniza
610'

Puerto
San
Quintin

Old
Highway 1

Fish
Camp

Rio
SantaMaria

Bahia
Falsa

Flood
Damage

Punta Azufre

5

6

7

PACIFIC
OCEAN

8

4

Breaker
Zone

Beach - Landing

3

Bahia
San Quintin

Monte Mazo - 160'

4

Punta Entrada

1 Flash

Cabo San Quintin

OLD RAILROAD CAUSEWAY AREA AT BAHIA SAN QUINTIN (Looking E) -- The Ernesto's and Old Mill Motels may be seen on the shore above the causeway.

sea breaks considerably in front of the hotel area making swimming a bit dangerous.

There are numerous rows of tamarisk and other trees bordering the flat agricultural lands north of the Hotel La Pinta San Quintin. When viewed from the sea the area appears to be heavily forested.

EL SOCORRO SAND DUNES -- Arroyo El Socorro is a minor stream channel that meets the sea 9 miles ESE from Cabo San Quintin. Directly north of the arroyo a narrow, lateral strip of sand crosses the landscape some 200 feet above sea level. A patch of light color shows on the steep slopes of the

---

arroyo south of the narrow strip. When illuminated by the sun, these light-colored areas stand out as good landmarks. This sandy area bears 80 degrees from Cabo San Quintin and is labled "Patch of White Sand" on U.S. Chart 21060.

BADLANDS -- As at the north end of Section C, the geographic change from low-lying, to steep coastal topography does not occur neatly at Punta Baja where I would like it to. Instead the southern end of the coastal plain ceases, and the land rises some 600-feet in elevation at a point some 13 miles north of Punta Baja. From this point south to the mouth of the Rio del Rosario the seaward facing land is heavily eroded into what geologist refer to as badlands.

HOTEL LA PINTA SAN QUINTIN (Looking SE) Note the heavy surf conditions in this area.

The bare, light gray-to-buff soil creates a landmark that shows clearly from the sea.

RIO DEL ROSARIO -- The Rio del Rosario is one of Baja's major drainages. It has formed a valley 1/2 to 1 mile wide which runs many miles inland. This broad valley is clearly in evidence at the south end of the badlands area. The river itself turns NE a few miles inland so that only the canyon's western extremity is visible from the sea. The village of El Rosario is situated on the Transpeninsular Highway 4 miles upstream. There is no anchorage or landing at the mouth of the river. However, the town may be reached for supplies from the anchorage at Punta Baja.

SAN QUINTIN LAND FRAUDS

The American speculators who started the development of Ensenada sold out to an English firm in 1888. As with the Americans, the new group's motive was land fraud on a grand scale. They concentrated their activities at Puerto San Quintin which was advertised as being capable of "holding all the fleets of Europe put together," a tall endorsement for a shallow lagoon composed mostly of area which dries in patches at low water.

The English commenced to dredge the harbor and built a large flour mill, as their announced intention was to sow wheat over a substantial acreage. A railroad was planned from San Quintin to Yuma, Arizona, and some 15 miles were actually constructed. By 1892 the entire enterprise had been abandoned. Today's travelers can still view a section of railroad causeway, old milling machinery, and an English cemetery on the shores of the lagoon (See BAHIA SAN QUINTIN AREA Chart).

EL ROSARIO

The village of El Rosario is the site of the first mission established by the Dominican order in Baja in 1774. The headquarters was moved 30 years later to a location on the north bank of the Rio del Rosario downstream from the community and about 2 miles from the sea. Its ruins may be visited on a short side trip from the Transpeninsular Highway. The antiquity of the current U. S. nautical chart is indicated by the fact that it notes the presence of this long-abandoned mission, but omits reference to an existing town of several thousand people.

There is a substantial area of tillable land and abundant water at El Rosario. This was not the case at the far more arid sites chosen for missions by the Jesuits to the south. It was thus able to produce exportable quantities of grain, olives, dried beef, and similar products. Historian Tomas Robertson notes that ships anchored offshore to take on these products. He speculates that the anchorage area was at Punta Baja. Logic would say that he is correct in this view.

The terrain north of the river mouth is considerably more eroded than that to the south. There is also a sharp contrast in soil coloration. Geologic maps show a fault line paralleling the Rio del Rosario. Land movement along this fault no doubt accounts for the differences in soil color and erosiveness on the two sides of the canyon.

PUNTA BAJA -- Punta Baja forms the southern terminus of the Northern Reach (See Chart in Chapter 8). It is located at the extremity of a narrow, mile-long peninsula which runs almost due north-south. This projection of land is relatively flattopped rising only 50 to 100 feet above sea level. At its end is a latticework navigation light tower. The light and the long, level terrain provide a distinctive profile.

SECTION D
ISLA DE SAN MARTIN

ISLA DE SAN MARTIN -- Isla de San Martin lies 3 miles off the mainland coast and some 10 miles NW of Cabo San Quintin. It is circular in shape, and is dominated at the center by its notched 471-foot cinder cone. This double peaked summit is readily apparent when viewed from several directions and makes an unmistakable landmark.

Isla de San Martin's circular shape is interrupted abruptly on the SE side by a remarkable above-water hook of lava rock. Its straight and orderly conformation leads one to conclude it could be a man-made breakwater. This hook of rock forms Caleta Hassler, a small but good

anchorage sheltered from the prevailing NW winds (See Photo). However, should the wind become more northerly, the cove is swept by swells. On one occasion I entered Hasslers in company with a modest 10 knot northerly breeze. The sailboats at anchor were rolling badly. Under these conditions far smoother anchorage was taken off the mouth of the small lagoon south of the rock hook.

There is good holding ground in 4 - 6 fathoms for at least 1/4 mile in both directions from the lava rock hook at Caleta Hassler. Arriving skippers should check this entire area to determine the calmest anchoring location under the prevailing swell conditions. Also be alert to the fact that swells refracting around the island's south side may break over the low spot in the rock hook (See Photo) imparting considerable roll to vessels anchored immediately to the north. Thus, what might seem to be the best anchoring location may actually be the worst. The anchorage NW from the rock hook is touted as a good anchorage in SW storm conditions.

A mussel farm was established in Caleta Hassler a short time after the photo in this book was taken. As a result, much of the anchoring area in the cove is taken up with

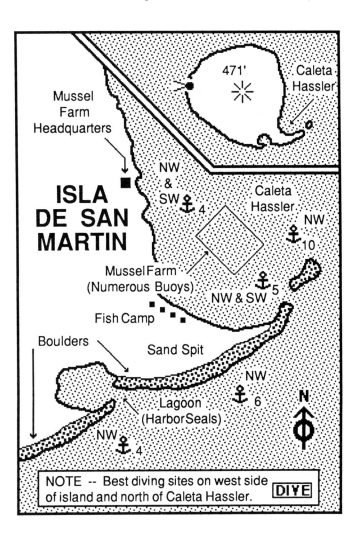

CALETA HASSLER -- ISLA DE SAN MARTIN (Looking NW) -- Here the island's peak is shrouded in low clouds that are often present in this area. Note that the rock reef is breached by the sea at high tide. Photo was taken before installation of the mussel farm buoys noted in the text. Swells can be seen coming around both sides of the island in the photo's lower right segment.

lines of round floats supporting underwater ropes wrapped with mesh tubing. The tubes contain thousands of maturing mussels. The mussel farm floats are invisible on dark nights, and vessels entering the cove under such conditions can easily snarl a prop or rudder. Anchorage east of the floats is possible in 10-fathoms, and to the NW, in 4 fathoms.

All island anchorages are romantic, but a stop at Hasslers may be your first opportunity to visit a Mexican fish camp. The camp is located on the sand beach at the head of the cove. Its inhabitants have been known to sell crab and lobster to visiting cruisers. Floats attached to crab pots ring the island. Be careful to avoid these when anchoring in the area west of the rock bar.

PUNTA BAJA (Looking 125 Degrees) -- Note the points low-lying profile.

A colony of harbor seals makes its home in the small lagoon SW of the camp. They are worth a visit. (Previous guidebooks report elephant seals here. The local fishermen report that they are not now present.) These animals are very sensitive to the presence of humans so the lagoon should be approached slowly and quietly.

Isla de San Martin is mantled with rough lava rock. Thus, any extensive hiking will prove difficult. However, a tour through the terrain inland from the harbor seal lagoon will be rewarding. The rocks are heavily encrusted with lichens

THE FISH CAMP AT CALETA HASSLER (Looking SE)
Several of the cinder cones near Bahia San Quintin
are visible in the left background.

ISLA DE SAN MARTIN (Looking 270 Degrees) -- The
island's profile is typical of a shield volcano. The twin
peaks of its high point form the island's most distinctive feature.

SAN QUINTIN CINDER CONES (Looking E from Isla
de San Martin)

and there are numerous species of low growing
cacti, succulents, and shrubs. Many places here
would be the envy of rock gardening enthusiasts.

ROCA BEN -- Charts 21004 and 21060 show
Roca Ben (Ben's Rock) lying 2.5 miles south of
Isla de San Martin along with the notation
"Breaks Occasionally." The rock lies 1 1/2
fathoms below the sea surface. In a 1987 letter
to *Latitude 38 Magazine*, veteran skipper Skip
Allen reports as follows concerning an encounter with Roca Ben: "The depth sounder
began a precipitous rise from the steady 50
fathoms it had been showing. In less than a
minute it was reading 15 fathoms and continued
to drop. Just as we began to alter course one of
the biggest waves I've ever seen rose out of the
calm sea not 50 yards abeam. It broke in a roar-
ing smother of foam 50 yards across and 100
yards long. -- Unfortunately this February 5, a 57-
foot charter powerboat was fishing over Ben's
Rock when a similar wave came through. The
boat was rolled over and sunk, and nine lives
were lost. Beware of Roca Ben!" Nuff said.

Chart 21060 also shows another unnamed rock
6 miles southward from Roca Ben.

CHAPTER 8
THE NORTHERN BIGHT
PUNTA BAJA TO PUNTA EUGENIA

CHAPTER SUMMARY

Chapter 8 describes the Northern Bight. It is the largest of three broad indentations in Baja's Pacific coast. Its southern portion is named Bahia de Sebastian Vizcaino in honer of the expedition leader who thoroughly investigated the peninsula's Pacific coast in 1602-03.

One distingushing characteristic of the Northern Bight is the fact that it is bypassed by most coastal cruisers, both north and south bound. The merits of proceeding in this manner are presented early in this chapter, along with an arrary of navigation alternatives. While this section of coast is infrequently visited, it does contain numerous anchorages and points of interest. It is thus described with the same thoroughness as other portions of the coast.

SECTION			DESCRIPTION
NO.	FROM	TO	
A	Punta Baja	Punta Blanca	Coastline is steep-to with few indentations and thus few protected anchorages. The one anchorage, San Carlos, is a good one.
B	Punta Blanca	Punta Rosarito	Coastline is steep-to but with numerous protected points that form fair to good anchorages.
C	Punta Rosarito	Punta Malarrimo	Low-lying coast at edge of the Desierto Vizcaino. Continuous sand beaches, gentle offshore gradients.
D	Punta Malarrimo	Punta Eugenia	A short segment of steep-to coastline but with only slight indentations and no protected anchorages. Faces the prevailing winds.

SECTION A
PUNTA BAJA TO
PUNTA BLANCA

It is 78 miles from Punta Baja to Punta Blanca. The intervening coastline is rocky with few sandy beaches. It is backed by terrain of moderate steepness. There are a few prominent points of land, and with one exception (Punta San Carlos) the bights on their SE flanks are not sufficiently concave to form protected anchorages.

Punta Baja is the approximate break point between two vegetative regions. To the north lie the chaparral brushlands (California Vegetative Region) typical of northern Baja and southern Alta California. Starting at Punta Baja is the Sonoran Desert Region. This region continues south to near the tip of the peninsula (See discussion in Chapter 5 concerning the plants found in the Sonoran Desert).

PUNTA BAJA AREA -- At Punta Baja the peninsular coast makes a right angle turn from north-south to east-west. The narrow neck of land forming the point itself is aligned almost due north-south. It thus poses a far superior barrier to the prevailing NW swells than do many other Pacific promontories. The bay easterly from Punta Baja is Bahia del Rosario. It provides good anchorage as there is minimal swell refraction. Most vessels anchor abreast of the Punta Baja fishing village, but equally good protection is afforded for a considerable distance in either direction.

The Bahia del Rosario anchorage does have two negative qualities. The quiet waters in the lee of the point have made an ideal location for the deposition of ocean-borne sand. The offshore gradients are thus quite gradual with the 4 fathom point lying 1/4 mile from the shore. Making a trip to the village in the ship's tender becomes quite a chore if it is not motor driven. Also, the anchorage offers little protection from the prevailing wind due

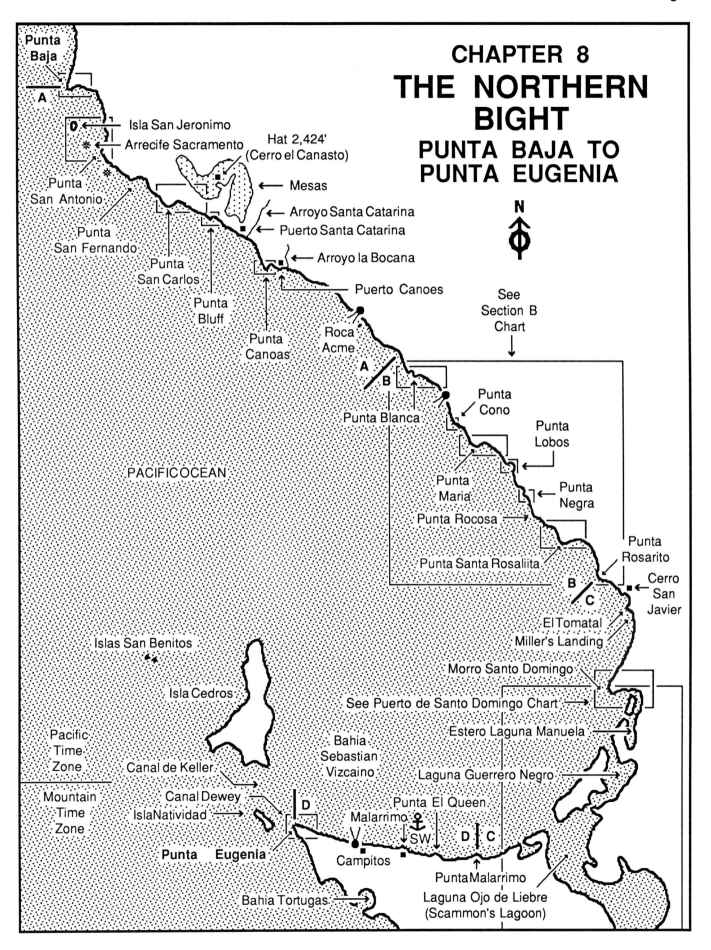

CHAPTER 8
THE NORTHERN BIGHT
PUNTA BAJA TO PUNTA EUGENIA

N

Punta Baja

A

Isla San Jeronimo

Arrecife Sacramento

Hat 2,424'
(Cerro el Canasto)

← Mesas

Punta San Antonio

← Arroyo Santa Catarina

Punta San Fernando

← Puerto Santa Catarina

Punta San Carlos

← Arroyo la Bocana

Punta Bluff

Puerto Canoes

Punta Canoas

Roca Acme

See Section B Chart

A

B

Punta Cono

Punta Blanca

Punta Lobos

Punta Maria

Punta Negra

Punta Rocosa →

PACIFIC OCEAN

Punta Santa Rosaliita

Punta Rosarito

B

C

Cerro San Javier

El Tomatal

Miller's Landing

Islas San Benitos

Morro Santo Domingo

Isla Cedros

See Puerto de Santo Domingo Chart →

Estero Laguna Manuela

Pacific Time Zone

Bahia Sebastian Vizcaino

Laguna Guerrero Negro

Canal de Keller

Mountain Time Zone

Canal Dewey

D

Punta El Queen

Isla Natividad →

Malarrimo

D | C

SW

Punta Eugenia

Campitos

Punta Malarrimo

Laguna Ojo de Liebre
(Scammon's Lagoon)

Bahia Tortugas

to its low-lying configuration, and the distance from shore to the anchoring ground.

There are no stores or other commercial outlets at the small Punta Baja fishing village located near the landward end of the Punta Baja promontory. However, it is probable that one of its residents can be hired to drive visitors to Highway 1 and the community of El Rosario over a good standard secondary road. The ocean cruiser may also seek assistance from tourists in recreational vehicles who occasionally camp and fish at Punta Baja. Small boats may be launched with some difficulty from a steep road leading to the sea at the village.

The anchorage at Punta Baja is one of the more frequently used stopover points on Baja's Pacific coast as it lies at the north end of the lengthy open sea crossing

EXPLORING ASHORE AT ISLA SAN JERONIMO

Isla San Jeronimo is a good place for onshore exploring. Hiking is easy as the terrain is gentle and there is little vegetation, a marked contrast to the difficult land-scape at Isla San Martin to the north. Especially interesting are the numerous small coves on the north and west shores where tidepool vegetation and sea life are abundant. I have observed elephant seals in these pools, a fact that is not reported in current literature concerning this species. The elephant seal is recovering from near extinction and may be expanding its territory. The island also serves as a rookery for several species of sea birds. The island itself is made up of a variety of sedimentary rock.

of the Northern Bight. It provides north-bound vessels with welcome relief from the uphill pound into the Pacific swell.

NAVIGATION ALTERNATIVES -- The best boating waters in Baja California are near Cabo San Lucas or in the southern reaches of the Sea of Cortez. Many coastal cruisers wish to proceed to these areas with minimal delay. This requires setting a course from Punta Baja towards Isla Cedros and making an ocean passage that completely bypasses the Northern Bight coastline. This alternative offers a logical course of action for many cruisers and I do not argue against it. However, I do offer three alternatives for those who do make this choice. Cruising close to shore along the Northern Bight coastline offers a fourth course of action. Each of these four possibilities is briefly discussed below.

ISLA CEDROS, EAST SIDE -- Most coastal cruisers leaving Punta Baja have Bahia Tortugas as their next major destination. The most direct course to this haven passes along the eastern coast of Isla Cedros. Anchorage may be taken en route at several places along this shore, and the island's village is an interesting place to visit. Isla Cedros' eastern, or lee, shore also provides calmer waters than the western side.

ISLA CEDROS, WEST SIDE -- For those making a round trip along Baja's Pacific shore, consider traversing the island's western shore on the journey south, and reserve the eastern, or lee, shore for returning home. Laying a course along the eastern shore of Isla Cedros is the obvious north-bound choice because of the calm waters present on this side of the island. There will be plenty of rough sea ahead. A convenient rest stop along the western route may be taken at Bahia del Sur at the SW tip of the Island. This is one of the most well protected anchorages along Baja's Pacific shore, and the best one at Isla Cedros.

ISLAS SAN BENITOS -- Paying a visit to this group of islands and its colonies of elephant seals is to me one of the high points of a voyage along Baja's Pacific coast. The time to do this is on the way south. From here it is a relatively short hop back to Bahia del Sur and Cedros Village, or directly on to Bahia Tortugas. Taking in both Islas San Benitos and the southern portion of Isla Cedros on the way south is my recommended course of action for those who wish to build a reasonable amount of leisure time into their south-bound trip.

TRAVERSE THE BIGHT -- There are two reasons why you might choose to travel close in along the shore of the Northern Bight. First, should you be seeking solitude, this is a good place to visit. As noted, it is bypassed by most ocean cruisers. The Transpeninsular Highway is many miles inland and there are no coastal roads of consequence. The only communities directly on the coast lie at the end points (Punta Baja and Punta Eugenia) and at Santa Rosaliita.

The long beat north along the Pacific coast can be a wearing one when returning home from the winter in Baja. The second reason for choosing the close-in route is to break the northern run into shorter segments with overnight stops along the Northern Bight. Obviously, the total trip will be longer.

There is also an intermediate north-bound alternative. This is to set one's course from Punta Eugenia, or Isla Cedros, toward the anchorage at San Carlos rather than directly at Punta Baja. Refuge can be taken at San Carlos to shorten the crossing, or in the event the weather should kick up. The total distance involved in this alternative is very little more than in a direct crossing.

ISLA SAN JERONIMO -- Isla San Jeronimo is in clear view from Punta Baja. The 3/4-mile long island is 9 miles south from this point and 5 miles offshore. Its long access runs essentially north-south, but the southern portion of the eastern shore faces SE and provides good protection from the prevailing NW swells. A fish camp of tightly packed buildings is located here at the head of a slight indentation.

Good prevailing wind anchorage may be taken 200 yards offshore from the fish camp in 4 fathoms. It is fre-

ISLA SAN JERONIMO (Looking 160 Deg.)

quently used by coastal vessels. Skippers should expect to encounter some degree of wave refraction coming from both ends of the island. However, my experience is that this anchorage provides better wind protection than that at Punta Baja. There is also a good landing at the fish camp. In taking shelter here, you may care to pay tribute to Juan Rodriguez Cabrillo who anchored his vessels at Isla San Jeronimo on August 20, 1542, only 50 years after Columbus's first voyage to the new world.

There is a small cove along the island's NE shore (See ISLA SAN JERONIMO Chart). I believe this area would provide a satisfactory anchorage in SW storm condi-

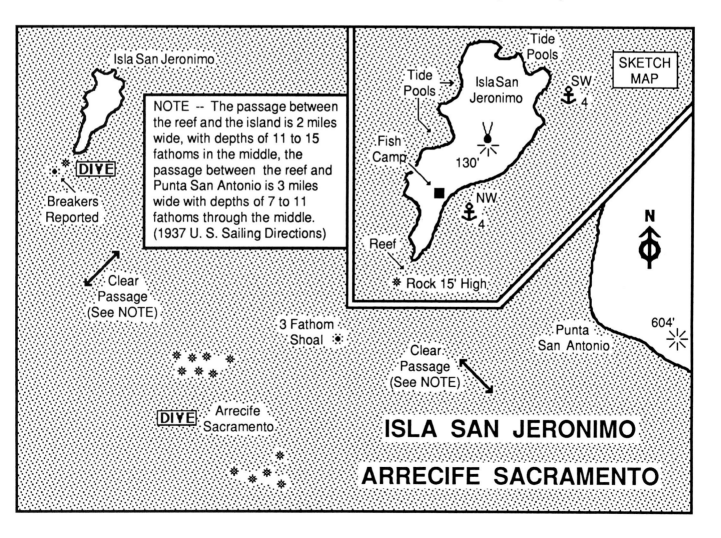

ISLA SAN JERONIMO FISH CAMP (Looking S)
Photo was taken from the island's lighthouse. The fish camp may be seen on the island's SE shore with *La Patricia* at anchor offshore.

tions. Four fathoms may be sounded 150 yards offshore. I have traversed along the island's eastern shore from the above noted NE cove to the anchorage off the fish camp. Water depths of 4 - 6 fathoms and gentle bottom gradients were sounded in all places. It is thus possible to anchor anywhere in this area. Finding this situation was not unexpected as Chart 21005 indicates water depths of only 8 - 12 fathoms in the entire channel between the island and the peninsular coast.

One of Baja's older lighthouses is situated on the island's 130-foot highpoint. I have observed that the light from this structure is rather dim. A similar condition has been seen at several other of the lighthouses of similar vintage. In clearing San Jeronimo, give adequate birth to the reef of rocks which extends for some 1/2 mile from the island's

southern tip. The presence of this reef gives added swell protection to the island's fish camp anchorage.

ARRECIFE SACRAMENTO -- The two most notorious hazards to navigation along Baja's Pacific coast are Arrecife Sacramento (Sacramento Reef) and the rocks lying off Punta Abreojos at the southern end of the Middle Reach. Arrecife Sacramento covers an area over 2 miles long centered 4 miles west of Punta San Antonio and 3 1/2 miles south of Isla San Jeronimo. The reef derived its name from the 271-foot side-wheeler *S.S. Sacramento* which it sent to a watery grave in 1872.

The reef is particularly hazardous to vessels approaching Isla San Jeronimo or Punta Baja from the south after the long passage from Isla Cedros. Such skippers should give the area a

PUNTA SAN ANTONIO (Looking S)

wide birth, particularly at night. Two large areas of breakers usually occur over the reef if substantial swells are present. This observation conforms with the distribution of the reef's rocks in two groups as shown in the ARRECIFE SACRAMENTO Chart. At other times I have observed no sign of their presence. See this same chart concerning clear passages north and east of the reef. I have traversed the passage between the reef and the peninsular shore on several occasions with no problems.

PUNTA SAN ANTONIO -- The substantial change in coastal alignment that occurred at Punta Baja is short lived, and the shore's north-south trend is quickly resumed. A more lasting change to NW-SE occurs south of Punta San Antonio. It might easily be argued this is the appropriate place to designate as the upper end

THE LIGHTHOUSE ON ISLA SAN JERONIMO

of the Northern Bight. I have chosen Punta Baja for this honor because its protected anchorage is such an obvious destination point. In contrast there is no bay on either side of Punta San Antonio, and it is of no use as an anchorage. The land inland from the point is low and of no particular distinction (See Photo).

PUNTA SAN FERNANDO -- Five miles SE from Punta San Antonio is another point which lacks significant distinction (See Photo). Punta San Fernando does have a shallow indentation on its eastern side, and one previous guidebook designates it as an anchorage. However, the northerly indent of the bight would indicate it would be an indifferent haven at best. I have never used it. There is a small fish camp near the mouth of an arroyo at the head of the cove indicating that it does provide some degree of protection, at least for landing purposes.

PUNTA SAN CARLOS AREA -- Punta San Carlos is a far more substantial promontory than the two points noted above. It lies 26 miles SE of Punta Baja. The point's immediate shore is a moderately steep bluff about 50 feet high. However the land for some 1/2 mile inland is level and is the site of a natural surface airstrip. Wave action has created a small islet off the southern extremity of the point. Under moderate swell conditions, the sea breaks heavily here and for several hundred yards further south into the ocean. This area is extensively used for

PUNTA SAN FERNANDO (Looking SE) -- Note that the shore of the bight above (east) of the point is fully rimmed with breakers, a good indication that it is swept by refracted swells and provides little protection from the prevailing weather.

wind surfing, and is reported to be one of the best locations for this sport in North America.

Bahia San Carlos is a substantial bay to the east of the point (See Photo). It creates a sizeable anchorage. On one occasion I have shared this haven with some twenty-five Mexican fishing vessels that were resting here over the weekend.

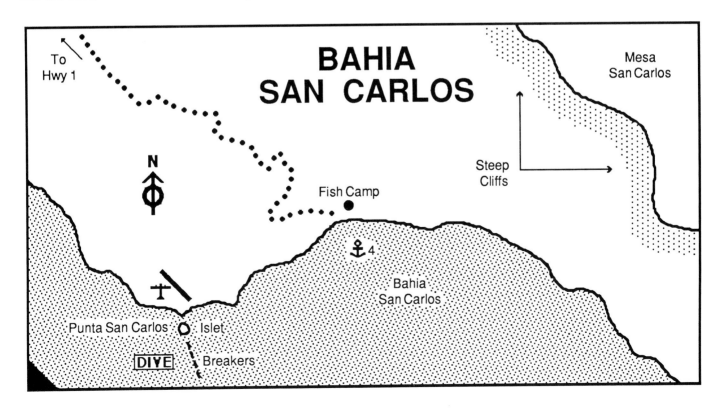

BAHIA SAN CARLOS (Looking E) -- Note Mesa San Carlos along the upper edge of the photo. The size-able erosion scars along the mesa's flanks make excellent landmarks from the sea. Windsurfing activities center around the low islet which lies directly off Punta San Carlos.

4-fathoms 400 yards offshore. One previous guidebook recommends anchoring immediately east of the islet off Punta San Carlos. However, I observed no discernible difference in swell action at any point between this islet and the fish camp. Holding ground is available at any point in this area in 4 fathoms.

North and east of the bay lies massive Mesa San Carlos. It may be used as a guide in locating the anchorage. The mesa's 1,600-foot high rim approaches to within about 1 mile of the coast NE of the anchorage. Previous literature reports that high velocity winds can sweep down these slopes making the harbor untenable. I have not experienced such winds.

There is a substantial stand of cardon (giant cactus) on the steep slopes below the rim of the mesa bearing 10 degrees from the fish camp. This species is typical of the larger desert plants which make Baja's Sonoran Desert one of the most fascinating areas of arid vegetation in the world. Most of the larger species grow principally at higher elevations in the interior. The rapid elevational rise of the mesa at this point brings the environmental conditions needed by the cardon to within view of the coast.

There is a fish camp at the head of the cove which is served by a low standard road.

I have been in Bahia San Carlos on four occasions and found it windy most of the time. Wind surfers advise that substantial winds are one of the reasons the area is prized for their sport. The close proximity of high mesa walls a short distance inland no doubt contribute to these conditions.

On one recent visit I entered Bahia San Carlos in steady 25-knot winds and found it swept with wind-waves. The calmest spot was directly off the fish camp where anchorage may be had in

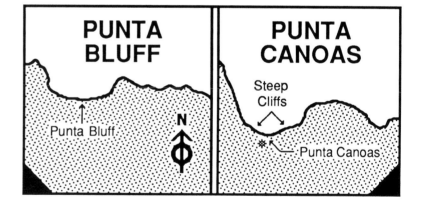

PUNTA SAN CARLOS (Looking 285 Degrees).

Motorists in SW United States may view many mesas whose bases are thousands of feet in elevation. Here, near Bahia San Carlos, is the best location of which I am aware on the North American coast where such massive tablelands can be seen rising directly from sea level. Mesa San Carlos has already been mentioned. To the SE is Mesa Santa Catarina. The two dominate the coastal skyline for a distance of over 15 miles. Note the strata of hard rock which forms the upper surface of these mesas. It is this hard cap rock which gives these formations their table-like structure.

Topographic maps show that the two mesas are actually joined near their inland edges. The steep-sided arroyo that divides the two lobes of what is really one mesa is named El Canasto (The Hamper). This canyon is readily apparent from the sea. A rounded peak is situated 7 miles inland near the eastern end of Mesa San Carlos. This is 2,424-foot high Cerro El Canasto. It is referred to as Hat on Chart 21060. Although an excellent landmark from some distance at sea, it is obscured by the rims of the mesas from close inshore.

PUNTA BLUFF -- Punta Bluff (Punta Escarpada) is a minor point of land 7 miles SE of Punta San Carlos. The point is approximately 1 mile west of a line running due south from Hat Peak (Cerro El Canasto).

In his *Baja Cruising Notes*, Vern Jones recommends that the bight east of Punta Bluff "is a far better lee with better protection from the prevailing NW winds than its bigger brother, Bahia San Carlos." For this reason a chart of Punta Bluff has been included in this book so that the two areas may be compared. My own observations do not concur with Vern's, but I pass on his views for your consideration.

I entered the bight at Punta Bluff the morning following the 25-knot wind situation described for Bahia San Carlos. The moderate swells present swept the potential anchorage area with little or no decrease from their intensity in the open sea. Holding ground did appear to

PUNTA BLUFF (Looking 300 Degrees).

be present in 4 fathoms 200 yards offshore. This close-in position combined with the steep bluffs of the point no doubt give better wind protection than at San Carlos. However, swells rank as the priority in my mind, and I would not anchor here except in very calm seas.

PUERTO SANTA CATARINA -- Arroyo Santa Catarina is a major stream channel that runs along the base of the eastern flank of Mesa Santa Catarina. It reaches the sea due south of the mesa's eastern rim, and 13 miles SE of Punta San Carlos. A fish camp lies about 1 mile NW of the mouth of the arroyo. A smaller 1,300-

PUERTO SANTA CATARINA

The coastline is relatively straight near the mouth of the Arroyo Santa Catarina, and it offers no protection from incoming ocean swells. Yet this desolate area bears the name Puerto (Port) Santa Catarina, and for many years it was the site of port facilities serving several mines located in the interior. Topographic maps show five abandoned copper and iron mines in the region 10 to 20 air miles inland to the NE.

But the port's most famous customer was the onyx mine at El Marmol. This mine is 51 miles by rough dirt road from Puerto Santa Catarina. It lies on the eastern side of the Transpeninsular Highway and is less than 15 air miles from the Sea of Cortez. Should you be the owner of an ashtray or other item made from Baja onyx, you can marvel at the fact that the heavy rock from which it is made was probably hauled almost totally across the Baja peninsula and transported from this remote segment of coast.

The *1937 U.S. Sailing Directions* reports the presence of a wharf projecting from the beach, and that lighters would move cargo from here to vessels anchored nearby in the open roadstead. *Baja Sea Guide* notes a pier capable of accommodating vessels of 20-foot draft as late as 1957. Then the development of plastics greatly reduced the market for onyx. Today there is little left at Santa Catarina but memories.

foot mesa whose high point is labled Bracket Peak on Chart 21060 is situated some four miles due east. A prominent patch of sand dunes is located a short distance NW of this mesa.

PUNTA CANOAS -- Punta Canoas is a prominent rounded point 20 miles SE from Punta San Carlos. Its seaward face consists of vertical cliffs of light-colored sedimentary rock. These cliffs are backed by a substantial area of gentle terrain. The overall configuration reminds one of a diminutive Punta Colnett (See Photos).

PUNTA CANOAS (Looking 280 Degrees) -- Note the vertical cliffs.

PUNTA CANOAS (Looking E) -- The point's level top fronted by vertical cliffs give it a distinctive appearance. In this regard it is similar to Punta Colnett except that the talus slopes present at Colnett are missing at Punta Canoas.

To the east of the point lies a small bay. Reference to the charts will show that this bight is somewhat larger than that at Punta Bluff but the two areas have otherwise similar characteristics, i.e., the 4 fathom point lies 200 yards offshore, steep cliffs offer wind protection, and the anchorages are swept by swells with little or no decrease from those in the open sea. It is thus interesting to note that Vern Jones reports that the anchorage at Punta Canoas is poor, but that Punta Bluff is good. I have found both of them to be of poor quality.

PUERTO CANOAS -- Easterly from Punta Canoas the coast runs almost due east-west. Four miles easterly from the point is the broad, easily discernible mouth of an arroyo named La Bocana (See Photo). There are fish camps on either side of its channel. The westerly camp shows clearly to sea, while the easterly encampment lies largely behind a coastal dune. This area bears the proud name of Puerto Canoas. The offshore water depths are shallow and landing here would be undertaken with some difficulty. Obviously the local fishermen manage to accomplish this feat.

ROCA ACME -- The coast from Punta Canoas SE to Punta Blanca has little to distinguish it. Thus, the coastal cruiser will welcome any significant landmark. Twenty-foot-high Roca Acme provides this service about halfway between these two points. The rock is actually an islet labled Islote Piedra de San Jose on Mexican maps. It lies about 1/3 mile offshore and is the home of a substantial colony of sea lions. A concrete navigation light tower is constructed on a bluff northward from the islet (See Photo). Several small houses lie NE of the light. This is Puerto San Jose. The *1937 U. S. Sailing Directions* notes that it was formerly "a shipping point for properties in the interior."

PUERTO CANOAS (Looking NE) -- The fish camp at the base of the horizontally banded cliffs show poorly from the sea. The flat-bottomed arroyo and salt water lagoon to the left is La Bocana. The presence of such a lagoon fronted by a barrier beach is typical wherever a sizeable stream channel meets the sea in arid Baja California.

ROCA ACME AND PUERTO SAN JOSE (Looking E) -- The islet at the extreme right of the photo is Roca Acme. The concrete navigation light lies north of the rock.

ROCA ACME (Looking N) -- Note navigation light on shore to the left of the rock.

During a visit to Roca Acme in calm seas I recorded four fathoms of water halfway between the rock and the navigation light. *Baja Sea Guide* reports that the waters in this area can provide a smooth anchorage that is frequented by commercial fishing boats. During the visit in question I did in fact find calm seas. During a subsequent visit moderate swells were running and heavy breakers were in evidence between the islet and the navigation light indicating the presence of a reef in this area. The waters on the leeward (east side) of this reef were calmer than the open sea but were sufficiently agitated to discourage my venturing further into them. This area is a calm sea anchorage at best.

There is a series of minor points southward between Roca Acme and Punta Blanca but they are of no particular distinction. Two miles NW from Roca Acme binoculars will disclose a stand of datilillo plants inland about 1 mile. The datilillo is a small tree which resembles the Joshua tree of SW United States. It is one of the dominant plants in the interior of the central portion of the Baja peninsula but is infrequently seen along the coast.

SECTION B
PUNTA BLANCA TO
PUNTA ROSARITO

There have been relatively few prominent points of land in Section A to the north. In Section B the coast continues its basic NW - SE trend, but there are many distinguishable promontories. This is so much so that it requires some care in navigation to properly determine one's location.

There are also several anchorages in the fair-to-good category. The four best are Bahia Blanca, Bahia Falsa, Bahia Playa Maria, and Bahia Santa Rosalilita (on the shore of which there is a substantial village). The first three of these were entered within a 2 1/2-hour period in moderate

PUNTA AND BAHIA BLANCA (Looking E) -- Punta Blanca is in the photo's lower left corner. Note its dark coloration.

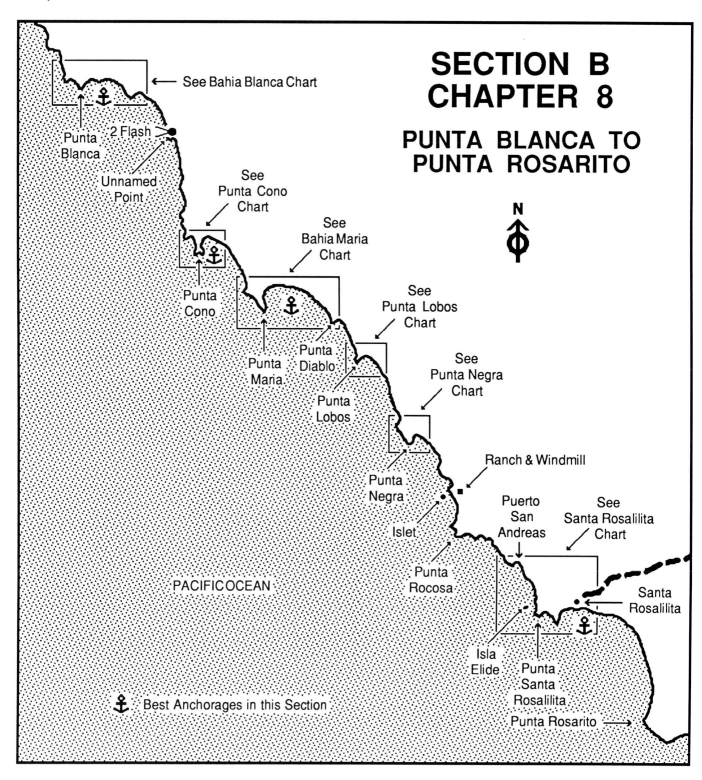

SECTION B
CHAPTER 8

PUNTA BLANCA TO
PUNTA ROSARITO

NW swells conditions. Both Bahia Falsa and Bahia Playa Maria clearly had calmer water conditions than Bahia Blanca and would appear to be better anchorages.

PUNTA BLANCA -- In my first visit to Punta Blanca I approached from the SE and anchored in Bahia Blanca to the east of the point. It was noted that the face of the point in view from this anchorage consisted of <u>dark colored rock</u>. Punta Blanca means "White Point." We

anticipated that the coloration would lighten upon rounding the point in the morning, but being of little faith, I noted in the log, "God save us from Punta Blanca, a dark colored point."

Sadly, I must report that salvation did not descend upon us. Indeed, Punta Blanca is a point made up of dark colored rock. The point is low and level and rises inland to a gently rounded plateau (See Photo).

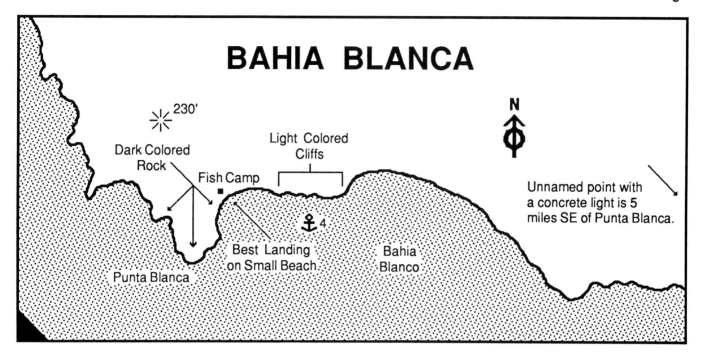

BAHIA BLANCA

230'

Dark Colored Rock

Fish Camp

Light Colored Cliffs

N

Unnamed point with a concrete light is 5 miles SE of Punta Blanca.

Best Landing on Small Beach

Punta Blanca

Bahia Blanco

4

BAHIA BLANCA -- To the east of Punta Blanca is a sizeable bay some 1/2 mile deep and 2 miles in breadth. The best landing is on a small beach at the head of the cove directly adjoining the fish camp. East of this landing, the shore consists of a 1/2-mile-long cliff of light colored rocks (See Photo). It is perhaps this light colored area that has caused the bay and point to bear the name "blanca." The cliffs stand out well and create a good landmark when approaching from the south. The bay is swept by swells refracting around Punta Blanca, but it provides a fair to good anchorage in 4 fathoms 400 yards offshore. I have found the calmest spot to be off the eastern end of the cliffs but any location in this general area appears acceptable.

UNNAMED POINT - Five miles SE from Punta Blanca lies a rounded rocky point which has no

UNNAMED POINT SE OF PUNTA BLANCA

name on any available chart or map (See Photo). Its significance lies in the presence of a concrete light tower. The point and light provide a landmark when approaching Bahia Blanca

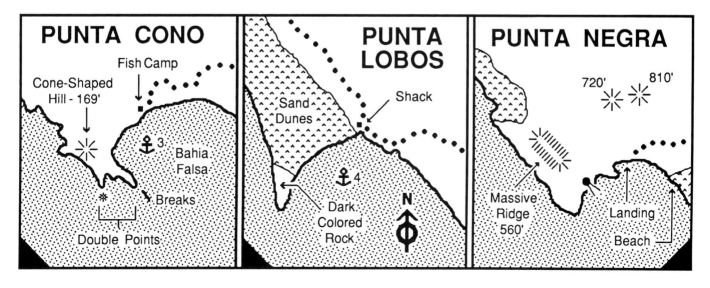

PUNTA CONO

Fish Camp

Cone-Shaped Hill - 169'

3

Bahia Falsa

Breaks

Double Points

PUNTA LOBOS

Sand Dunes

Shack

4

Dark Colored Rock

N

PUNTA NEGRA

720'   810'

Massive Ridge 560'

Landing

Beach

PUNTA CONO (Looking NE) -- Bahia Falsa lies beyond Punta Cono's double points. Only the SE portion of the point's cone-shaped hill is visible at the photo's left edge.

PUNTA CONO (Looking 75 Degrees)

from the south. There is no apparent reason for the location of the light here except that it is approximately halfway between the fish camps at Bahia Blanca and Bahia Falsa. Perhaps it represents a compromise solution to having a light at both camps.

PUNTA CONO -- Punta Cono is a double-pointed headland located 10 miles SE of Punta Blanca (See Photo). Both of the rocky points project southward. "Cono" is the Spanish word

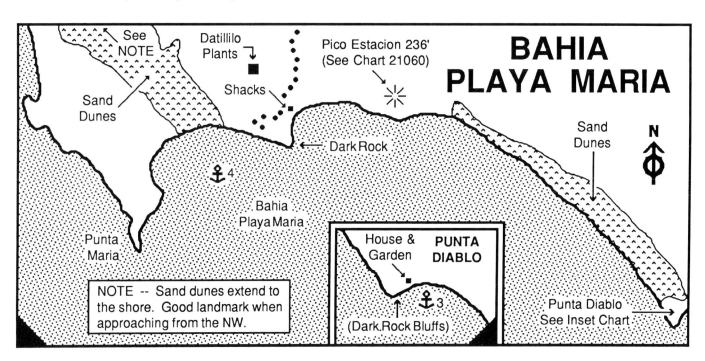

BAHIA PLAYA MARIA (Looking E) -- The end of Punta Maria is cut off in the photo.

for cone. True to its name, the promontory exhibits a small 169-foot tall, cone-shaped, light brown hill about 1/2 mile NW from the double points. It creates a small but readily discernible landmark. It is this hill and the low-lands to the NE that create a distinctive profile from any distance at sea (See profile photo).

The circular-shaped cove formed east of Punta Cono is named Bahia Falsa (False Bay). It is a bit over 1/2 mile in both depth and breadth. There is a small fish camp at the head of the cove. I have not anchored here but have entered the cove to a depth of 3 fathoms and observed that the swell conditions appeared calmer than those at Bahia Playa Maria to the east.

PUNTA MARIA AREA -- Punta Maria is a low-lying point of dark colored rock which comes to a very sharp point. It is situated 4 miles SE from Punta Cono. Bahia Playa Maria lies to the east of the point (See Photo). It is nearly 1 mile deep and 2 1/2 miles in breadth, making it the largest of the bays in Section B. There are extensive areas of sandy soil and dunes on the shores of the bay. (See BAHIA PLAYA MARIA Chart.) Fair to good anchorage may be taken in 4 fathoms 300 yards off the beach.

PUNTA DIABLO & PUNTA LOBOS -- Two points lie SE of Punta Maria which are not named on U.S. Chart 21060. These are Punta Diablo 4 miles SE (see BAHIA PLAYA MARIA Chart), and Punta Lobos 5 1/2 miles SE. Both points consist of dark colored rocks backed by areas of sandy soil and dunes (See Photos).

The cove to the east of Punta Diablo is too small to form an effective anchorage for ocean cruising vessels although there is good holding ground in 3 fathoms which could be used in calm seas as the area receives some protection from Punta Maria.

The bight east of Punta Lobos is larger and holding ground is available in 4 fathoms 250 yards offshore. However, this cove is swept by refracted NW swells far more than Bahia Falsa or Bahia Maria.

PUNTA NEGRA -- Now that the cartographers have treated us to the dark colored rock at Punta Blanca

PUNTA DIABLO (Looking E) -- Note sand dunes inland from the dark colored point.

PUNTA LOBOS (Looking E) -- The small islet lying 200 yards from the point on its western shore is an aid to identifying this flattopped point.

(White Point), one should be well braced for Punta Negra (Black Point) which is composed of light colored rock. Punta Negra is the southern end of a massive light-to-medium brown ridge. It is clearly lighter in color than many of the promontories to both north and south.

A small rounded cove is formed on the east side of the point. A concrete navigation light is constructed on the SE face of the promontory offering guidance into the cove. It is visible only when approaching from the south. Chart 21060 incorrectly shows the light as being on the SW side of the point. (See PUNTA NEGRA Chart and Photo.) The beach at the head of the cove is used as a fishermen's landing but the cove itself is badly swept by refracted swells. It would make a fair weather anchorage in 4 fathoms 250 yards offshore.

PUNTA NEGRA (Looking NE) -- See text concerning error in the location of the navigation light as shown on Chart 21060.

Some 3 miles SE of Punta Negra and 2 miles NW from <u>Punta Rocosa</u> is a <u>small islet</u> as shown on Chart 21060. A cluster of ranch buildings and a windmill are situated on a bench a short distance north of the islet.

PUNTA ROCOSA -- Punta Rocosa (Rocky Point) is in fact a rocky promontory. It is formed by a change in coastal direction from north-south to east-west. There is no pronounced bay on either side of the point. The most conspicuous feature is a <u>notch</u> near sea level several hundred feet inland from the point (See Photo). This indentation creates a distinctive profile when approaching from the north. It is not in evidence from the south unless one's vessel is close inshore. The point is formed of sedimentary layers tilted at a sharp angle.

When viewed from some distance away, a substantial area of <u>light colored soil</u> may be seen surrounding the darker rock of Punta Rocosa. This light area creates a <u>distinctive landmark</u> for up to 25 miles seaward on clear days.

PUERTO SAN ANDREAS -- A small bay lies 3 miles NW from Punta Santa Rosalilita. This is Puerto San Andreas. The relative absence of swells on the beach near this camp (See Photo) would seem to indicate that this is a better landing site than the more heavily used but swell-swept beach east of the village at nearby Bahia Santa Rosalilita.

ISLA ELIDE -- Isla Elide is a substantial islet lying 1/3 mile offshore NW of Punta Santa Rosalilita. At its eastern end are the remains of several <u>buildings</u> reported to have been once used as a weather station (See Photo). Should one have become confused with the profusion of promontories along this section of coast, Isla Elide provides an <u>unmistakable landmark</u>.

PUNTA SANTA ROSALILITA AREA - The point and bay are labeled Santa Rosalia on Chart 21060. I use the correct Santa <u>Rosalilita</u> in deference to the presence of a sizeable town located here whose name is spelled in this manner.

<u>Sandy soil</u> dominates the terrain at low-lying, <u>double-pointed</u> Punta Santa Rosalilita; however, the seaward edge of the two points are low bluffs of dark colored rock. (See SANTA ROSALILITA AREA Chart). The westerly of the two points is labeled as Punta Santa Rosalilita although the easterly projection is a bit more prominent. Punta Santa Rosalilita is tipped by a

PUNTA LOBOS (Looking 110 Degrees).

PUNTA NEGRA (Looking 320 Degrees).

PUNTA ROCOSA (Looking 115 Degrees).

PUNTA ROCOSA (Looking SE) -- Note the notch inland from the point (See Text).

Chapter 8

PUERTO SAN ANDREAS (Looking E) -- One building marks the site of this landing place. Note the linear sedimentary rock layers.

ISLA ELIDE AND PUNTA SANTA ROSALILITA (Looking SE) -- The mottled, dark colored patches seen several places on the island are groups of birds.

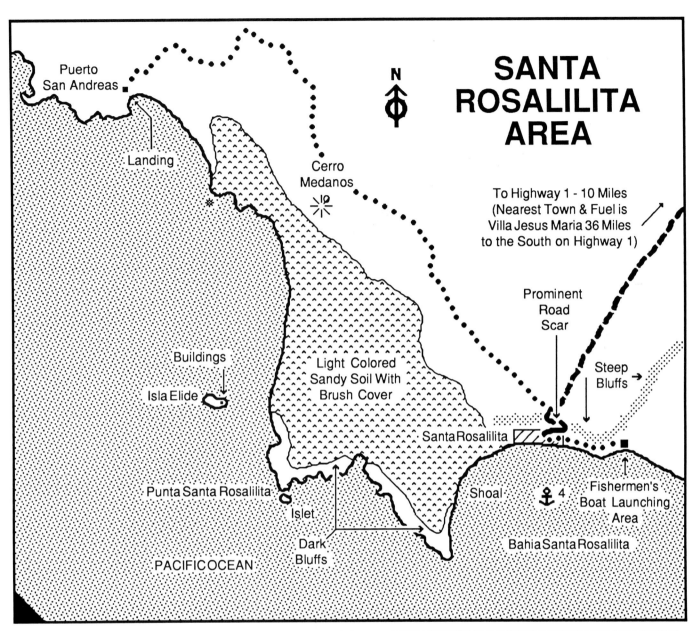

SANTA ROSALILITA AREA

Puerto San Andreas

Landing

Cerro Medanos

To Highway 1 - 10 Miles
(Nearest Town & Fuel is
Villa Jesus Maria 36 Miles
to the South on Highway 1)

Prominent Road Scar

Steep Bluffs

Buildings

Isla Elide

Light Colored Sandy Soil With Brush Cover

Santa Rosalilita

Punta Santa Rosalilita

Islet

Shoal

4

Fishermen's Boat Launching Area

Dark Bluffs

PACIFIC OCEAN

Bahia Santa Rosalilita

SANTA ROSALILITA VILLAGE (Looking NE) -- Note the scar created by the road traversing the bluff behind the community (See Text). The landing used by local fishermen is situated to the right of the small point near the right edge of the photo.

PUNTA SANTA ROSALILITA (Looking 110 Degrees).

here that boats are transported into the water astride carts fashioned from the axle of a pickup truck. The battering the boats take in the launching process is interesting to behold.

The village lies near sea level at the base of a bluff. Two branches of the dirt road that serves the community run steeply down this bluff creating a considerable scar. The resultant light coloring stands out from the surrounding vegetation and makes a good <u>landmark</u> (See Photo).

closely detached islet some 100 yards in length. The land inland from the points rises slowly to form a low, lens-shaped plateau.

East of Punta Santa Rosalilita lies <u>Bahia Santa Rosalilita</u>, the largest of the bays in Section B. It forms a <u>fair to good anchorage</u>. Most of the anchorages discussed in this section have shallow water depths directly eastward from the protecting point. This situation is even more aggravated here, no doubt due to windblown sand coming from the dunes to the west. The best anchorage is abreast the Santa Rosalilita village in 4 fathoms 1/2 mile offshore.

The <u>Santa Rosalilita community</u> is made up of some fifty houses and other buildings (See Photo). There are no stores or gas station, but supplies can no doubt be obtained in some manner by the persuasive mariner. Fishermen launch their vessels from the beach 1/2 mile east of the village. The offshore gradient is so shallow

PUNTA ROSARITO -- As viewed on a chart, Punta Rosarito would appear to be a dominant point of land. While it is a sizeble projection, the point is low and sandy and does not stand out well when approaching in either direction (See Photo). The offshore gradient is shallow as indicated by a line of <u>breakers</u> that front the point for approximately 2 miles. Some distance inland from the point can be seen the ruins of a multi-roomed adobe building.

SECTION C
PUNTA ROSARITO TO
PUNTA MALARRIMO

Punta Rosarito is the approximate end of the mountainous terrain of Section B, and the start of the flat lands at the edge of the <u>Desierto Vizcaino</u>. There are a few isolated hills on the coast to the south in Section C, but the majority of the shore consists of one, long,

PUNTA ROSARITO (Looking SE) -- A low-lying sandy point whose off-lying breakers are visible from the sea.

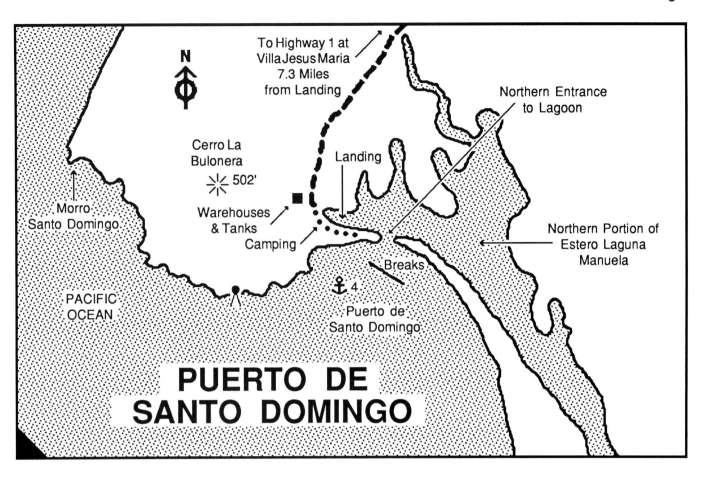

To Highway 1 at
Villa Jesus Maria
7.3 Miles
from Landing

N

Cerro La
Bulonera
502'

Landing

Northern Entrance
to Lagoon

Warehouses
& Tanks

Camping

Morro
Santo Domingo

Breaks

Northern Portion of
Estero Laguna
Manuela

PACIFIC
OCEAN

4

Puerto de
Santo Domingo

PUERTO DE SANTO DOMINGO

sandy beach backed by extremely flat desert topography. The coastline gradually sweeps westerly forming Bahia Sebastian Vizcaino. The Section contains the entrances to three major lagoons and one fair coastal anchorage at Puerto de Santo Domingo.

MINOR POINTS -- Two unnamed points of land lie at 5 and 7 miles south of Punta Rosalilita. While it projects only a short distance seaward, the northernmost of these two points is backed by a massive east-west running ridge. The high point on this ridge, Cerro San Javier, is 705 feet in elevation and 1 1/2 miles inland. It is a dominant feature in the coastal landscape in this area. The elevation 581 feet shows near the point on Chart 21060.

The southerly point has markedly different topography from its massive neighbor to the north. It is low and backed by a patch of sand dunes. In the lee of the dunes rests the El Tomatal fish camp, and lobster trap floats are present offshore. A small grove of palms trees grows 300 yards from the shore in the arroyo north of the camp. It is only 2.9 miles by low standard road from these trees to Highway 1. As a result recreation vehicles may sometimes be observed in this area.

South of the fish camp is the site of Miller's Landing. This was the second of Baja's onyx/marble loading points. This one served the El Marmolito quarry located

some 10 air miles to the east. No remnants of these activities are visible from the sea.

MORRO SANTO DOMINGO -- A long, straight, dune-backed beach stretches south from Miller's Landing for 13 miles. It is covered with low-growing shrubs and thus does not appear sandy from the sea. At the southern end of this beach is Morro Santo Domingo. One mile inland from the point is Cerro La Bulonera. This 502-foot high hill is readily distinguishable from the sea because of the extensive flat terrain which extends from it in all directions.

From a distance, the land inland from Morro Santo Domingo appears dark in color due to the presence of low-growing vegetation. From closer in, one can see alternating patches of dark lava rock and sandy areas on the southern and western slopes (See Photo). This alternating light and dark coloration provides a distinguishing characteristic. A concrete light tower is constructed 1-1/2 miles SE of the point.

PUERTO DE SANTO DOMINGO -- A shallow bay is formed eastward from Morro Santo Domingo. At its head is a narrow entrance to the northern end of Estero Laguna Manuela (See Photos). Shoal draft boats may enter through this channel with careful attention to the state of the swells, or breakers, at the seaward side. The estero extends for over 10 miles to the south be-

MORRO SANTO DOMINGO (Looking SE) -- Photo shows the southern section of Morro Santo Domingo which supports the navigation light (See Chart). Note the alternating patches of dark lava rock and light sandy areas (See Text).

hind coastal barrier beaches. A larger entrance to the lagoon is located 2 1/2 miles south of the northern channel (See Photo).

A landing inside the northern entrance is used as a base of operations for fishermen living at two inland communities. Lightweight trailer boats may be launched here, although the beach gradient is very slight. Structures for the propagation of oysters are located in the shallow waters of the lagoon.

On one occasion I anchored in Puerto de Santo Domingo in 3 fathoms bearing 85 degrees from the concrete navigation light. In due course, breakers developed along the shoals at the mouth of the lagoon entrance. I found myself almost in their midst and promptly moved offshore to 4 fathoms. This new location offered minimal protection from refracted swells which sweep the bay. I would rate this as an indifferent anchorage. It is this experience that led to the development of my 4 fathom minimum anchorage rule.

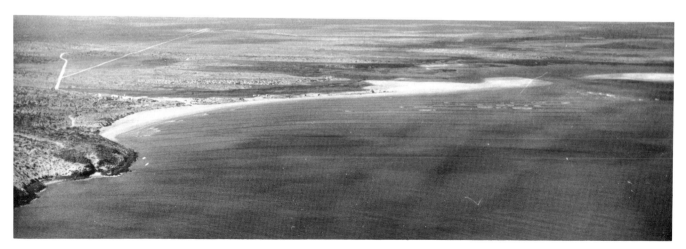

PUERTO DE SANTO DOMINGO (Looking E) -- Photo shows the anchoring area SE of Morro Santo Domingo. At the right is the northern entrance to Estero Laguna Manuela. Note the low, level terrain of the Desierto Vizcaino. The road in the photo's left portion leads to Highway 1.

NORTHERN ENTRANCE TO ESTERO LAGUNA MANUELA (Looking NE) -- Close inspection will reveal trucks on the shore of the lagoon at the landing site used by local fishermen.

LAGUNA GUERRERO NEGRO -- Nine miles south of Morro Santo Domingo is the entrance to Laguna Guerrero Negro (Black Warrior Lagoon) (See Photo). It is the middle of the three large lagoons that lie inside the coastal barrier beaches in this Section. The entrance does not show well from the sea.

Large, abandoned salt loading port facilities (Puerto Venustiano Carranza) lie several miles inside the lagoon

entrance (See Photo). These apparently came into disuse due to the difficulty of keeping the entrance channel free of sand. In some years whales are able to enter through this channel, while in others the water is too shallow for their use. It stands to reason, if the whales have difficulty penetrating the lagoon through this channel, it is not the place for one's yacht. I have been advised by a Scammon's Lagoon tugboat skipper that the channel is suitable only for pangas and that it is

SOUTHERN ENTRANCE TO ESTERO LAGUNA MANUELA (Looking NE).

ENTRANCE TO LAGUNA GUERRERO NEGRO (Looking SE) -- This entrance is suitable only for shallow-draft vessels and with local knowledge.

blocked with sand at low water. The pilot buoy shown outside the lagoon entrance on Chart 21060 is no longer present.

A fish camp is situated inside Laguna Guerrero Negro west of the abandoned port facility (See Photo). Trailer boats may be launched here, or tour boats rented to observe whales that frequent the lagoon.

SCAMMON'S LAGOON -- The entrance to famous Scammon's Lagoon is located 24 miles south from Morro Santo Domingo. The lagoon's Spanish name is Laguna Ojo de Liebre, which translates to "Rabbit Springs." There is a spring of water lying 15 miles into the desert from the lagoon which bears the name "La Cantina" (The canteen). (It still shows on the Auto Club road map.) Early visitors apparently observed numerous rabbits drinking from this water source. Scammon's Lagoon's fame as a California gray whale calving grounds and whale hunting center are related in Chapter 5.

The currently used salt loading port facility (Puerto El Chaparrito) is located easterly from the mouth of the lagoon (See Photo). Here salt is loaded onto large bar-

PUERTO VENUSTIANO CARRANZA Looking SE) -- This salt loading facility has been abandoned in favor of a new port in Scammon's Lagoon.

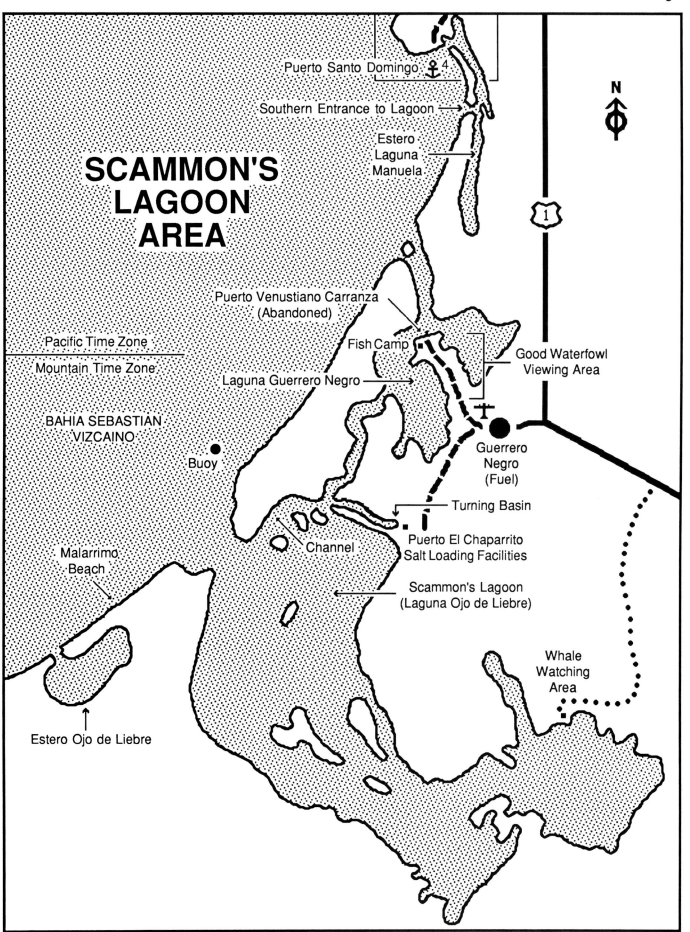

SCAMMON'S LAGOON AREA

Puerto Santo Domingo ⚓4

Southern Entrance to Lagoon →

Estero Laguna Manuela →

N

Puerto Venustiano Carranza (Abandoned)

Fish Camp

Good Waterfowl Viewing Area

Pacific Time Zone

Mountain Time Zone

Laguna Guerrero Negro →

BAHIA SEBASTIAN VIZCAINO

• Buoy

Guerrero Negro (Fuel)

Turning Basin

Puerto El Chaparrito Salt Loading Facilities

Malarrimo Beach

Channel

Scammon's Lagoon (Laguna Ojo de Liebre)

Whale Watching Area

Estero Ojo de Liebre

LAGUNA GUERRERO NEGRO FISH CAMP (Looking SE) -- Note the fishing pangas moored near the camp.

ges and towed to a deep water port at the SE corner of Isla Cedros, some 50 miles from the mainland coast. The channel to the loading port is marked with a variety of poles. In the sea off the mouth of the lagoon is a buoy consisting of three smaller buoys welded together. It is topped with a pole bearing a light.

I was granted a cordial interview by the public relations director of the salt company at Guerrero Negro. This official asked me to please not convey any information that would encourage recreation vessels to enter Scammon's Lagoon. I am advised that the channel is narrow and that there is no anchoring room near the port

ENTRANCE TO SCAMMON'S LAGOON (Looking E) -- The entrance buoy noted in the text is located northerly from the entrance near the left edge of the photo.

SCAMMON'S LAGOON INNER CHANNEL (Looking SE) -- The salt loading port is located at the edge of the turning basin at the left end of the channel.

facility. This can be seen from the photos in this book. Obviously the salt company does not wish to have its operations complicated with the presence of visitors. It was made clear that this situation applys to all vessels, including Mexican fishing boats. It is not directed solely at tourists.

I feel duty-bound to honor this request. I shall note, however, that in the calm weather that prevailed during my visit offshore, there were no breakers at the mouth of the lagoon. I observed a Mexican fishing boat towing one of its disabled fellows into the channel with no difficulty. The salt barges and tugs that regularly enter the lagoon are of deeper draft than most yachts. Should

you care to follow in their path, you're on your own. However, I recommend you do so only in the event of emergency.

ESTERO OJO DE LIEBRE -- The coastline continues as a sand dune-backed beach (Playa Malarrimo) for 13 more miles SW from the mouth of Scammon's Lagoon. At this point the terrain again becomes mountainous. Near the midpoint of this area is the entrance to a small lagoon shown as Estero Ojo de Liebre on Mexican maps (See Photo). This estuary is not shown on Chart 21060. Its narrow channel is completely rimmed by breakers, yet I have observed a Mexican fishing panga riding the swells into the lagoon.

SCAMMON'S LAGOON SALT LOADING DOCK (Looking S) -- This photo is a close-up of the salt loading port turning basin area.

SCAMMON'S LAGOON (Looking SW) -- The lagoon entrance is in the photo's upper right portion. Inside the lagoon, the channel hugs the edge of the barrier beach which separates the lagoon from the sea. Two loaded salt barges may be seen in the channel.

SECTION D
PUNTA MALARRIMO TO
PUNTA EUGENIA

The seemingly endless sand beach that forms the inner curve of Bahia Sebastian Vizcaino comes to an abrupt end approximately 2 miles east of Punta Malarrimo. From here west to Punta Eugenia the coastline is steep and mountainous, the result of the sea's interface with the slopes of the Sierra Vizcaino. This range of mountains forms the sharp-pointed peninsula which terminates at Punta Eugenia.

PUNTA MALARRIMO -- Punta Malarrimo (incorrectly spelled Mal Arrimo on Chart 21060) lies 30 miles eastward from Punta Eugenia. The point makes only a minor projection into the sea, but is nevertheless very prominent due to the steepness of the slopes that rise inland. When viewed from the vicinity of Isla Cedros, it

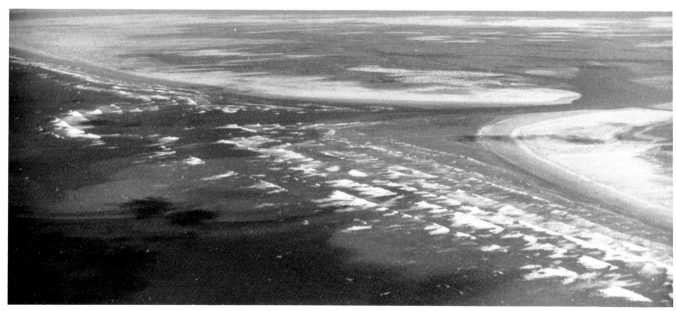

ENTRANCE TO ESTERO OJO DE LIEBRE (Looking E).

marks the end of the coastal mountains and the beginning of the flat desert lands to the east.

I am advised that the broad sweep of the coast in this vicinity causes offshore currents as high as 10 to 12 knots. Mexican skippers refer to anchoring here as "anchoring on the beach." Need I say more?

MINOR POINTS -- There are several inconsequential points of land between Punta Malarrimo and Punta Eugenia. Three of these will be mentioned. None of these are named on the Chart 21060.

Punta el Queen is the easterly of the three points. A fish camp of about 12 shacks lies on the shore of the bight east of the point (See Photo). A low standard road leads from here to the coastal village of Malarrimo to the west.

Ten miles west of Punta Malarrimo is an unnamed point. The coast indents east of the point forming a shallow bight. The point is backed by a sizeable bench of flat land which is the site of the Village of Malarrimo (See Photo). It consists of about 15 small dwellings.

A bar extends NE from the point causing a series of breakers. Shoal draft vessels can anchor in the lee of the point protected to some degree by the point and the bar. Commercial fishing vessels anchor farther offshore essentially without protection in prevailing NW weather. The holding ground is good.

Further west, and 17 miles from Punta Malarrimo, is another point similar to the one noted at the Malarrimo

FIRST ENTRANCE INTO SCAMMON'S LAGOON

Captain Charles M. Scammon arrived off the mouth of the body of water which now bears his name about the first of December, 1857. He commanded the brig *Boston* which was accompanied by a small schooner. The Captain's account of his first entrance into the lagoon notes that it was "heretofore unknown to whalers," but that he had "previously ascertained its presence."

The *Boston* was anchored outside the lagoon in the open ocean. Small boats and the tender were dispatched to sound out the entrance. Two days had passed when word was received that there was sufficient water to allow the brig to enter. In the afternoon, both vessels proceeded into the channel in company with a brisk breeze, but this failed when they were in the shallowest portion. They were forced to anchor. Night came and a heavy swell began to break around the boats. No one slept. It was not until the following noon before sufficient wind arose to carry the two ships into the lagoon.

Long months at anchor while whaling inside the lagoon fouled the ship's bottoms. Thus the outward passage to the sea was at a snail's pace. The loaded hulls were so low in the water that their keels stirred the sandy bottom and left a whitened wake astern. One has to admire the seamen who made these voyages even though their endeavors were to result in the near extinction of the California gray whale.

PUNTA EL QUEEN (Looking S) -- Small boats could no doubt be launched from the steep road at the fish camp seen here.

VILLAGE OF MALARRIMO (Looking SE) -- The area of 4 rectangles located adjacent to the village are shallow basins constructed for the propagation of shrimp.

VILLAGE OF CAMPITOS (Looking SE) -- The concrete navigation light is located on the point of land near the village.

PUNTA FALSA AND ISLOTE CHESTER ROCK (Looking SW) -- Punta Falsa is in the upper left portion of the photo. The white breaks above Chester Rock are over the reef noted in the text.

Village. It is again the site of a small village (Campitos) of the same size as Malarrimo (See Photo). A concrete navigation light tower painted with horizontal red stripes is located 1/4 mile west of the point. Both Campitos and Malarrimo are connected by road with the town of Bahia Tortugas.

The conformity of the coastline east from Punta Eugenia indicates that this area would provide good protection from SW storms. This fact is also noted in the *U. S. Sailing Directions* and in previous guidebooks The bights at the villages of Malarrimo and Campitos would appear to be the best locations. I have never anchored in these locations in such weather.

PUNTA FALSA -- Punta Falsa (False Point) (See Photo) is another minor promontory. It is the northernmost point of land on the Vizcaino peninsula. It lies 2 miles NE from Punta Eugenia. It derives its name from the fact that it can be mistaken for this latter point when approaching from the east. Two prominent islets, Chester Rock (See Photo) and Piedra Negra, are situated NE of the point at a distance of 2/3 miles from shore. *U. S. Sailing Directions* note "The passage between the two islets, and that between the islets and the shore are filled

with kelp. No hidden dangers have been found, but these passages are not recommended."

The *U. S. Sailing Directions* also calls attention to a dangerous oval-shaped reef lying 1/2 mile northward from Punta Falsa. It is "3/4 miles long, and 1/2 mile wide, sur-

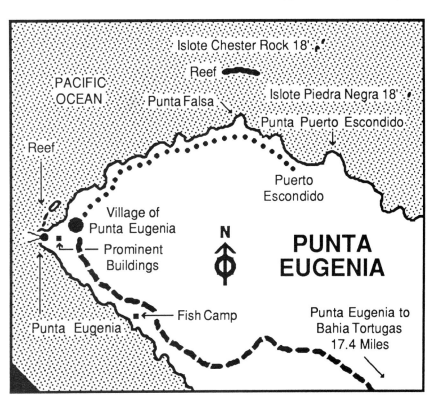

PUNTA EUGENIA PENINSULA (Looking SW) -- Punta Falsa is the farthest right point in the photo with Punta Eugenia at the center-top.

rounded by kelp; near the middle of the reef is a rock, awash, over which the sea breaks heavily."

PUNTA EUGENIA AREA -- Steep bluffs some fifty feet high lie on both sides of Punta Eugenia. Above the bluffs the land flattens for several hundred yards inland. One of Baja's old lighthouses resides on this flat near the end of the point. About 100 yards inland from the light are situated several sizeable buildings.

Most yachts plying Baja's Pacific coast approach Punta Eugenia on a course taking them to or from Isla Cedros. They thus may not see the thirty or more colorfully painted houses of the Village of Eugenia that is tucked

into a coastal depression several hundred yards NE of the point (See Photo). A rocky reef parallels the coast about 200 yards off the village, creating a reasonably well protected harbor. Shoal draft boats may enter this shelter through a passage between the rocks located near the southern end of the reef.

Divers scour the rocks on the shores of Punta Eugenia for abalone. Their boats are hauled onto the beach with a cable device powered by an automotive engine that has been defrocked from its former calling. The road to the Punta Eugenia area has been greatly improved in recent years. Thus, this device will no doubt be put to use launching tourist trailer boats in the future.

PUNTA EUGENIA (Looking NE) -- Chester Rock may be seen near the top of the photo.

CHAPTER 9
PACIFIC ISLANDS
ISLAS CEDROS, SAN BENITOS, & NATIVIDAD

CHAPTER SUMMARY

There is something romantic about even the thought of a desert island in a foreign land. Several islands have been encountered in the proceeding chapters, but they may have been to small, and too close to the U. S./ Mexican border to meet the requirements of the adventuresome spirit. But here, NW of Punta Eugenia, these needs can be fulfilled.

Many ocean cruisers making the Baja passage visit the peninsular port of Bahia Tortugas to obtain fuel for their vessels. (See NAVIGATION ALTERNATIVES early in Chapter 8.) May I suggest that the islands described in this chapter are the best places on Baja's Pacific coast to refuel the spirit. Each has a permanent community of hardworking Mexicans earning their livelihood from the sea. Should your agenda call for turning the ship's crew into tourists anywhere along Baja's Pacific coast, I recommend that this is the place to put them ashore.

SECTION		DESCRIPTION
NO.	NAME	
A	Isla Cedros	By far the largest of Baja's Pacific islands. Sizeable community, salt loading dock, coniferous forests, and good anchorages.
B	Islas San Benitos	A group of 3 small islands grouped to form a good central anchorage. Elephant seal colonies.
C	Isla Natividad	Forms the west side of Canal de Dewey. Has a small town and good anchorage.

SECTION A
ISLA CEDROS

To the mariner hell-bent to or from Cabo San Lucas, Isla Cedros offers one outstanding attribute; it provides the only opportunity along Baja's entire Pacific shore to navigate in the lee of a protective shoreline. The island is aligned due north-south and is 20 miles in length. Vessels cruising close-in off the easterly shore may enjoy waters that are sheltered from the main force of the prevailing NW swells. This calming effect extends to a lesser degree to the Keller and Dewey channels.

Fair-to-good anchorage may be taken at Isla Cedros village and at many other places along the eastern shore of the island. However, this shore is not free from swells refracting around both Punta Norte and Punta San Agustin. Under these conditions, such open roadstead anchorages can impart considerable motion to small

vessels. Skippers seeking respite near Punta Morro Redondo may encounter swells refracted from both ends of the island. The island's anchorage that is best protected from NW swell conditions is located easterly from Cabo San Agustin.

FISH CAMPS -- Isla Cedros village is the headquarters for fishermen who conduct their operations from five separate camps on the island's more remote shores. Their locations are shown on the chart in this chapter. Most of these contain structures somewhat more substantial than most of Baja's other fish camps.

NOTE -- The balance of the material concerning Isla Cedros is presented in a clockwise direction starting at Punta Norte.

PUNTA NORTE -- Much of Isla Cedros is made up of sedimentary and volcanic formations. In contrast, the ex-

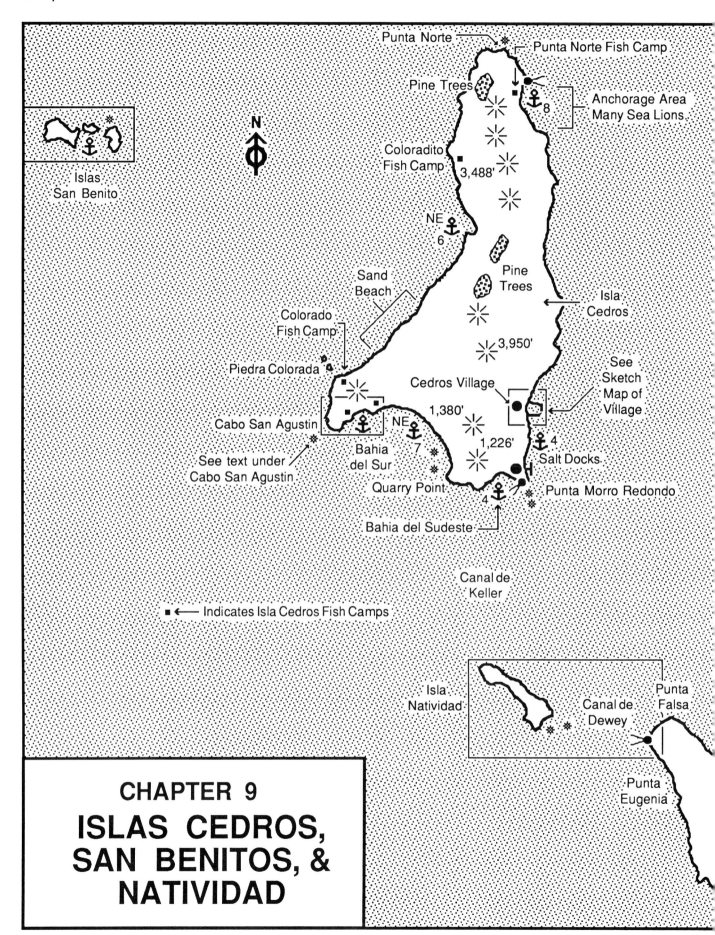

Punta Norte
Punta Norte Fish Camp
Pine Trees
Anchorage Area
Many Sea Lions
8
Coloradito
Fish Camp
3,488'
Islas
San Benito
NE
6
Sand
Beach
Pine
Trees
Isla
Cedros
Colorado
Fish Camp
3,950'
See
Sketch
Map of
Village
Piedra Colorada
Cedros Village
Cabo San Agustin
1,380'
NE
7
See text under
Cabo San Agustin
Bahia
del Sur
Salt Docks
1,226'
4
Quarry Point
Punta Morro Redondo
4
Bahia del Sudeste

Canal de
Keller

■ ← Indicates Isla Cedros Fish Camps

Isla
Natividad
Canal de
Dewey
Punta
Falsa

Punta
Eugenia

CHAPTER 9
ISLAS CEDROS, SAN BENITOS, & NATIVIDAD

PUNTA NORTE (Looking NW) -- Punta Norte is the point in the upper portion of the photo.

treme northern tip, Punta Norte, is composed of granite, an igneous rock. Punta Norte is worth a close-in look. It is not as colorful as the Morro Hermoso coast to the south, but the topography is extremely steep, rugged, and scenic (See Photo). It is so inhospitable that it provides no site for the construction of a navigation light which one would expect at the end of such a prominent cape.

PUNTA NORTE FISH CAMP -- A small flat point of land projects from the coast approximately 1 mile SE from the steep terrain of Punta Norte. The extremity of this point is the site of a white, four-sided, navigation light tower built in 1931 (See Photo). Good anchorage may be taken in 8 fathoms about 1/4 mile south of this point, and directly offshore from the small Punta Norte fish camp. A good landing site is present here near the remains of an old masonry pier and adjoining water cistern. These structures, and the remnants of a nearby road, served a copper mining operation that flourished inland about 1910.

SEA LION ANCHORAGES -- Southward from the Punta Norte fish camp the coast forms a slight indentation for a distance of about 3 miles. Along this shore are several narrow sand and shingle beaches which serve as homes for large numbers of sea lions and elephant seals (See Photo). Anchorage may be taken in most places

along this shore in from 4 to 10 fathoms, 100 to 200 yards offshore. The northernmost portions of this area provide anchoring sites that are superior to a position

PUNTA NORTE FISH CAMP (Looking S) -- The concrete lighthouse may be seen at the tip of the flat point to the left of the wrecked freighter. This wreck had disappeared when the site was visited 7 months after the picture was taken. -- The Punta Norte fish camp lies in a grove of tamarisk trees near the shore above, and slightly to the left, of the light. The good NW wind anchorages off the sea lion beaches (see text) are in view above the village.

NAVIGATION LIGHT SE OF PUNTA NORTE -- ISLA CEDROS

directly off the Punta Norte fish camp, and I believe these are the best such sites on the eastern shore of Isla Cedros.

On one occasion I made the crossing from the main Baja Peninsula to the Punta Norte anchorage area. As the island was approached, NW winds of 25 knots and substantial swells were encountered. I was concerned that this weather would make the above described anchorages untenable. Instead we found light wind, calm seas, and only modest refracted swells.

The above noted light wind may be interrupted by strong gusts from directly offshore as the result of NW flowing air being funneled down canyons on the island's eastern shore. Anchoring positions off the shingle beaches at the mouths of the canyons offer the shallowest water depths but are most effected by these

ASHORE AT PUNTA NORTE

Two trails leave the Punta Norte fish camp at its northern edge. The seaward fork proceeds to the nearby lighthouse over flat terrain. Travelers taking this route may observe typical Sonoran Desert vegetation. There are excellent examples of century plants and prickly pear cactus.

A far more strenuous adventure lies at the end of the inland trail. It leads in about 2 miles to the long-abandoned copper mine which was worked during the first decade of the 20th century. The trail briefly be-

comes a road, and then reverts to a trail. However, a majority of the trip consists of simply working one's way up a canyon bottom that bears 240 degrees from the Punta Norte lighthouse.

At the end of a two-hour trek, hikers are rewarded with a substantial open-pit mined-over area with various rusting remnants of machinery, tanks, ore carts, etc. The mine lies at the lower edge of the island's Bishop pine and juniper forest. Several of these trees are in the mining area.

OLD MINING MACHINERY INLAND FROM PUNTA NORTE.

winds. Locations between the beaches have deeper water but are less subject to the wind.

The area in question is sea lion heaven. Every beach has one or more large colonies, and anchoring here is tantamount to locating off a dog pound. The animals' barking and carrying on is considerable. They may also cavort around one's vessel. The sound of bubbling water under the hull at night can be disconcerting unless you are aware of the cause.

Logic tells one that shelter from SW storms should be available at the north end of Isla Cedros. I believe that this area would provide good protection from such weather.

ISLA CEDROS VILLAGE -- The topography in the southernmost portion of Isla Cedros is more gentle than the balance of the island. This area provides the site for Isla Cedros village and

CONIFEROUS FORESTS

Those readers who have suffered through the Author's Preface in my book *The Magnificent Peninsula* will be aware that I am a forester. Thus, I am compelled to subject you to the following dissertation:

Cedro is the Spanish word for cedar. In many parts of the world, junipers are referred to as cedars even though technically they are not. Knowing this can give one a great sense of superiority, even when sitting soaking wet in the cockpit of a sailboat wondering when the next following sea will invite itself aboard. There are numerous low-growing junipers on Isla Cedros. These were identified by the very earliest explorers who prized them as firewood for their galley stoves. The island was thus given the name Cedros, which it still bears.

Far more impressive than the junipers, are the island's stands of Bishop pine (Pinus Muricata). The Bishop is a relatively scarce species of pine that frequents the Pacific coast of the Californias. The high elevations in the northern portion of Isla Cedros constitute the southern extreme of its range. These trees may be seen at several places along the main skyline ridge along the island's eastern shore. On the western side, several stands extend some distance down the steep mountain slopes where they are clearly visible from the sea. These sites are noted on the chart in this chapter.

its breakwater-enclosed harbor (See Photo). These are located 16 miles south from Punta Norte and 4 miles north of Punta Morro Redondo.

Isla Cedros harbor was constructed about 1980. Unfortunately the area enclosed is rather small, and the dock extending from the fish cannery takes up considerable space. When commercial fishing vessels are present there is little room for visiting yachts although they are permitted to anchor when space is available. Under storm conditions, I am certain that pleasure craft would be welcome to raft alongside commercial vessels in the harbor.

Water depth at the harbor entrance is about 8 fathoms. Soundings decrease toward shore and appear to reflect the original bottom unaltered by dredging. Good anchorage may be taken directly north of the harbor in 6-10 fathoms, or to the south in 4-6 fathoms. There are landing beaches adjoining both of these anchorages. The southern landing is the least affected by NW swell action as it lies in the lee of the harbor breakwater. However, landing here brings one into the back residential side of town. Going a-

shore at the north landing brings the visitor more quickly to the *downtown* area.

Cedros village supports a Port Captain, post office, small restaurant, medical clinic, several doctors, and a variety of stores. There is a general store (El Puerto Mercantil) where one may purchase a wide variety of household and personal goods. Replenishments for the ship's liquor locker are also available nearby. There is a salt water conversion plant at the cannery and additional fresh water is piped to town from springs in the island's interior. Diesel and gasoline is obviously available at Cedros, but it is not supplied to visiting yachts except in emergencies. A low flattopped ridge is situated immediately west of the center of town. It contains the cemetery. A climb up to this vantage point will give the visitor a good spot from which to survey the community and take pictures of one's vessel at anchor.

A sizeable fish cannery is situated on the shore of the harbor. Several varieties of fish are processed, with the ground-up remains coming to rest in bags labled *Harina de Pescado*. The words mean *fish flour*, but there can be little doubt that the contents are used as fertilizer. The cannery also produces the town electricity from several massive diesel generators. The community is well illuminated at night, with the cannery and the technical school south of town being the most prominent features (See Photo).

The above-noted technical school is situated on the shore adjoining the anchorage south of the harbor. Weary mariners need to brace for the morning and

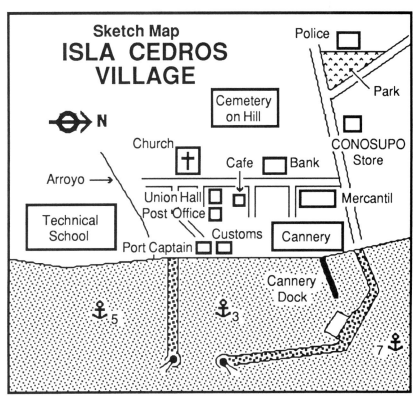

Sketch Map
ISLA CEDROS VILLAGE

Police

Park

CONOSUPO Store

Cemetery on Hill

Church

Cafe

Bank

Mercantil

Arroyo →

Union Hall

Post Office

Customs

Cannery

Technical School

Port Captain

Cannery Dock

⚓ 5

⚓ 3

⚓ 7

N

ISLA CEDROS VILLAGE AND HARBOR (Looking NW) -- The fish cannery is the group of large buildings at the landward end of the pier within the harbor. The group of larger buildings to the left of the harbor is the technical school.

GEOLOGIC NOTE

Low cliffs lie along the shore of the Isla Cedros harbor area. The material at their base consists of sedimentary strata tilted 15 to 30 degrees from the horizontal. These are overlaid by horizontal layers. It is clear that the lower rocks were tilted, raised above sea level, and had their upper surface eroded after they were originally deposited. The upper material was then laid down at a later time. The contact between these two deposits is called an "angular unconformity." Having absorbed this weighty knowledge, I'm sure you are exhausted and will be compelled to retire to the ship's bar.

---

evening flag ceremonies, complete with drums and bugles. The school serves about 200 pupils, ages 11 to 17. They come from many places in Baja and live at the school or in town. They are taught a variety of technical subjects, including navigation and other skills related to making a living from the sea.

The population of Cedros village was given as 200-400 in the 1971 edition of the *Baja Sea Guide*. By the early 1980s, there were some 6,000 people. Every time I visit the community it appears to have grown considerably. Thus even the remotest villages have shared in Mexico's exploding population.

SALT DOCKS -- Just north of Punta Morro Redondo is the deep water port and storage area (See Photo) for the salt producing industry

VESSELS ANCHORED INSIDE THE BREAKWATER HARBOR AT CEDROS VILLAGE (Looking W).

ISLA CEDROS SALT DOCKS (Looking NW) -- Note the loaded salt barge moored at the right of the photo.

based at Scammon's Lagoon to the east. This combined operation is certainly one of the largest, if not the largest, industrial operation in Baja California. Fair anchorage may be taken far enough north of the docks so as not to interfere with vessels using this facility. The loading operation may be viewed from the deck of your vessel, or you may take a shore excursion by landing adjoining the anchorage, or by securing a taxi ride from Isla Cedros Village to the north.

Salt is produced in extensive evaporation ponds located near Scammon's Lagoon on the Baja peninsula. It is then transported to Isla Cedros in large barges. You may find these barges and their tugs secured on several mooring buoys lying close offshore awaiting their turn at the unloading docks. Each barge contains an internal, gravity-fed conveyor belt system which moves salt to a continuing series of belts on the docks, and eventually to the top of enormous mounds of salt several hundred yards inland. During unloading periods you may be able to witness a bulldozer inching its way up the seemingly impossibly steep sides of the salt mounds. Once atop the mound, it is used to spread out newly arrived salt.

An ore carrier loading dock with along-side depths of 15 fathoms adjoins the unloading facility. It can accommodate one large ocean-going vessel at a time. Others may be seen waiting at anchor in the roadstead. These ships are conveyor-belt loaded from the stockpiles ashore. There are five large black tanks south of the dock facilities. These store bunker oil used to fuel the dock operation. Inland from the docks are various shops, offices, and residences. There is also a small

hospital with x-ray and operating facilities. Further inland is the island's airstrip.

Under NW wind conditions I have found the anchorage here to be less satisfactory than that off Isla Cedros village, due in part to swell refraction coming from around the southern end of the island. Under such conditions, I have been warmly welcomed to raft alongside one of the moored tugs, and to partake in a feast of barbecued steaks on the aft deck. Should you find that such an offer is not readily forthcoming, you might ask the ladies in the crew to appear on deck fondly waving with one hand, while holding a cerveza in the other. Get back to me if it works. The old playboy scam has worn thin.

PUNTA MORRO REDONDO -- Punta Morro Redondo is the SE extremity of Isla Cedros (See Photo). Its profile is low, as is most of the island's southern segment. Near the tip is a navigation light, radar tower, and a small building. The southern end of the island's airstrip begins immediately inland from the light. The sea breaks at several points along a reef of rocks which extends about 1/4 mile to the south. It should be given a wide birth in rounding the point.

It is off the above-referenced reef where Francisco de Ulloa encountered Indians fishing during his history-making voyage in 1540. The events which took place in this vicinity are noted in Chapter 4 MARITIME HISTORY.

BAHIA DEL SUDESTE -- Approximately 2 1/2 miles west of Punta Morro Redondo is an unnamed point. It is

MORRO REDONDO (Looking NE) -- The salt storage area and port facilities are clearly visible.

the seaward end of the north-south aligned low ridge which is situated westerly from Isla Cedros village and the salt docks. Between these two points the coast makes a shallow indent named Bahia del Sudeste (Southeast Bay). Fair anchorage may be taken here in calm weather. My observation is that this location is even less desirable than the anchorage off the salt docks when significant swells are refracting around the southern end of Isla Cedros.

An additional promontory is located 1 1/2 miles westerly from the above-noted unnamed point. It likewise bears no name, so to ease its pain, we hereby christen it Quarry Point. Providing this title takes little imagination, as it is clear that the rock used to build the breakwaters at Isla Cedros village was secured from this location. Quarry Point is composed of dark colored rock which stands in contrast to the adjoining landscape. This dark coloration, and the quarry scar, make good landmarks.

BAHIA DEL SUR -- It is a straight-line distance of 6 miles from Quarry Point NW to Cabo San Agustin. The coastline makes a substantial indentation between these two points. This is Bahia del Sur (South Bay).

Good anchorage may be obtained NE from Cabo San Agustin. In seeking protection from north, or NW weather, this is the best location offered by Isla Cedros. This counsel was provided to me by the tugboat skipper who hosted the above-referenced barbecue. My own observations, and the fact that the area has been selected as the location for two of the island's five fish camps, substantiate this fact.

The best anchorage appears to be off the San Agustin Fish Camp (See BAHIA DEL SUR Chart). Directly at the water's edge, and 200 yards SW from the camp, lies a 100' high, cone-shaped hill. It is dark in color in contrast to the surrounding light brown terrain. While small in stat-

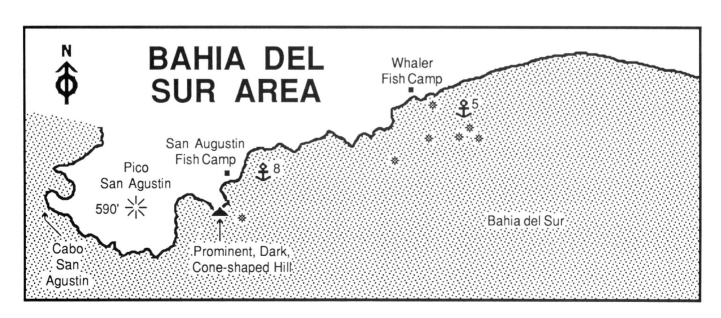

BAHIA DEL SUR, ISLA CEDROS (Looking NE) -- The dark, cone-shaped hill noted in the text is in view left of the photo's center. The San Agustin fish camp may be seen immediately to the right of the top of the hill.

ure, this pinnacle stands as a clear landmark from as far away as Isla Natividad (See Photo).

I have entered Bahia del Sur in 30 knot NE winds. In rounding Quarry Point from the south these winds continue unabated as they are funneled through low passes in the mountains to the east. However, at the head of the bay (bearing 260 degrees from the cone-shaped hill at the Cabo San Agustin fish camp) was a sizeable area of calm water where anchorage may be taken in 7 fathoms 300 yards offshore. The contrast from the 30 knot wind only a short distance away is remarkable.

CABO SAN AGUSTIN -- Cabo San Agustin is a prominent point of land. It is bold and rocky. It lies midway in stature between the massive granite cliffs at Punta Norte and the modest low-lying profile of Punta Morro Redondo. The extremity of the cape is closely backed by 590' high Pico San Agustin.

U. S. charts indicate two rocks surrounded by a large bed of kelp are located about 1 mile SW of Cabo San Agustin. The *1937 U. S. Sailing Directions* reports that this reef breaks in heavy seas. I have been in this general location in calm seas with absolutely no surface indication of these rocks and there was little kelp. Depth soundings did markedly decrease from the surrounding area indicating the presence of an under water obstruction. Use caution when navigating in this vicinity.

THE DARK, CONE-SHAPED HILL NEAR THE SAN AGUSTIN FISH CAMP (Looking NW)

CABO SAN AGUSTIN (Looking 100 Degrees)

PIEDRA COLORADO -- What is shown on the chart as Piedra Colorado (Red Rock) is actually two sizeable, low-lying islets and at least one other smaller rock. The buildings of the Colorado fish camp may be seen on the point of land adjacent to the islets. The shoreline NE from the fish camp is relatively

ISLAS SAN BENITOS (Looking E) -- Note lighthouse located on the west side of Benito del Oeste.

ASHORE ON BENITO DEL OESTE

Visitors going ashore on this island may easily visit numerous tidepools along the relatively level area of land NE from the village. Elephant seals are often present. More energetic hikers will be rewarded with fine views by taking the trail that leads from the village to the island's main lighthouse. At one time this trail was wide enough for the passage of small wagons. It still provides an easy route for foot travel. Allow one hour to arrive at the lighthouse.

The island's vegetation is scant, due at least in part to the ravages of the resident donkeys. Perhaps it will improve when they have passed on.

---

free of indentations and is the location of an extensive sandy beach, by far the longest on Isla Cedros.

WEST SIDE ANCHORAGE -- North of the above-noted beach is a small cove. In approaching this area from Islas San Benito my depth sounder indicated a water depth of 50 fathoms 2 miles offshore. Soundings gradually reduced to 6 fathoms at a point 200 yards off the cove. We were experiencing NE winds of 10-15 knots. Under these conditions the waters at this point were quite calm. I suspect that winds from the NE to SE quadrant are infrequent in this region. However, I dutifully report, that under such conditions, the area in question appears to offer a reasonable anchorage.

COLORADITO FISH CAMP -- North of the above-described anchorage the coast becomes steep and rocky, terminating in the extremely rugged terrain at Punta Norte. Six miles south of this point is a very small sloping bench near the mouth of an arroyo. On this bench is located a closely packed group of 10-12 shacks. This is the Coloradito fish camp. Several willow trees can be seen in the arroyo indicating that a source of fresh water may be available. My log contains the following notation: "If ever I saw a lonely looking place, this is it."

SECTION B
ISLAS SAN BENITOS

It is a straight-line distance of 132 miles across the Northern Bight from Punta Baja along the east coast of Isla

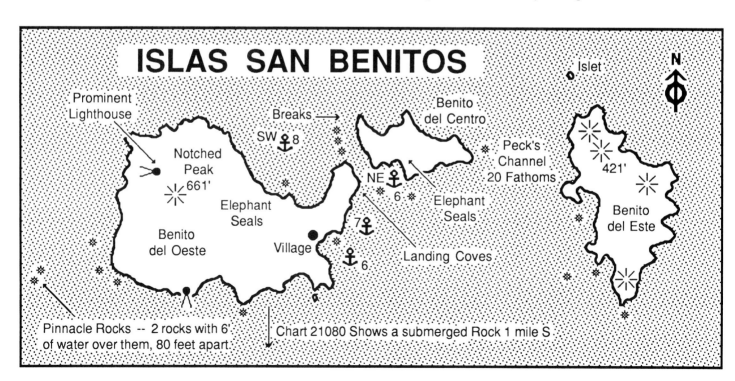

ISLAS SAN BENITOS

Prominent Lighthouse

Notched Peak 661'

Elephant Seals

Benito del Oeste

Village

SW 8

Breaks →

NE 6'

7

6

Benito del Centro

Peck's Channel 20 Fathoms

Elephant Seals

Landing Coves

Islet

Benito del Este 421'

N

Pinnacle Rocks -- 2 rocks with 6' of water over them, 80 feet apart

Chart 21080 Shows a submerged Rock 1 mile S

MAIN ANCHORAGE, ISLAS SAN BENITOS (Looking SW) -- The village on Benito del Oeste may be seen at the base of the high ground above and to the left of the photo center. The shoal channel between Benito del Oeste and Benito del Centro is to the right.

Cedros to Punta Eugenia. Should you choose to visit the Islas San Benitos en route, the voyage would be lenghtened as follows: Punta Baja to Islas San Benito 100 miles; Islas San Benitos to Punta Eugenia 38 miles; total 138 miles. The difference in distance between the two alternatives is only 6 miles.

A long-out-of-print U. S. government chart of these islands shows considerable detail. It is now reproduced in the *Chart Guide* folio noted in PART 1. The data from this chart has been used to supplement my own observations in preparing the material presented below.

ANCHORAGES -- The three islands of the Benitos group lie in a general east-west alignment. They partially enclose a bay which provides varying degrees of protection from the west, north, and east (See Photo). The entire bay would be fully exposed in the event of southerly storms. There is good protection from the prevailing NW weather. Under these conditions, the best anchorage is close-in off the village on Benito del Oeste in 5 to 10 fathoms.

I have visited Islas San Benitos in company with NE winds of 20 knots. I anticipated that the best anchorage under these conditions would be along the western side of Benito del Este. Unfortunately this shore is swept by significant swells coming south through Peck's Channel. The best anchorage proved to be south off Benito del Centro (See ISLAS SAN BENITOS Chart).

COVE ON THE NE SIDE OF BENITO DEL OESTE (Looking S) -- See text concerning the potential use of this cove in the event of SW storms. The village is in view left of the photo's center.

VILLAGE AREA, BENITO DEL OESTE (Looking S) -- The best anchorage in the prevailing weather is in the area west of the village. The small coves near the bottom center of the photo make good landing sites.

A smaller bay is formed on the NE shore of Benito del Oeste (See Photo). Its alignment would indicate that it would provide protection in the event of SW storms. The U. S. chart shows generally shallow water depths in the general area, and my depth sounder indicated depths of 8 to 12 fathoms over a considerable area roughly 200 yards offshore. The chart also indicated rocky bottom conditions, but, as they say, "any port in a storm."

PECK'S CHANNEL -- A passage of navigable water runs between Benito del Centro and Benito del Este (See Isla del Este Photo). It has a total width of over 1/2 mile. The U.S. chart shows a least depth of 13 fathoms

between the islands. In passing through this channel my depth sounder frequently indicated 20 fathoms. The far narrower channel between Benito del Centro and Benito del Oeste is foul.

BENITO DEL OESTE -- The westerly island is by far the largest of the three. A village of about 20 dwellings and a very small two-towered church lies adjoining a small cove and landing at the eastern end (See Photo). An adjoining cemetery contained four graves in 1983.

The fishermen living here have been known to come alongside visiting yachts with yet-to-be-dispatched samples of the local lobster population. It is under such

ISLA BENITO DEL ESTE (Looking NW) -- Peck's Channel lies to the left of the island.

ELEPHANT SEAL BEACH, BENITO DEL CENTRO (Looking SW) -- The seals are lying on the beach near the center of the photo. The shoal channel between this island and Benito del Oeste is to the right -- The NE wind anchorage noted in the text lies to the left of the off-lying rock above the seal beach.

circumstances when proper training of the ship's crew will pay dividends. A properly schooled commissary officer will show little interest in lobsters (langosta) and will maintain that they would certainly make everybody ill. However, consideration will be given to acquiring those on hand, at a reasonable price, and as a gesture of international friendship. The balance of the crew should be kept below decks where excessive salivation will not prejudice the negotiations.

The island has also long been home to a resident population of donkeys. In the past these animals were used to transport fuel to the lighthouse located on the island's peak. Their services were no longer required after the advent of the present solar-powered system, but the kind-hearted villagers were loath to send them to their rewards. As an alternative, they chose to deprive the male donkeys of their reproductive capacities. These friendly creatures are often the first to greet those visiting the island. Be kind to them, for their days are numbered. There were six animals in 1983 but only three remained in 1987.

BENITO DEL CENTRO -- The central island is the smallest of the three. Its terrain is gentle with a maximum elevation of only 82 feet. The southern side facing the anchorage contains numerous groups of elephant seals (See

Photo). They are best viewed from the water using the ship's tender. Going ashore is almost certain to unduly disturb the animals.

BENITO DEL ESTE -- The easterly island offers no special features but is of reasonably gentle terrain and makes a good place for hiking although it is infrequently visited.

THE VILLAGE, BENITO DEL OESTE (Looking E)

ELEPHANT SEALS, ISLAS SAN BENITOS -- Here a small colony of elephant seals are sunning themselves in one of the landing coves NE of the village on Benito del Oeste.

LIGHTHOUSE, ISLA NATIVIDAD (Looking NW).

SECTION C
ISLA NATIVIDAD

Isla Natividad (Christmas Island) forms the western side of Dewey Channel. Cabrillo anchored in its lee for three days in August 1542.

A sizeable village of about 75 dwellings is situated on the SE end of the island (See Photo). As have other coastal towns, it has grown considerably from the "several dozen huts" described by the 1971 *Baja Sea Guide*. The village is the site of a steepled church which provides a good landmark when approaching along the island's SW facing shore. A tall 50' high white navigation light tower and a sizeable white building at its base are located on the ridge NW of the community.

The village has a diesel-operated generating plant and it is well illuminated at night. There is also a school and a water cistern on a high point inland. Water is transported from the main peninsula and pumped from the shore to this reservoir.

The island's best anchorage during prevailing NW weather conditions is in 6 fathoms 400 yards off the village. NW swells refracting around the island's SW side break heavily off its southern point. This action provides some swell protection for the anchorage from this direction. The anchorage's other flank receives swell protection from Roca Plana and a reef between this rock and the island.

In approaching this anchorage pay close attention to Roca Lawry. The *1937 U. S. Sailing Directions* describes it as "a circular rocky shoal about 1/2 mile in diameter with a depth over it of 1 1/2 fathoms, and 6 - 10 fathoms around." Roca Lawry breaks only very occasionally. I have pass-

ISLA NATIVIDAD, NW END (Looking N) -- The off-lying islet is Roca Maria.

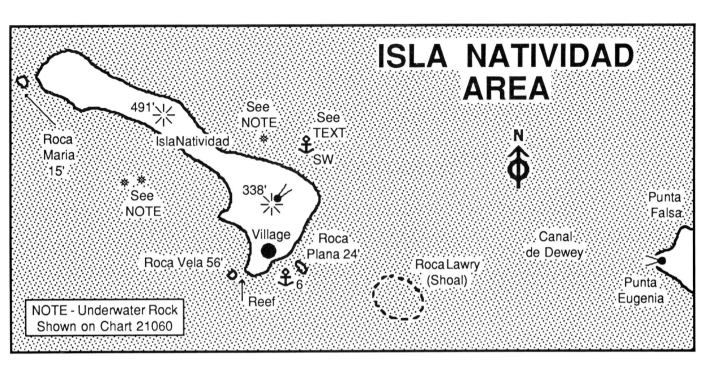

ed between Roca Lawry and Roca Plana with minimum depth soundings of 11 fathoms.

Logic would indicate that Isla Natividad's NE coast would provide refuge in SW storm conditions. I have traversed

this entire shore in fair weather sounding depths of from 6 to 12 fathoms 200 to 400 yards offshore. Depths become more shallow as one proceeds SE. I believe a vessel can be anchored anywhere off this shore. Be alert for a submerged rock as shown on Chart 21060.

ISLA NATIVIDAD, SW SIDE (Looking NW) -- A portion of the village may be seen at the right edge of the photo.

ISLA NATIVIDAD, SE END (Looking N) -- Note the lighthouse on the ridge above left from the village. Roca Plana is on the right side of the photo.

BAJA CALIFORNIA

WHERE THE DESERT MEETS THE SEA

CHAPTER 10
THE MIDDLE REACH
PUNTA EUGENIA TO PUNTA ABREOJOS

CHAPTER SUMMARY

Chapter 10 describes the Middle Reach It is the most interesting segment of the Baja peninsula's Pacific coast. Its shores embrace the fueling port of Bahia Tortugas, along with several other good anchorages and sizeable villages. The largest of these are Punta Asuncion and Punta Abreojos.

Many ocean cruisers lay their courses close inshore along this area. Punta Abreojos is frequently used as an overnight stop before or after crossing the Middle Bight.

For many years the Middle Reach coastline was the most isolated area along Baja's Pacific shore, and domestic water was in very short supply. Both of these conditions have now changed. A road constructed to highway standards, but not yet fully paved, has been completed from Highway 1 to Bahia Tortugas. It will no doubt be fully surfaced in the future. Good standard secondary roads serve all the principal communities.

Prior to 1987, the principal towns had salt water conversion plants. Now a major water pipeline has been constructed from deep wells located in the desert to the east. It serves all the coastal towns. Large water reservoirs constructed of rock may be seen at these communities.

SECTION			DESCRIPTION
NO.	FROM	TO	
A	Punta Eugenia	San Cristobal	Steep topgraphy along the west-facing slopes of the Sierra Vizcainos. Bahia Tortugas is the only reliable Pacific fueling port.
B	San Cristobal	Punta Abreojos	Low-lying coast backed by the Dieserto Vizcaino. Occasional high peaks. Several good anchorages.

SECTION A
PUNTA EUGENIA TO
SAN CRISTOBAL

The peninsula formed by the Sierra Vizcaino is by far the largest promontory of land in all of Baja California. Section A is a 38-mile segment of coast along the SW flank of this range. In places, the mountain slopes fall directly into the sea. In others, there are intervening areas of more gentle terrain, but the mountains are not far inland and they dominate the landscape.

A sizeable portion of all vessels making the Baja Passage cruise close-in along this section of coast in order to

pay a call at Bahia Tortugas. This refuge is the only reliable fueling point on Baja's Pacific coast.

CANAL DE DEWEY -- On August 2, 1542, Juan Rodriguez Cabrillo and his small fleet passed through Canal de Dewey, the channel between Punta Eugenia and Isla Natividad (See the ISLA NATIVIDAD AREA Chart in Chapter 9). Today, many ocean cruisers follow this same course. The Cabrillo log clearly describes this overall area, but it errs in its advice to plot a course toward the western side of the channel. Mariners should in fact favor the eastern side of the passage. This is due to the presence of the Roca Lawry shoal that lies off the eastern end of Isla Natividad. It breaks only occasionally in calm seas and is thus difficult to detect.

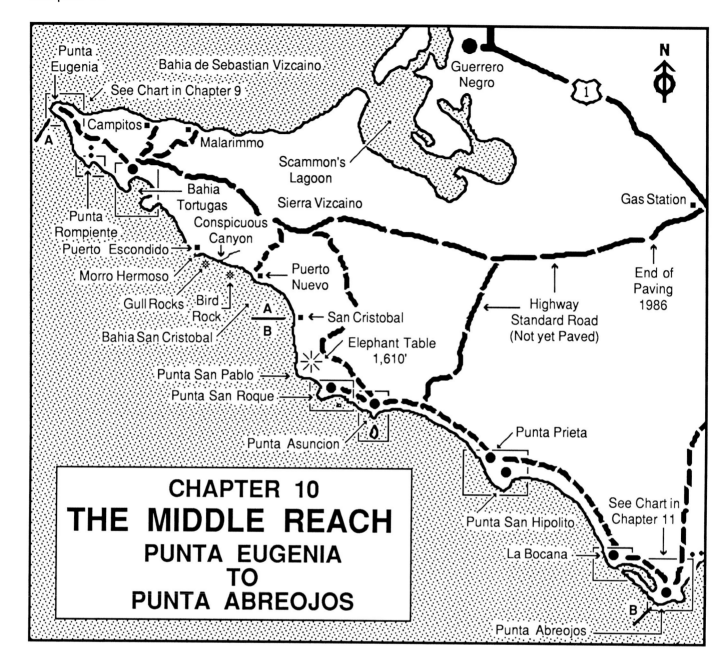

CHAPTER 10
THE MIDDLE REACH
PUNTA EUGENIA
TO
PUNTA ABREOJOS

Canal de Dewey is also the favored passage for the California gray whale as these animals closely follow the contours of the coast in their annual migration. I have found the waters in this area between Punta Eugenia, Isla Natividad, and Isla Cedros to abound in whales, dolphins, and sea birds. I have also observed the waters immediately north of the Punta Eugenia light to be deep green in color. This is no doubt due to the presence of large amounts of plankton resulting from upwelling from the ocean's depths.

The shelter provided by Islas Cedros and Natividad results in seas considerably calmer than those in the open ocean to the west; however, be alert to considerable south setting currents in the area. These are the result of the prevailing southerly coastal currents encountering the broad sweep of the Vizcaino peninsula and

the constricted channels caused by the presence of the islands.

PUNTA EUGENIA / SE FACE -- (Punta Eugenia itself is described at the end of Chapter 8.) Mariners passing through Canal de Dewey may not see the Village of Punta Eugenia which lies on the side of the point facing Bahia Sebastian Vizcaino. It may be seen when viewed from north of the point. Sometimes it is fully illuminated at night.

The Punta Eugenia lighthouse, the village school, community hall, and other buildings are clearly in view on the level terrain behind the point. The Loberia fish camp is situated about 1 mile SE from the point. The secondary road which runs between Punta Eugenia and Bahia Tortugas closely parallels the shore NW from the camp.

PUNTA ROMPIENTE -- Punta Rompiente is the first major point of land SE (9 miles) of Punta Eugenia (See Photo). The point is relatively low and the ridge which lies inland and to the north is only about 225 feet in elevation. For this reason it is considerably less prominent than Punta Prieta (See PUNTA ROMPIENTE Chart). This latter point lying approximately 2 miles to the NW of Punta Rompiente projects only slightly into the sea but is backed by peaks and ridges that rise from 600 to 700 feet.

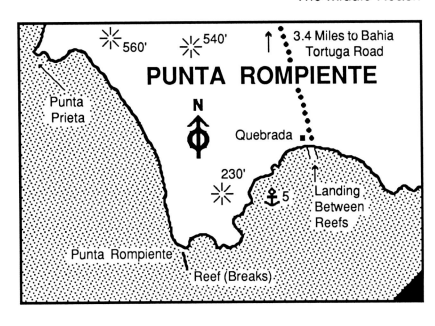

Rompiente is the Spanish word for reef or shoal. Punta Rompiente earns its name because the sea breaks heavily off the point, indicating the presence of submerged rocks. The Mexican topographic map refers to the point as El Muertito, which roughly translates as "Little Death." Might I suggest we give Punta Rompiente a wide berth. (CAUTION -- The *U.S. Sailing Directions* notes that a ship struck an obstruction 1 1/2 miles WNW of Punta Rompiente in 1965.)

QUEBRADA -- A sizeable bay indents east of Punta Rompiente. On the low bluffs at its head is a small fish camp. Two rocky reefs some 100 yards apart project into the sea in front of this camp. Black sand beaches between the reefs are used as a landing by local fishermen. This spot bears the name Quebrada (See Photo). The word is an adjective meaning, among other things, "navigable waters between reefs." Few places are better named.

The bay east of Punta Rompiente provides one of the better open bay anchorages on Baja's Pacific coast because relatively deep water is present very close to the head of the bay. Ground tackle can be dropped in 5 fathoms within only 100 yards of shore. The calmest waters lie between the fish camp and Punta Rompiente. The hills north from Punta Rompiente also provide reasonable protection from the prevailing wind. Unfortunately the anchorage is infrequently used by ocean-cruising yachts because of the close proximity of Bahia Tortugas.

An arroyo proceeds north from the head of the bay. It is surrounded by gentle terrain. The soils in this area are decidedly lighter in color than the surrounding land. When illuminated by the sun, this coloration provides a good landmark for vessels approaching from the south or west.

BAHIA TORTUGAS -- With the exception of Bahia Magdalena, Bahia Tortugas is the largest port on Baja's Pacific coast. The various place names and points of interest in the area are indicated on the chart in this chapter. Bahia Tortugas is the name used on most current Mexican and U.S. maps; however, the name Port San Bartolome persists on the U.S. maritime charts. (Chart 21081 is a large scale rendition of the bay.)

Bahia Tortugas provides a very good anchorage (See Photos). In moderate seas there is virtually no swell action. Unfortunately a sizeable arroyo runs inland NW from the anchorage directly in line with the prevailing winds. In addition, the bottom gradient off the village is shallow, and the 3-fathom point lies some 1/3 mile offshore. As a result it can be windy, with wind-waves being generated between shore and the anchorage.

The wind, and wind-waves become more aggravated in the event of SW winds which precede storm fronts. Under these conditions, the anchorage off the village is

PUNTA ROMPIENTE (Looking E) -- Note the large area of light colored soil mentioned in the text.

QUEBRADA FISH CAMP (Looking N) -- Note the area of light colored soil mentioned in the text.

on a lee shore. When this occurs, many skippers seek protection across the bay under Cabo Tortolo. This location reduces the wind-wave problem but has only modest effect on the wind itself, which sweeps in over the low ground to the SE. Water depths are shoal in this area. Thus, to secure a 4-fathom anchorage one's vessel must be positioned fairly near Cabo Tortolo as shown by the location of the anchor on the BAHIA TORTUGAS Chart.

The above-noted chart is drawn to the 1/50,000 scale used for most of the harbor charts presented in this book. In comparing their relative size, one can see that Bahia Tortugas is a large harbor. Its overall configuration is just what is demanded by our visions of a faraway, romantic hideaway. However, in terms of providing protection for small craft, it would have been preferable if the original designer would have provided a more diminutive cove, with better protection from the wind;

BAHIA TORTUGAS (Looking SW) -- Kelp Point is at the top-center of the photo. The group of large buildings at the left edge of the town may be brightly lighted at night making it difficult to pick out the navigation light located nearby.

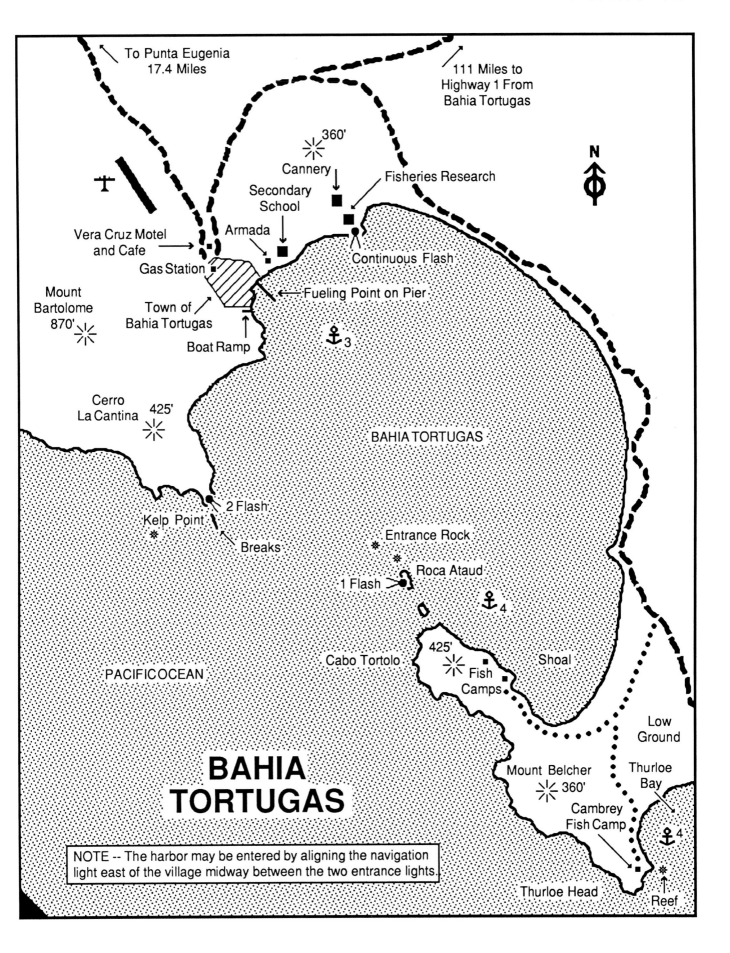

To Punta Eugenia
17.4 Miles

111 Miles to
Highway 1 From
Bahia Tortugas

N

360'
Cannery

Secondary
School

Fisheries Research

Armada

Vera Cruz Motel
and Cafe

Gas Station

Continuous Flash

Fueling Point on Pier

Mount
Bartolome
870'

Town of
Bahia Tortugas

Boat Ramp

⚓3

Cerro
La Cantina   425'

BAHIA TORTUGAS

2 Flash

Kelp Point

Breaks

Entrance Rock

Roca Ataud

1 Flash

⚓4

PACIFIC OCEAN

Cabo Tortolo

425'
Fish
Camps

Shoal

Low
Ground

Thurloe
Bay

Mount Belcher
360'

Cambrey
Fish Camp

⚓4

**BAHIA
TORTUGAS**

NOTE -- The harbor may be entered by aligning the navigation
light east of the village midway between the two entrance lights.

Thurloe Head

Reef

BAHIA TORTUGAS ENTRANCE (Looking SE) -- Kelp Point is at the photo bottom with Cabo Tortolo and its off-lying rocks at the top.

but then who are we to argue with this particular *Designer*.

The Town of Bahia Tortugas provides the following services: gas station, grocery stores, liquor store, motel, cafes, medical clinic, doctor, fresh water, post office, telegraph, airport with commercial flights, and a fuel dock.

The last mentioned facility projects some 200 yards into the bay. It is built of pilings with the walking surface some 15' above water line; thus one cannot simply come alongside and stride ashore. In addition there is only about 6' of water at the end of the dock at low tide.

Diesel is stored in barrels near the end of the dock. Skippers desiring fuel should position their vessels close-in, adjoining the barrels on the NE side of the dock. Secure the boat with an anchor from one end and a line thrown to the dockhands from the other (See Photo). If there are no dockhands in evidence, you face the added step of summoning their presence.

Gasoline is normally not stored on the dock because of it volatility. The dock crew will obtain it for you from the gas station located at the other end of town. Allow for the appropriate time delay. Messages concerning your fueling needs can be conveyed through the time-honored processes of shouting and the waving of arms.

The fueling operation has long been the enterprise of a Mexican gentleman named Adan Gerardo, who has come to be known as Gordo. When applied to an individual, this word refers to a person of some rotund proportions. The business is now run by Gordo's son, a smaller version of his father. He reports that Gordo has

BAHIA TORTUGAS VILLAGE (Looking NW) -- Visiting yachts are anchored in the lower left portion of the photo. Fishing pangas are strategically moored closer to the village to provide a navigation challange to those approaching the fuel dock.

moved to the luxuries of Ensenada. Treat these folks with kindness, for without them, the Pacific coast of the Baja peninsula would be littered with abandoned yachts, and the fishing business at Cabo San Lucas would wither away.

There is a <u>detachment of marines</u> at Bahia Tortugas, and a Mexican Navy frigate calls here on occasion. Visiting vessels may be boarded and inspected by navy officials, particularly if you linger in the harbor for several days as do many coastal cruisers. This is not the place to display firearms or other goods that you have aboard which do not conform to Mexican law.

THURLOE HEAD -- Thurloe Head is situated 2 1/2 miles SE from Cabo Tortolo, the southern headland of Bahia Tortugas. When approaching from the south, one may see the town of Bahia Tortugas over the low isthmus which connects Thurloe Head with the main peninsula. The careless skipper could mistake this isthmus area as the entrance to Bahia Tortugas with less than satisfactory results.

A small bay (<u>Thurloe Bay</u>) is formed to the east of Thurloe Head. I have not anchored here but have entered to a depth of four fathoms. The best position is 300 yards offshore, a short distance north from the reef adjacent to the Cambrey fish camp (See Photo). This reef provides some protection from incoming refracted swells. The anchorage is rarely used by visiting yachts

BAHIA TORTUGAS PIER (Looking E) -- Note the two yachts tied to the pier's fueling point with bow anchors out.

because of the nearness of more satisfactory protection in Bahia Tortugas.

MORRO HERMOSO -- <u>Hermoso</u> is the Spanish adjective for beautiful. It aptly describes the 15-mile-long segment of mountains that rise steeply from the coast SE from Bahia Tortugas (See Photo). Its northern

THURLOE HEAD & BAHIA TORTUGAS (Looking N) -- Thurloe Head is at the lower right of the photo. Note the low isthmus of land which connects the point to the mainland. This lowland allows SW wind to sweep into Bahia Tortugas. The Reef noted in the text may be seen in the extreme right edge of the photo.

MORRO HERMOSO & GULL ROCKS (Looking NW) -- The Morro Hermoso promontory is at the left of the photo, with Gull Rocks to the right.

terminus starts at a point 4 miles SE from Thurloe Head. (The promontory labled Morro Hermoso on Chart 21080 lies near the middle of this mountainous area.) The steep slopes are all but devoid of vegetation and display many patches and bands of colorful rock. Many travelers will be reminded of the formations displayed in Death Valley National Monument in the United States.

One may readily discern a distinct line about 50 feet above sea level on the steep slopes at numerous places along the shores of Morro Hermoso. This line marks the position of sea level as it was at a relatively recent time in the geologic past. Close inspection with binoculars will disclose water-worn rocks marking the location of former shingle beaches.

PUERTO ESCONDIDO -- About 1/2 mile NW from the Morro Hermoso promontory is a small cove. At its head is located a 6-8 shack fish camp on several levels of a sloping bench. This is Puerto Escondido (See Photo). A road may be seen switchbacking up the barren slopes above the camp. It eventually arrives at

PUERTO ESCONDIDO (Looking NE).

PUERTO NUEVO (Looking NE) -- The dark patches in the sea are kelp.

Bahia Tortugas. Fishing pangas are often moored in the cove, and small boats may be landed or launched here, where the road meets the sea.

CONSPICUOUS CANYON -- Chart 21080 indicates a conspicuous canyon 4 miles SE of Morro Hermoso; however, it constitutes only an indifferent landmark.

OFFSHORE ROCKS -- Approximately 1 1/2 miles SE of Morro Hermoso is a group of offshore rocks named Gull Rocks (See Photo). Their seaward faces are whitened with birdlime. An additional 4 miles to the SE brings one to a a prominent solitary pinnacle called Bird Rock. It lies only a few feet offshore and is difficult to distinguish from the adjacent cliffs.

Gulls are of course birds, and birds are likewise gulls, but these are two separate landmarks. Northbound skippers have been known to mistake one for the other and thus misjudge their landfall at Bahia Tortugas to the NW. Who would do such a foolish thing? Don't ask.

PUERTO NUEVO -- Slightly over 2 miles SE from Bird Rock, and 8 miles from Morro Hermosa, can be seen a village of some twenty buildings (See Photo). This is Puerto Nuevo (New Port). A road runs parallel to the shore inland from the community. It is a distance of 8.2 miles on this road to the main road which runs between Bahia Tortugas and Highway 1. There is no protected cove and landing of small boats would be difficult.

SAN CRISTOBAL -- The steep mountainous terrain of Section A comes to an end at a point some 3 1/2 miles SE of Puerto Nuevo. An arroyo bearing the name San Cristobal arrives at the coast a short distance to the NW of this point. A very broad bay (ensenada) forms an indentation from Morro Hermosa to Punta San Pablo. This is Bahia San Cristobal.

A short distance SE from the arroyo is the San Cristobal fish camp (See Photo). The camp is largely obscured from the sea by a small point of land, but the access road to the camp can be seen winding its way uphill and makes a good landmark.

SECTION B
SAN CRISTOBAL TO
PUNTA ABREOJOS

From San Cristobal to Punta Abreojos is a distance of about 70 miles. Near the midpoint of this section is a massive coastal mountain which lies inland from Punta San Pablo. With this exception, the coast of this section is backed by terrain considerably lower than that to the north. There are several good anchorages, including those at Punta Asuncion and Punta Abreojos.

The divisional point between Sections A and B is also the approximate place where the numerous kelp fields of the colder northern waters come to an end. There is abundant kelp at Kelp Point at Bahia Tortugas, and a scattering of plants between there and San Cristobal. Farther south, there is very little. The scientific literature lists Punta San Hipolito as the extreme southern limit of the species' range.

SAN CRISTOBAL FISH CAMP (Looking NE) -- Note the access road above the camp as noted in the text.

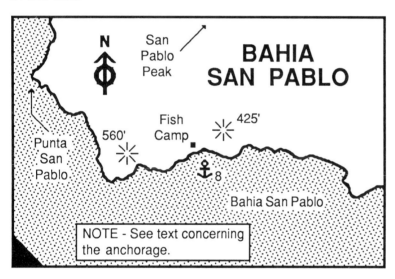

PUNTA SAN PABLO (Looking 125 Degrees).

PUNTA SAN PABLO -- At Punta San Pablo the coast makes a ninety-degree change in direction from north-south to east-west. A sizeable bay, Bahia San Pablo, is formed easterly from the point. I believe this bay would provide only an indifferent anchorage as the coast does not indent sufficiently in a northerly direction eastward from the point. On the other hand, the bay's deep water allows anchoring in 8 fathoms only 100 yards offshore near the fish camp. Steep cliffs would also provide protection from the prevailing winds. Thus the area would no doubt prove a satisfactory anchorage in fair weather, but it has not been included in the anchorage chart in Chapter 3 because of the absence of adequate northerly indent .

Inland from Punta San Pablo lies a massive group of mountains whose high points rise over 1,800 feet (See Profile Photo). Their steep slopes rim the coast for a distance of 8 miles north, and 3 miles east from the point. The high point bears the name San Pablo Peak. The name given to these formations on Mexican maps is Sierra la Pintada. Pintada translates as spotted or mottled, and is indicative of the fact that these mountains display the same colorful rock formations as does the Morro Hermoso range to the north. The point itself is made up of very dark rock. Also in view is the same wave-cut beachline noted for Morro Hermoso.

Northeasterly from the high peaks of San Pablo Peak is a 1,600-foot-high mesa. It is 5 1/2 miles

BAHIA SAN ROQUE (Looking NE) -- A portion of the village of San Roque is visible at the head of the Bay. Punta San Roque is out of the photo to the left.

from the coast and is named Elephant Table (Cerro El Elefante). Its flattop profile makes it a prominent landmark.

PUNTA SAN ROQUE -- The SE headland of Bahia San Pablo is Punta San Roque. It is backed 1/2 mile to the NE by a substantial hill rising to an elevation of 518 feet. The village of San Roque is situated on a bench about 1/2 miles easterly from the point. It contains more than two dozen buildings including a school and church. On the hillside east of the community is a cross made from white stones. San Roque is the northern-most of six villages that lie between here and Punta Abreojos.

Bahia San Roque is a small bay formed east of Punta San Roque (See Photo). Unlike the larger Bahia San Pablo, it has a significant northerly indent and forms a good anchorage. The bay offers relatively deep water depths allowing vessels to be anchored in 4 fathoms well into the cove and only 150 yards offshore. One cannot often anchor this close to shore along this coast.

ISLA SAN ROQUE (Looking NE).

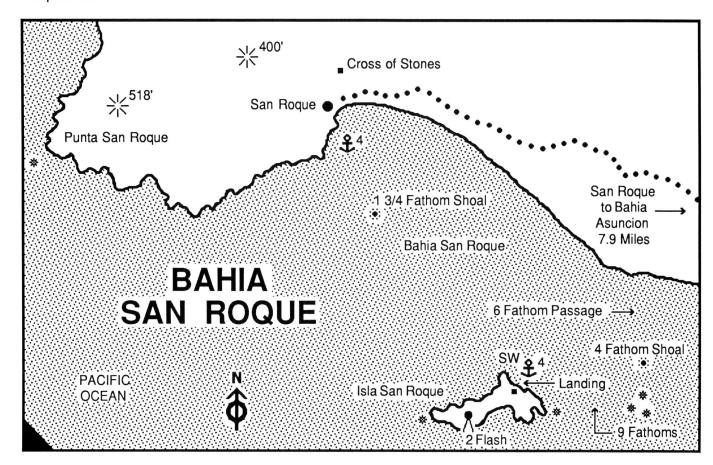

ISLA SAN ROQUE -- Isla San Roque lies 1 mile off the coast SE from the village of San Roque. It is about 3/4 mile in length. Its profile is low, with a maximum elevation of only 50 feet (See Photo). An old U.S. chart showing a group of rocks 2/3 miles east of the island indicates there are 6 fathoms of water between these rocks and the main coast, and a 9-fathom passage between the group of rocks and the island. I have ven-

tured through the latter passage with a minimum sounding of 11 fathoms.

The lay of the land would indicate that protection from the swells created by SW storms could be found on the NE side of Isla San Roque. There is a small cove at this point which provides protection from the prevailing NW swells. This anchorage would provide little relief from

ISLA & PUNTA ASUNCION (Looking NW) -- Isla and Punta San Roque are in view above the island. The village of Bahia Asuncion is visible at the extreme right of the photo.

the wind because of the island's low, flat profile. A small building, cistern, and the remains of other apparatus are located here. These no doubt served as the generator site for the island's navigation light prior to the advent of solar power.

ISLA ASUNCION -- Isla Asuncion is some 3/4 miles in length and lies south of Punta Asuncion (See Photos). Its main ridge is higher than the land inland from Punta Asuncion. It thus shows before the point when one approachs from a distance.

ISLA ASUNCION (Looking 75 Degrees) -- The prevailing wind anchorage lies on the island's far side.

A water cistern, building foundation, and other apparatus lie on the island's eastern side. They were apparently the base of operations for a lighthouse which has long since been abandoned. <u>Good anchorage</u> is afforded off this area. Numerous sea lions haul out on the island's eastern shore.

PUNTA ASUNCION -- Punta Asuncion lies 46 miles SE from Bahia Tortugas. The point is low and level. Numerous buildings may be seen as part of the point's profile in approaching from the sea. <u>Isla Asuncion</u> lies due south (See Photos). There are numerous rocks and shoal ground between the island and the point. This combination of point, shoals, and island projects seaward in excess of 2 miles. As a result, the easterly lying bay (<u>Bahia Asuncion</u>) makes a substantial northerly indent. The result is a <u>good anchorage</u>.

Vern Jones's *Baja Cruising Notes* reports a 5-fathom-deep passage between the point and the island. An out-of-print U. S. Chart shows 2 1/2-fathom depths in this same area. (See BAHIA ASUNCION Chart.) I have never taken this route.

The <u>town of Bahia Asuncion</u> occupies much of the eastern side of the Punta Asuncion promontory. The older residential portion of the community lies about 1 mile north of the point. An old cannery building is situated directly on the shore near the town center. This area is distinguished by the presence of numerous trees which have been planted along the town's dirt streets. At the community's northern edge is a modest building where mother-of-pearl buttons are made from sea shells. Most of these improvements are obscured from view when approaching Punta Asuncion from the NW.

A newer, and more sizeable, fish cannery, a 40' tall water tower, and several other buildings are constructed near the point south of the main portion of the community. These facilities are located on high ground and are clearly in view from the sea in all directions.

Bahia Asuncion is a community of over 2,000 people. There are several small grocery stores, a cerveza outlet, telegraph office, gas station, fresh water, and an airfield that provides commercial flights to Ensenada.

Punta and Isla Asuncion project from the coast in a due north-south direction. They create a major barrier to the prevailing NW swells in the same way as does Punta Baja to the north. As a result, <u>good anchorage</u> may be taken for a considerable distance along the eastern shore of the point off the village. Should you wish to visit the

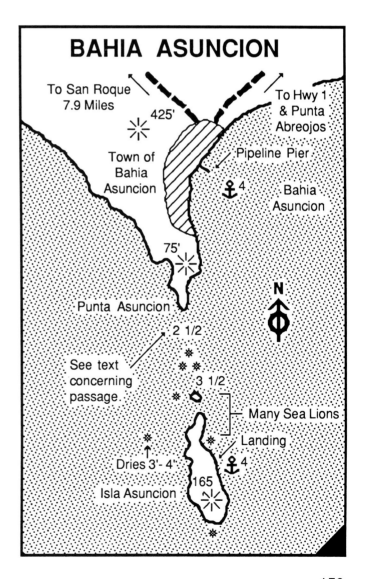

ISLA & BAHIA ASUNCION (Looking NE) -- Isla Asuncion is in the right foreground.

town, the best anchorage is in 4-fathoms, 400 yards off a narrow pier and salt water intake pipe which extends 200 feet seaward from the old cannery. This anchorage is opposite the town landing where a dirt street leads to a sandy beach.

PUNTA PRIETA -- The coast SE from Punta Asuncion to Punta Abreojos is low and level. Punta Prieta lies on this shore 15 miles SE from Punta Asuncion (See Photo). Punta Prieta is low, and its seaward projection is so minimal that it is not distinguishable from offshore. The small village of Punta Prieta is built a short distance SE of the point. The town owes its existence to the presence of a 200-yard-long reef which extends seaward near the NW end of the community (See Photo). It provides modest protection for a black shin-

gle beach 200 yards to the SE which is used as a landing. Small boats reach the beach through a crevasse in the offshore shelf. The skyline inland from the community is dominated by a large, dark-colored mesa whose high point bears 35 degrees from the village.

Adjoining the landing at Punta Prieta is a mechanical marvel consisting of an old automobile engine and a cable used to haul boats up from the beach. It is similar in design to that present at the village of Punta Eugenia to the north. As at Punta Eugenia, abalone fishing is a principal source of revenue for the fishermen of Punta Prieta.

PUNTA SAN HIPOLITO -- It is an additional 4 miles SE from Punta Prieta to a more substantial, but still low-lying, point of land. This is Punta San Hipolito. To the east lies Bahia San Hipolito (See Photo). It has a northerly indent of about 1 1/4 miles and thus forms a fair anchorage. The most protected spot is opposite the village which lies at the head of the bay. The small fishing community of San Hipolito offers no commercial services. The beach in front of the village is rocky but offers a good landing site.

About 1/4 mile west from the point is a 30' high concrete light tower with red and white stripes. Between this tower and Punta los Lobos lies the wrecked bow section of a coastal freighter. Its mast and crow's-nest lean skyward providing a good perch for the gulls. The combination of the light and wreck makes for easy identification of the point. Keep in mind that future storms could change the location of the wreck. (The locations of Punta San Hipolito and nearby Punta los

PUNTA PRIETA VILLAGE (Looking NE) -- Note breakers on the reef which protects the town's beach from NW swells.

Lobos shown in this book are those given on Mexican topographic maps.)

ESTERO LA BOCANA -- A minor point of land projects seaward 17 miles SE from Punta San Hipolito. Two miles farther SE is the shallow mouth of Estero la Bocana (See Photos). This very shallow lagoon parallels the coast for 7 miles to the western edge of the community of Punta Abreojos.

A sandy beach on the left, and just inside the entrance to Estero la Bocana, is used as a landing by the fishermen from the adjacent community of Estero la Bocana. The main body of the town lies about 1/2 mile west of the mouth of the lagoon. It contains some 100 dwellings and warehouses and projects inland for about 1/2 mile.

Chart 21080 correctly shows a 1-mile-long reef of rocks projecting from the coast directly offshore from the village. The sea breaks heavily here even in calm weather. The chart also shows that shallow water is present southward from this reef. I have sailed across this shoal area more than 3 miles offshore and sounded only 6 fathoms.

PUNTA PRIETA & PUNTA SAN HIPOLITO (Looking SE) -- Punta Prieta is the minor point in the right foreground with the village of Punta Prieta in view above the point. Punta San Hipolito is at the upper right.

PUNTA ABREOJOS -- At Punta Abreojos the coast makes a major 90-degree change in direction. Usually such places are bold and rocky promontories. In total contrast, Punta Abreojos is low and sandy. It is little more than the SE end of the barrier beach that separates Estero la Bocana from the sea.

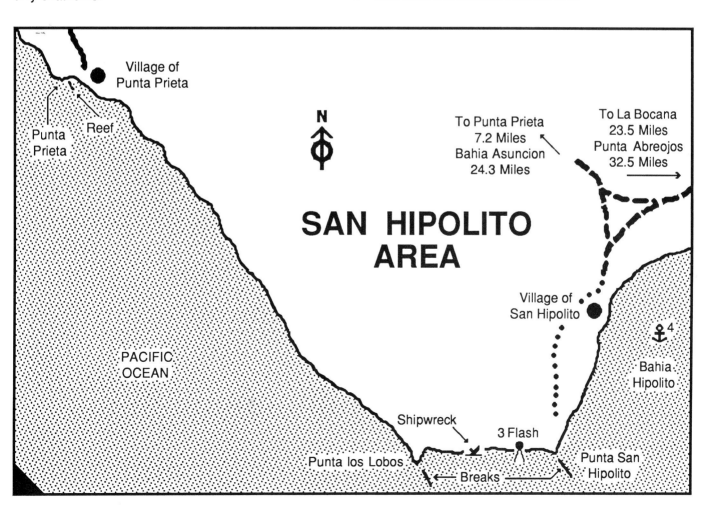

Village of
Punta Prieta

Punta
Prieta   Reef

N

To Punta Prieta
7.2 Miles
Bahia Asuncion
24.3 Miles

To La Bocana
23.5 Miles
Punta Abreojos
32.5 Miles

**SAN HIPOLITO
AREA**

PACIFIC
OCEAN

Village of
San Hipolito

Bahia
Hipolito

Shipwreck

3 Flash

Punta los Lobos

Breaks

Punta San
Hipolito

BAHIA SAN HIPOLITO (Looking NE) -- Punta los Lobos is the sharp point near the photo's right margin.

ESTERO LA BOCANA

N

To Bahia Asuncion 47.7 Miles

Village of Estero la Bocana

To Punta Abreojos 9.0 Miles

Landing

Large White Building

Reef (Breaks)

Estero la Bocana

The fame of Punta Abreojos stems not from its prowess as a point but because of its offshore hazards. These were discovered by Cabrillo on July 25, 1542. The account refers to "very dangerous reefs of rock called Abreojo." These hazards are several in number, and are shown on the PUNTA ABREOJOS AREA Chart in Chapter 11. It is imperative that the mariner consult Chart 21080 in approaching the anchorages NE of Punta Abreojos.

ROCA BALLENA -- Roca Ballena is a long, low, above-water obstruction visible only from close range. Even in calm seas there are numerous breakers at, and in the vicinity of, the rock. There are obviously various nearby below-water hazards. (Vern Jones's *Baja Cruising Notes* reports that one of these submerged rocks is actually Roca Ballena, and the above-surface rock is known locally as La Lobera.)

Chart 21080 and Vern Jones's book indicate it is possible to pass between Roca Ballena and the peninsular shore in approximately 5 fathoms. Vern recommends making such a passage only in fair weather. I see little advantage in laying such a course and have not taken this route; however, I have observed other vessels being taken through this passage with no ill effects.

LA RECHINADORA -- Chart 21080 shows an unnamed submerged rock about 1 mile SW of Roca Ballena. It is known locally as La Rechinadora. As with Roca Ballena, there is an extensive line of breakers at this location. I have passed south of this hazard some 3 3/4 miles offshore and sounded only 8 fathoms.

BAJO WRIGHT -- In contrast with the above two hazards, Bajo Wright (Wright Shoal) breaks only

ESTERO LA BOCANO & VILLAGE (Looking NW) -- The estero mouth is at the right of the photo.

very occasionally or not at all in calm seas. On one occasion I became confused by the abundance of light towers on Punta Abreojos and approached on a direct course for Bajo Wright. (See the discussion of the Punta Abreojos area in Chapter 11 concerning navigation lights.) I was saved from an encounter with this obstruction by my depth sounder. I have passed between Punta Abreojos and this shoal with a minimum sounding of 6 1/2 fathoms.

BAJO KNEPPER -- While Bajo Wright breaks occasionally, I have never observed any sign of Bajo Knepper in calm seas. One may pass between the shoal and the adjoining shore with 6 fathoms minimum depth.

ESTERO LA BOCANA (Looking SE) -- The mouth of the estero lies SE of two unnamed points. The village may be seen stretching inland from the upper of these two points.

"Pray tell me, what is that poor creature you have there dangling by its antenna?" -- "A lobster you say." -- "What does one do with it?" -- "Eat it you say." -- "It looks very small and unappetizing, but, perhaps as a gesture of friendship, I will consider taking a dozen of your better ones, for shall we say, a six-pack of beer and a well used Playboy." -- "Throw in two Cokes you say." -- "Deal !" -- **"Tell the cook to hold the beans."**

CHAPTER 11
THE MIDDLE BIGHT
PUNTA ABREOJOS TO CABO SAN LAZARO

CHAPTER SUMMARY

The Middle Bight is a little visited segment of Baja's Pacific coast. Most skippers of ocean-cruising vessels lay their courses to proceed on a straight line between Punta Abreojos and Cabo San Lazaro. There is little reason to argue against such action. There is only one protected anchorage along the bight, although it (Bahia San Juanico) is a good one.

In addition the bight's shoreline offers little in the way of scenery for it lies at the edge of the flat Continental Borderlands geographic province. The low western edge of the Peninsular Range Mountains does closely approach the coast near the middle of the bight near Punta Santo Domingo. The topography near this central portion is thus somewhat different than for the flat areas in either direction. However, the difference is relatively minor, and I have chosen not to recognize this area as a separate section. There is thus no sectional breakdown in this chapter.

Most of the Middle Bight shoreline offers a clear example of a subsiding seacoast as discussed in Chapter 5 NATURAL HISTORY. Here, the immediate shore consists of coastal barrier beaches backed by shallow lagoons. The larger of these estuaries are accessible from the sea through narrow channels guarded by offshore shoals and breakers. Few ocean cruisers care to negotiate these treacherous passages.

The onshore waters of the Middle Bight are relatively shallow as is often the case off a low-lying, sandy coast. As a result, the area provides good habitat for shrimp. Groups of shrimp boats will often be observed.

While the Middle Bight contains relatively little of interest for the ocean cruiser, the coastal lagoons offer considerable potential for use by the owners of small, land-based boats and kayaks. There is relatively little such activity currently, but it is certain to increase in the future.

PUNTA ABREOJOS AREA -- Many vessels anchor off the village of Punta Abreojos before or after making the long passage across the Middle Bight.

ABREOJOS AREA LIGHTS -- The profusion of offshore hazards at Abreojos is matched by the number of navigation lights and lighthouse structures in the area. These are four in number. The word Abreojos means *Open Your Eyes*. One's eyes need to be kept open for the lights as well as the rocks. The lights are described below. The numbers used correspond to those shown on the PUNTA ABREOJOS AREA Chart. Wise skippers will keep alert to the possibility of change between these data and the arrival of their vessel.

(1) At the seaward extremity of Punta Abreojos is a latticework light tower of modern vintage. It displays a single flash.

(2) Some 200 yards inland, and northward from light #1, is a white concrete tower whose light displays three flashes. It is considerably taller than light #1. Neither of these two lights show on Chart 21100.

(3) The *original* (1939) Punta Abreojos lighthouse shown on Chart 21100 is constructed slightly over 2 1/2 miles inland and north of the point. It consists of a four-sided, concrete tower projecting above a sizeable caretaker's building, all painted white. A Mexican topo-

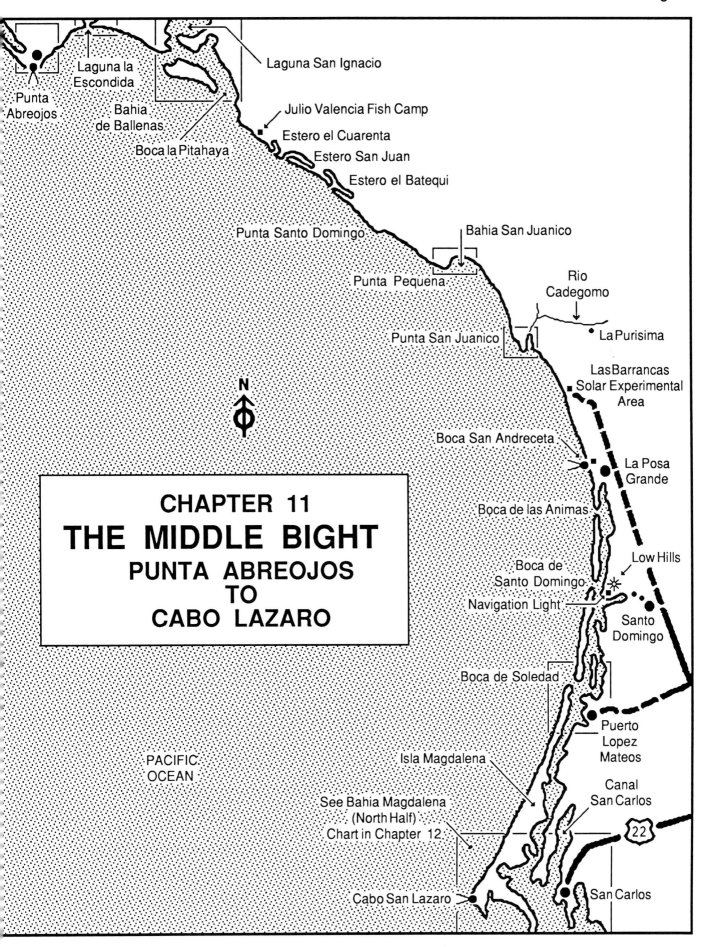

Laguna San Ignacio

Laguna la
Escondida

Punta
Abreojos

Bahia
de Ballenas

Boca la Pitahaya

Julio Valencia Fish Camp

Estero el Cuarenta

Estero San Juan

Estero el Batequi

Punta Santo Domingo

Bahia San Juanico

Punta Pequena

Rio
Cadegomo

La Purisima

Punta San Juanico

Las Barrancas
Solar Experimental
Area

N

Boca San Andreceta

La Posa
Grande

CHAPTER 11
THE MIDDLE BIGHT
PUNTA ABREOJOS
TO
CABO LAZARO

Boca de las Animas

Boca de
Santo Domingo

Low Hills

Navigation Light

Santo
Domingo

Boca de Soledad

Puerto
Lopez
Mateos

PACIFIC
OCEAN

Isla Magdalena

Canal
San Carlos

22

See Bahia Magdalena
(North Half)
Chart in Chapter 12

Cabo San Lazaro

San Carlos

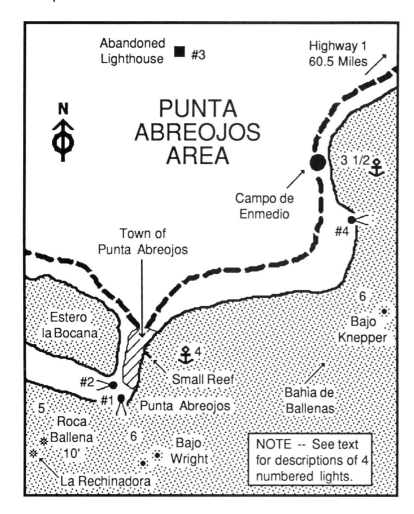

The topography in the Punta Abreojos area is low and level; thus, this lighthouse was constructed inland to gain elevation. In spite of these efforts, the chosen site is only 200 feet above the sea. Directly behind (north) of the light is a slightly higher hill, but it is composed of sand dunes and was apparently not a suitable construction site.

(4) A second latticework tower is located 2 miles NE of Punta Abreojos. Its light displays two flashes. Its purpose is to guide vessels to the anchorage off Campo de Enmedio. However, this light is visible from all directions because of the level terrain and the first time visitor may confuse it for light numbers 1 or 2.

PUNTA ABREOJOS ANCHORAGES -- The bight formed immediately east from Punta Abreojos provides a fair anchorage in 4 fathoms, 1/4 mile offshore. It is regularly used by commercial fishermen and coastal cruisers. Because of the low terrain, there is little protection from the prevailing wind (See Photo).

Landing may be made adjoining the village at a point where fishing pangas are usually drawn up on the beach. Offshore gradients are gentle as would be expected adjacent to a low sandy point. As a result, the sea breaks close inshore making landing here in the ship's tender a bit of an adventure. The local fishermen time the swells so as to ride in just behind the crest. On one occasion, my own calculations proved less precise. As a result, the last 100 feet were negotiated through the surf on foot towing an overturned rubber raft. The fishermen applauded. We aim to please.

A small rocky reef projects from the shore several hundred feet south of the above-described landing site. At low tide this reef provides some degree of protection from the swells, and a less *upsetting landing* may be secured.

PUNTA ABREOJOS (Looking NW) -- Estero la Bocana is seen extending NW from the village of Punta Abreojos. The landing site and small rocky reef noted in the text lie at the extreme right of the photo.

Reference to the PUNTA ABREOJOS AREA Chart will show a second cove NE from Punta Abreojos. This indentation provides a good anchorage, which is less affected by the prevailing NW swells than the one immediately east of Punta Abreojos. The offshore gradient is shallow with 3 1/2 fathoms lying 1/2 mile offshore. The small village of Campo de Enmedio is located on the low bluffs at the head of the bay (See Photo). The landing on the beach at this village appears superior to that at Punta Abreojos but I have not used it. Why do things the easy way, and of course, the cerveza outlet is located in the main village.

graphic map dated 1983 indicates this light as being "abandonado" (abandoned), and it displayed no light during my 1987 visit. However, as long as it remains in place it will provide a dominant landmark during daylight hours because it comes into view when Punta Abreojos and its lights are still below the horizon.

BAY ADJOINING CAMPO DE ENMEDIO (Looking NW) -- The small village of Campo de Enmedio may be seen at the head of the cove.

PUNTA ABREOJOS VILLAGE -- The village at Punta Abreojos contains some 50 houses. At the southern outskirts are several large tanks adjoining the town power plant. There is also a church, fish processing plant, town square, CONASUPO store, schools, clinic, and a marine detachment. At the outskirts to the NE end of town is a large structure enclosing a baseball field.

TRES VIRGENES VOLCANO -- In clear weather one may see the 5,670-foot-high Tres Virgenes Volcano bearing 35 degrees from the Campo de Enmedio anchorage. This mountain is situated only 10 miles from the Sea of Cortez north of Santa Rosalia. The land between Punta Abreojos and the volcano is the low-level Desierto Vizcaino.

LAGUNA LA ESCONDIDA -- (Laguna la Escondida is also known as Estero el Coyote.) Easterly from Punta Abreojos the coast makes a major change in direction, sweeping first to the NE, and then to the SE. The broad bay thus formed is <u>Bahia de Ballenas</u>. The offshore gradients are very shallow and the coast is so low that it is difficult to distinguish it from any distance at sea. At the head of this bay is the entrance to Laguna la Escondida (See Photo). This lagoon is 4 miles in length and 1 mile in width with the long axis lying parallel to the coast.

<u>Campo Rene</u> is a small group of cabins built along the shore of a small cove located westerly from the lagoon entrance. Both Mexican fishermen and tourists use a road cut on the shore of the lagoon as a place to launch

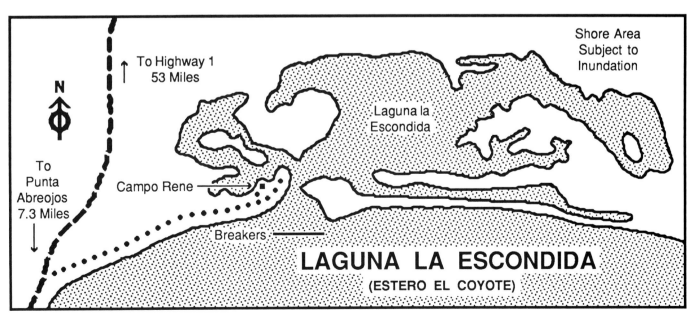

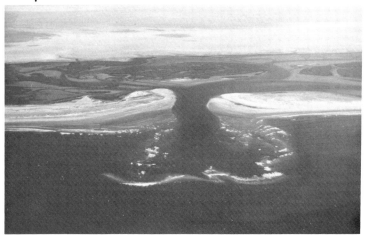

LAGUNA LA ESCONDIDA (Looking N) -- Campo Rene is located on the small cove situated inside and to the left of the estero entrance.

NOTE -- Northerly limit of boat access during whale calving season.

N

To San Ignacio
43 Miles

Yellow
Sand Hills
175'

Laguna
San Ignacio
Fish Camp

La Fridera
Fish Camp

Laguna
San Ignacio

See
NOTE

Punta Prieta

Lower
Lagoon

Punta
Bronaugh

To Bahia
San Juanico

Punta
Malcomb

Isla Arena

Estero la
Pitahaya

Boca la Pitahaya

**LAGUNA
SAN IGNACIO**

small boats. The cabins may be rented by tourists, and there is ample room for the parking of recreational vehicles.

Being located in the bight of Bahia de Ballenas, the estero entrance is somewhat more protected from NW swells than are the mouths of the numerous other lagoons that parallel the coast to the south. However, the entrance is difficult to locate from the sea. Small boat operators who have passed through it note that it "wasn't formidable; just one long continuous line of three foot surf." These boaters were led into the estero by local fishermen and report that the channel from the entrance to Campo Rene is a zigzag course in about 1 1/2 fathoms of water.

LAGUNA SAN IGNACIO -- Laguna San Ignacio is one of the principal calving lagoons used by the California gray whale. The entrance to the lagoon is approximately 16 miles east from Punta Abreojos (See Photos). Most Baja lagoons lie parallel to the seacoast. In contrast, the long axis of Laguna San Ignacio runs for 16

SAN IGNACIO LAGOON WHALE-WATCHING

San Ignacio Lagoon is the winter home of herds of California gray whales that have come to be known as "The Friendly Whales," as some individuals have initiated contact with humans by presenting their heads in and around small whale-watching boats. The shallow, 15-foot-deep upper reaches of the lagoon is "The Nursery" where most females give birth to their calves. Here they also find solitude from the males.

Each year commercial vessels make as many as 30 whale-watching trips into San Ignacio's Lower Lagoon. Such tours are available through agents who maintain offices at the sportsfishing docks near Shelter Island in San Diego. Such vessels are restricted to the waters south of Punta Prieta during the calving season.

Two fish camps are located on the eastern shore of the lagoon. Whale-watching literature indicates this area as the best available, land-accessible observation site. It may be reached over low standard roads from the town of San Ignacio on Highway 1. I have not made this trip.

SAN IGNACIO LAGOON (Looking NE) -- Punta Malcomb is on the right.

mouth of the lagoon. The best landmark is an area of yellow sand hills rising to an elevation of about 175 feet located approximately 5 1/2 miles north of Punta Bronaugh. See the LAGUNA SAN IGNACIO Chart.

The *U. S. Sailing Directions* notes, "No vessel should attempt to cross the bar, which is subject to frequent and sudden changes, without local knowledge. Good anchorage can be taken outside the entrance to the lagoon west of Punta Malcomb in depths of 5 to 6 fathoms." This anchorage is used by commercial vessels taking tourists on whale-watching expeditions. Numerous whales are present both inside and outside the bar during the calving season.

miles inland. In this regard it is similar to Scammon's Lagoon to the north. Topographic maps show that the land between these two lagoons is less than 100 feet in elevation; thus, an increase in sea level of about 100 feet would turn the mountainous area between Punta Eugenia and Punta Abreojos into an island.

As noted, the land on all sides of the Laguna San Ignacio is extremely flat, and it is difficult to locate the

JULIO VALENCIA FISH CAMP -- Julio Valencia fish camp consists of about twenty modest buildings located adjoining the flat sandy coast southeasterly from the entrance to Laguna San Ignacio, and approximately 25 miles from Punta Abreojos. The presence of pickup trucks indicates it is connected by road with the camps on the eastern shore of Laguna San Ignacio. This camp is not shown on any available maps, and the location shown on the map in this chapter is approximate. However, if this camp is in view, your

ENTRANCE TO LAGUNA SAN IGNACIO (Looking NW) -- The elongated area of breakers extends off Punta Malcomb.

PUNTA SANTO DOMINGO (Looking NE) -- The steep vertical cliffs seen here are a distinguishing characteristic of the point. The photo shows the two modest bights noted in the text.

BAHIA SAN JUANICO (Looking NE) -- Punta Pequena is out of the photo to the left. Note the village of Bahia San Juanico at the head of the bay.

vessel has clearly ventured SE from Laguna San Ignacio.

Several small lagoons lie parallel to the coast between this fish camp and Punta Santo Domingo. They are difficult to discern from the sea, and I have no information concerning them. Their names are shown on the chart in this chapter.

PUNTA SANTO DOMINGO -- For a distance of about 5 miles, the low sandy coastline prevailing in the area described in this chapter gives way to steep, dark colored, lava cliffs some 200 feet in height. The terrain immediately inland from the cliffs is level. An area of light sandy hills lies immediately to the NW. Near the middle of this area of cliffs is Punta Santo Domingo. The cliffs cease about 3 miles easterly from the point and the shore again becomes low and sandy.

The two modest bights formed east of the point do not have sufficient northerly indent to provide comfortable anchorage in the prevailing NW weather (See Photo). The area would no doubt be useful in the presence of NE winds under protection of the cliffs. Offshore gradients are very gradual, and with 4 fathoms lying less than 200 yards offshore in the easterly of the two bights.

PUNTA PEQUENA -- The low sandy coast starting SE from the Punta Santo Domingo cliffs continues to Punta Pequena and Bahia Juanico. Geologic maps

indicate that the point consists of lava rock, but its dark color is largely masked by its sandy surface. The navigation light near Punta Pequena is mislocated on Chart 21100. See BAHIA SAN JUANICO Chart for the correct location.

Pequena is the Spanish word for small. While the point is relatively flat, it is anything but small, as it projects some 2 miles seaward to form one of the best protected anchorages on Baja's Pacific coast. The bay so formed is named Bahia San Juanico (misspelled San Juanito on Chart 21100), ignoring the normal custom of naming bays after the point under which they are formed. There is a Punta San Juanico, but it lies some 15 miles to the SE, and there is no Bahia Pequena. If you understand all this, you are better than the author of the *Baja Sea Guide*, who let the resulting confusion lead him into misnaming two of his chapters. My mistakes will be more subtle.

BAHIA SAN JUANICO -- The northerly indent at many of the bays along Baja's Pacific coast is1 mile or less. This same dimension is almost 2 miles at Bahia San Juanico (See Photo). As a result the notes taken in my 1983 coastal survey proclaim, "The anchorage at Bahia San Juanico was as calm as we have had." While it is a good anchorage, the offshore gradient is very shallow and the 3 1/2 fathom point is 600 yards off the beach.

Obtaining a dry landing is a difficult task because of this shallow gradient. In returning to the sea, one needs to

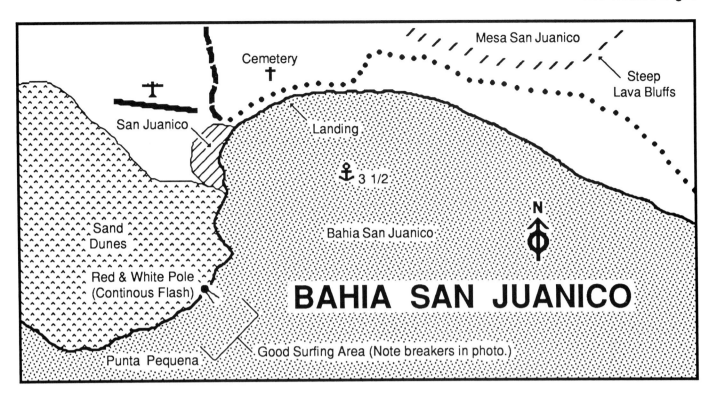

BAHIA SAN JUANICO

wade alongside the dingy to get into sufficient water to be outside of the low breakers. Local fishermen wear hip boots and wheel their boats out to deep water using a device made from the axle of a pickup truck. (The same system is used at Santa Rosalilita to the north under similar conditions.)

A visit to the town of San Juanico gives evidence that a road grader came by a few years ago, removed the vegetation, and leveled the terrain. Wide streets are laid out at right angles. There is a central plaza complete with bandstand, a small police building, basketball court, schools, clinic, and community building. The houses are of reasonable construction. An old cannery building stands abandoned with its machinery rusting away. The streets are lined with creosote-treated power poles delivering electricity from a diesel generator.

I am advised that the waters along the easterly side of Punta Pequena constitute a popular surfing area, and that the town is on occasion brimming with young people from the Estados Unidos doing their thing.

PUNTA SAN JUANICO -- It is 15 miles SE from Punta Pequena to a point backed by a sandy ridge which carries the name Punta San Juanico. The bay formed east of the point is very slight and provides little anchoring protection (See Photo). The point does provide protection for Laguna San Juanico, the drowned extremity of Rio Cadegomo. Several miles up this arroyo lies the community of La Purisima where the Jesuit fathers founded their sixth Baja mission in 1719.

A fish camp bearing the name La Bocana is located in the lee of Punta San Juanico. Fishing boats use the

KINO CROSSES BAJA

Famous Jusuit Padre Eusebio Francisco Kino and Admiral Isidro de Atondo led the first known party of Europeans to cross Baja California by land. They traveled over the mountainous peninsula starting from their base at San Bruno some 20 miles north of present-day Loreto on the Sea of Cortez. The Pacific shore was reached on December 30, 1684, at a point about three miles north of Punta San Jacinco. Their diaries clearly describe the sand dunes present in this vicinity. They explored the Laguna San Jacinco area and named it Puerto Ano Nuevo as they had arrived so close to New Year's Day. Kino's biographer, Herbert Bolton, retraced the expedition's tracks mile for mile in 1934. His report

leaves little doubt that Laguna San Jacinco was the western terminus of the expedition.

In the years to come, Padre Kino was instrumental in motivating the Jesuit colonization of Baja California which started thirteen years later at Loreto in 1697; however, the balance of his personal missionary efforts were to be carried out in NW Mexico and southern Arizona. So famous was he to become, that his statue is included as one of two representatives for the State of Arizona in the Statuary Hall collection at the U. S. Capitol Building. But his missionary career began in rugged Baja California.

LAGUNA SAN JUANICO (Looking W) -- Punta San Juanico is at the top left of the photo.

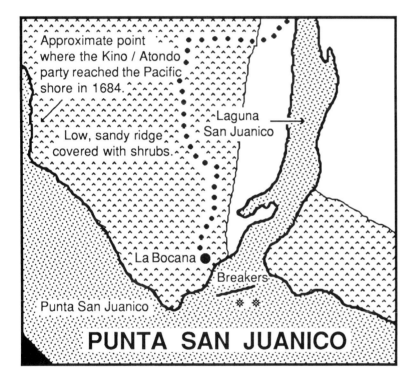

Approximate point where the Kino / Atondo party reached the Pacific shore in 1684.

Low, sandy ridge covered with shrubs.

Laguna San Juanico

La Bocana

Breakers

Punta San Juanico

PUNTA SAN JUANICO

LAS BARRANCAS (Looking E) -- Solar panels may be seen to the right of the group of large buildings at the photo's top-center.

beach on the eastern side of the mouth of the estero as a landing. South of Punta San Juanico the mountains recede inland and the coastline is backed by the broad, level Llano de Magdalena.

SOLAR EXPERIMENTAL AREA -- A large solar energy facility and associated buildings are located approximately 7 miles SE from Punta San Juanico (See Photo). This Las Barrancas development makes a good landmark from sea. In view behind the sandy bluff that borders the sea one may see large solar panels facing south, three tall cylindrical towers, a water tank on a steel tower, and two large glass buildings that appear to be greenhouses. There are also many houses and other buildings scattered about. A wide dirt road leads inland to the east.

BOCA DE SAN ANDRECETA -- A narrow estuary lies 12 miles south of Las Barrancas. This is the drowned seaward end of Arroyo Comondu (See Photo). Puerto San Andreceta is a small fish camp located immediately south of the mouth of this estuary. Pangas are often seen drawn up on the beach. While the camp is small it has a tall concrete light tower on a square concrete base with a flared top. It is painted with broad, red, horizontal stripes. Chart 21100 incorrectly shows this light located 2 miles north of its true location.

MAGDALENA LAGOONS -- I have never heard the term "intracoastal waterway" applied to the coastal lagoons and bays in this area, but why not? They are similar geologically to the extensive waterways that rim much of the subsiding coasts of the United States along the Gulf of Mexico and on the Atlantic shore from Virginia to Florida. The northern extremity of the Baja waterway is located approximately 4 miles south of Puerto San Andreceta. A shoal-draft boat launched here can travel southward through coastal lagoons and the waters of Bahia Magdalena and Bahia Almejas for a total distance of 125 miles.

The northern half of this waterway is made up of a 65-mile-long lagoon that varies in width from a few hundred feet to over 1 mile. The southern end of this shallow waterway blends into the deeper waters of Bahia Magdalena easterly from Cabo San Lazaro. Mexican maps provide a considerable array of names for different sections of the lagoons, but I have uncovered no single identifier which can be applied to the entire system. In the interest of simplicity, I shall refer to them as the Magdalena Lagoons.

With only minor exceptions, the main linear lagoon lies inland directly east from the coastal

BOCA DE SAN ANDRECETA (Looking N) -- The Puerto San Andreceta fish camp is in view below the mouth of the estero.

barrier beaches that separate it from the Pacific Ocean. These barrier beaches vary from about 1/4 to 1 mile in width. In most places the eastern edge of the main channel is lined with scores of islands and a myriad of secondary waterways and lagoons (See Photo). In addition, a second 15-mile-long channel (Canal San Carlos) lies inland from the the main system at its southern end. It adjoins Bahia Magdalena at the town of San Carlos.

We have already encountered many of Baja's coastal lagoons to the north of the Magdalena area, the largest being Guerrero Negro, Scammon's, and San Ignacio. The shoreline vegetation at these northern estuaries is close to nonexistent. In contrast, there are extensive areas of mangroves and low-growing shrubs adjoining the Magdalena Lagoons. Many of the so-called islands are little more than mangrove swamps, with no dry land. As a result, the area provides excellent waterfowl habitat, and the greenery is far more pleasant to the eye than flat desert.

The Magdalena Lagoons may be entered from Bahia Magdalena and through three breaches in the coastal bar to the north. Each of the latter entrances is fronted with breaking bars, and the passages are not suitable for coastal cruising vessels without considerable local knowledge. However, each provides an entrance for the California gray whale. These animals congregate both inside and outside of the openings.

The Magdalena Lagoons are visited by kayakers and owners of other small boats. These people set up camps on the sandy bars, and revel in paddling their frail craft among the whales and into the mangrove areas to observe waterfowl.

The principal access points for these boaters are the port communities of San Carlos and Puerto Lopez Mateos. These will be described in the pages to follow, as will the three coastal entrance points; however, detailed coverage of the lagoons is beyond the scope of this book. Should life and limb hold together, I hope to produce such material in the future. For now, what you see is what you get.

BOCA DE LAS ANIMAS -- Boca de las Animas is the northernmost of the three coastal entrances to the Magdalena Lagoons (See Photo). I have cruised close offshore in this area and have been unable to detect its presence. There is no navigation light or anything else man-made in view, and none are shown on the Mexican topographic maps. These maps indicate the opening is less than 300 yards in width.

The *U.S. Sailing Directions* notes "This entrance is fronted by a shallow bar and is available only to small craft with local knowledge." Boca de las Animas appears

TYPICAL SECTION OF THE MAGDALENA LAGOONS.

BOCA DE LAS ANIMAS (Looking SE)

to be the poorest place to enter the Magdalena Lagoons from the sea.

BOCA DE SANTO DOMINGO -- The middle coastal entrance to the Magdalena Lagoon system is Boca de Santo Domingo (See Photo). It is about 1/2 mile in width. From the sea one can see a white, concrete, navigation light tower painted with red, horizontal stripes lying south of, and inside, the lagoon entrance. It is not shown on Chart 21100. Its base is obscured by the coastal bar, but there appears to be a white building at its foundation.

About one mile south from the entrance a side lagoon projects inland to the east as shown roughly on the CHAPTER 11 Chart. There is a group of low hills on the

BOCA DE SANTO DOMINGO (Looking NE)

BOCA DE SOLEDAD (Looking N).

north side of this side lagoon. While they are only some 75 feet in height, they stand out from the flat terrain in all directions. The above-referenced light is constructed at the edge of the side lagoon and at the SE base of the hills. It is approximately 2 miles inland from the coast.

Comparison of the photo of Boca de Santo Domingo with that of Boca de las Animas would indicate that the former entrance is the deeper of the two. The presence of the lighthouse would indicate it is regularly used by local boats. However, I am compelled to recommend that this entrance be used only with shoal-draft vessels and in company with someone having considerable local knowledge.

The above-referenced secondary estuary proceeds inland some 5 miles to a place shown on road maps as La Banqueta. This site may be reached over a low standard road leading from the agricultural community of Santo Domingo. Santo Domingo is in turn connected to Highway 1 by a blacktopped road. La Banqueta may thus provide a suitable access point to the Magdalena Lagoon system for the owners of small boats. I have not visited this area.

BOCA DE SOLEDAD -- Boca de Soledad is the southernmost of the three coastal entrances to the Magdalena Lagoons (See Photo). It is over 1/2 mile in width, and is the deepest of the three channels; nevertheless, it is fronted by extensive shoals and should be entered only with local knowledge.

A latticework navigation light is situated near the end of the bar on the south side of the entrance. The light

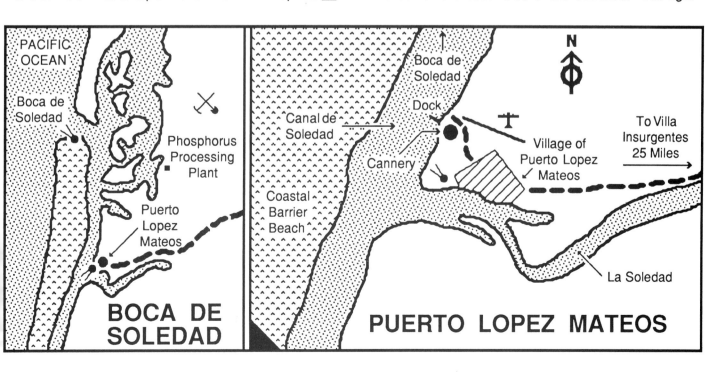

BOCA DE SOLEDAD

PUERTO LOPEZ MATEOS

PUERTO LOPEZ MATEOS (Looking SE) -- The group of large buildings on the shore behind the dock is the fish cannery. The community is within the trees further inland.

shown on Chart 21100 is located 4 1/2 miles too far south. I have been inside the lagoon at this point and was advised by a Mexican panga operator that the entrance channel lay offshore in a NE direction. This information is confirmed by small boat operators who entered the channel in 1986. They report, "Stay on the north side of the breaker line, line up the day/night marker onshore to the electric power generator poles on land, and you can head right down the slot to Puerto Lopez Mateos."

Puerto Lopez Mateos is a sizeable town situated 5 miles south from Boca de Soledad near the mouth of a side lagoon named La Soledad (See Photo). The town is incorrectly labled as La Soledad on Chart 21100. There

is a large fish cannery. Adjoining the cannery is a dock which projects about 100 feet into the main lagoon. It accommodates fishing vessels in the 50' range. Pangas may be rented here for trips to the area inside Boca de Soledad to view the California gray whale. The numerous trees growing in the town project above the coastal barrier beach. They and the town water tank may be seen several miles to sea.

The land north and east from Puerto Lopez Mateos contains substantial quantities of phosphorus. A large modern processing plant is constructed on the shores of a side lagoon as shown on the BOCA DE SOLEDAD Map (See Photo). This facility rises well above the coastal dunes and makes a good landmark. During my most recent visit in 1986, this plant did not appear operational; however, the plan is to haul enriched phosphorus ore by barge south down the Magdalena Lagoons to a deep-water port located at Punta Belcher inside Bahia Magdalena.

ISLA MAGDALENA -- Without question, there is no island in the world that has an outline anything like that of Isla Magdalena. To the offshore cruiser it is nothing more than a segment of the peninsular coast. But the presence of Bahia Magdalena and the Magdalena Lagoons to the east results in this piece of coast being, in fact, an elongated island. Most of its terrain is little more than several low coastal barrier beaches; but these extensive sandy areas are shaped by two of the isolated mountain peaks present on the seaward side of Bahia Mag-

PHOSPHORUS PROCESSING PLANT NE OF PUERTO LOPEZ MATEOS.

CABO SAN LAZARO (Looking N) -- Note the old lighthouse structure on the flat bench on the right side of the photo.

dalena. They, in turn, have become part of this odd-shaped island.

CABO SAN LAZARO -- Four isolated mountain ridges form the westerly rim of Bahia Magdalena. The northernmost of these is 4 miles in length. Its westerly extremity is Cabo San Lazaro and the highest point is Monte San Lazaro (See BAHIA SANTA MARIA AREA Chart in Chapter 12). One of the old original lighthouse structures is still in operation a few yards inland and SE from the Cape (See Photo). It is constructed on a small level spot at an elevation of about 200 feet. The lighthouse may be reached by trail leading from Estero San Lazaro on the eastern side of the mountain. (See discussion in Chapter 12.)

Cabo San Lazaro and nearby Bahia Santa Maria are the objectives of coastal cruisers crossing the middle bight from Punta Abreojos. The cape is visible from a distance of 40 miles. Currents are reported to set SE with a velocity of 1 to 1 1/2 knots along the low sandy beach north of Cabo Lazaro. Thus, vessels approaching from the north should keep well offshore until rounding the Cape. The breakers along this beach are something to behold.

There is a prominent large wreck stranded about 1/2 mile north of Cabo San Lazaro near the point where the rocky coast of the Cape gives way to the sand beach to the north. Another wreck lies on this beach 3 1/2 miles north of the Cape.

CHAPTER 12
THE SOUTHERN REACH
& BAHIA MAGDALENA
CABO SAN LAZARO TO PUNTA TOSCA

CHAPTER SUMMARY

The Southern Reach provides welcome elevational contrast to the monotonous low-lying plains that make up nearly half of the Pacific coast of the Baja Peninsula. What is not at first apparent is that these mountains are not part of the main peninsula but are a chain of four isolated ridges lying on two offshore islands. The peninsula coast itself is barely above sea level.

These mountain ridges have provided the anchor points for barrier beaches that appear destined to eventually tie these highlands into the main peninsula. But for now, they, and the connecting beaches, are islands, Isla Magdalena to the north, and Isla Santa Margarita to the south. Together they form the western edge of Bahia Magdalena, by far the largest protected body of water in Baja California.

The Southern Reach and Bahia Magdalena provide protected anchorages for coastal cruisers crossing the uninviting bights from both north and south. Bahia Santa Maria is the anchorage chosen by those who do not wish to enter Bahia Magdalena itself. However, there are several interesting places to visit inside this latter haven for those with more time available. Its protected waters, and the lagoons to the north, provide the land-based trailer boater with the best recreational waters on Baja's Pacific coast.

	SECTION		DESCRIPTION
NO.	FROM	TO	
A	Cabo San Lazaro	Punta Tosca	A 45-mile-long series of isolated mountain ridges and connecting sand spits that form the ocean side of Bahia Magdalena.
B	Bahia Magdalena		The northern deep-water segment of Bahia Magdalena.
C	Bahia Almejas		The southern, mostly shallow water, section of Bahia Magdalena.

SECTION A
THE SOUTHERN REACH
CABO SAN LAZARO TO
PUNTA TOSCA

It is 45 miles along the Southern Reach from Cabo San Lazaro to Punta Tosca. The four steep mountain ridges lying on Isla Magdalena and Isla Margarita make up most of the shoreline between these two points. Good an-chorage is available in Bahia Santa Maria near Cabo San Lazaro, with a lesser haven present easterly from Punta Tosca. The entrance to Bahia Magdalena lies near the center of the Reach.

Cabo San Lazaro and Punta Tosca are both turning points in the courses set by skippers of most cruise liners and other large commercial vessels plying the waters off the Baja peninsula; thus, such craft will frequently be seen from 2 to 10 miles offshore in this area.

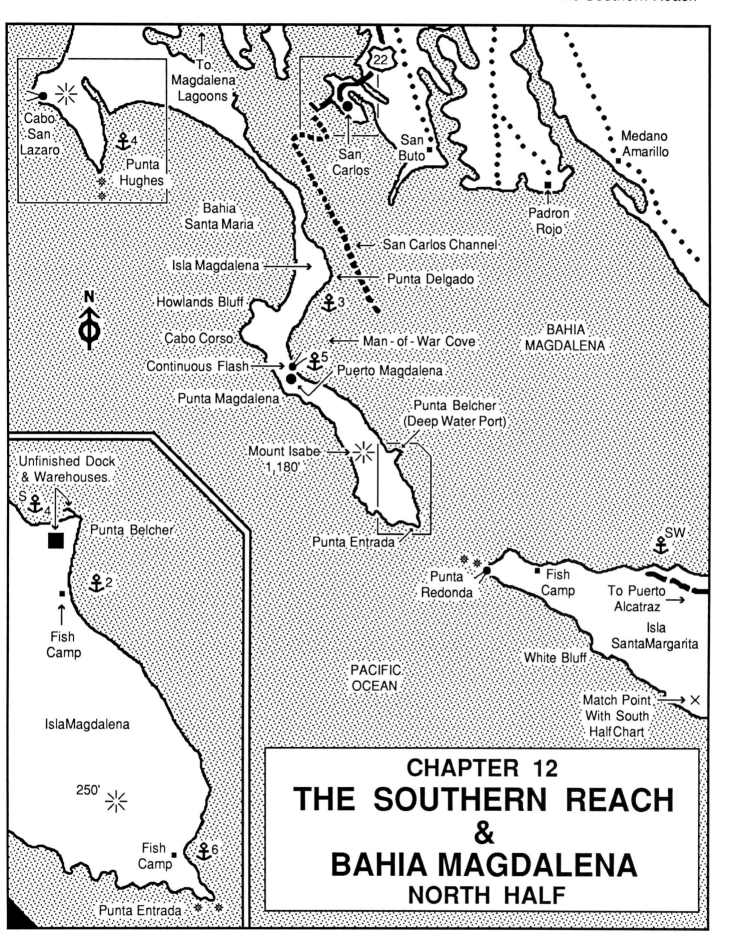

To
Magdalena
Lagoons

Cabo
San
Lazaro

⚓4
Punta
Hughes

Bahia
Santa Maria

22

San
Carlos

San
Buto

Medano
Amarillo

Padron
Rojo

Isla Magdalena →

San Carlos Channel

Punta Delgado

⚓3

Howlands Bluff

N

BAHIA
MAGDALENA

Cabo Corso

Man - of - War Cove

Continuous Flash →

⚓5
Puerto Magdalena

Punta Magdalena

Punta Belcher
(Deep Water Port)

Mount Isabe
1,180'

Punta Entrada

Unfinished Dock
& Warehouses.

S ⚓4

Punta Belcher

Punta Entrada

SW

Punta
Redonda

Fish
Camp

To Puerto
Alcatraz

Isla
SantaMargarita

⚓2

White Bluff

Fish
Camp

IslaMagdalena

PACIFIC
OCEAN

Match Point
With South
Half Chart

250'

Fish
Camp

⚓6

CHAPTER 12
THE SOUTHERN REACH
&
BAHIA MAGDALENA
NORTH HALF

Punta Entrada

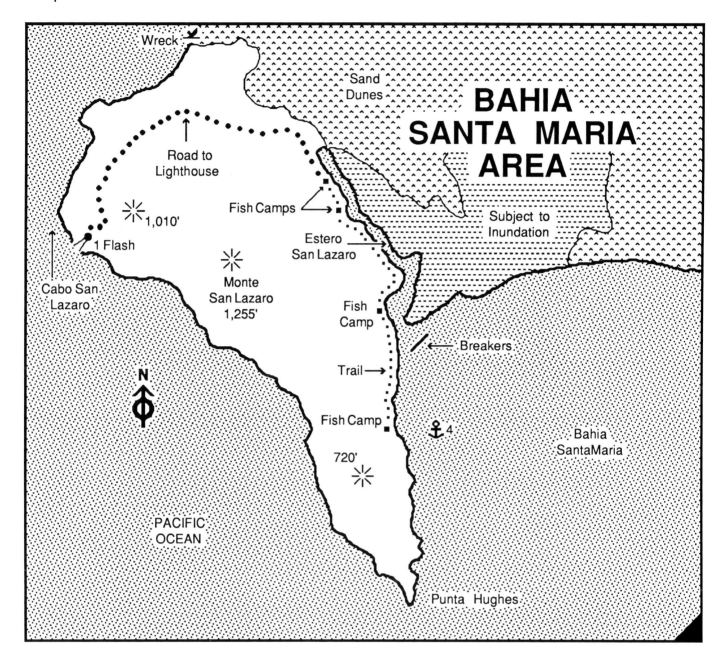

BAHIA
SANTA MARIA
AREA

Wreck

Sand
Dunes

Road to
Lighthouse

1,010'

Fish Camps

Estero
San Lazaro

Subject to
Inundation

1 Flash

Cabo San
Lazaro

Monte
San Lazaro
1,255'

Fish
Camp

Breakers

N

Trail

Fish Camp

720'

4

Bahia
SantaMaria

PACIFIC
OCEAN

Punta Hughes

PUNTA HUGHES -- Punta Hughes is the low-lying southern terminus of the 4-mile-long Monte San Lazaro ridge of complex metamorphic rocks (See Photos). As one would expect, this ridge continues underwater south of Punta Hughes, creating a shallow area often marked by the presence of lobster pots. This area should be given a wide berth in rounding the point into Bahia Santa Maria.

BAHIA SANTA MARIA -- The shore north of Punta Hughes runs true north and south, creating a northerly indent of almost 2 miles. The resultant bay, Bahia Santa Maria, thus affords good anchorage under prevailing weather conditions (See Photo). Unfortunately, NW winds are able to sweep unchecked over the flat sandy land at the head of the bay. As a result, most skippers choose to anchor midway between Estero San Lazaro

and Punta Hughes in order to garner some small degree of wind protection provided by the steep sides of the highlands north of the point.

Baja Sea Guide describes Bahia Santa Maria as having "a strange fascination; stark in its seclusion, primordial in its isolation, clean, unused, and rarely visited." The anchorage is still fascinating, due in large part to the towering land mass that rises to the west, although it is no longer unused or rarely visited. During the cruising season, there are often several vessels lying here after making the long sea passages to both north and south. The anchor lights of such craft serve as guides for those entering at night. Mexican fishing vessels also make heavy use of the bay. During moon-less nights, the glow of lights from no less than five communities can be seen rising to the east and SE above the sand barrier

CABO SAN LAZARO & PUNTA HUGHES (Looking SE) -- Punta Hughes is on the right. Note the Cabo San Lazaro lighthouse near the photo center.

ASHORE AT BAHIA SANTA MARIA

The energetic hiker will find a varied and interesting adventure ashore adjoining the Bahia Santa Maria anchorage. A well-used trail traverses the edge of the bluffs from the fish camp near the anchorage, to the camp at the mouth of Estero San Lazaro (See Photo). It passes through relatively sparse, low-growing cactus and other desert vegetation. The trail continues from the mouth of the estero to the upper of its two fish camps. This second trail segment passes along the edge of a mangrove swamp with its unique plant and animal life.

From the upper camp, a dirt road leads to the Cabo San Lazaro lighthouse. The desert vegetation along this route is unusually dense and festooned with a heavy growth of lichens, all the result of moisture-laden air which passes over the area from the sea. Also in view are massive sand dunes, and row after row of breakers off the beach north of Cabo San Lazaro. The wrecked freighter north of the Cape may also be visited.

The lighthouse itself offers flush toilets and wash bowls, all long in disuse. They are a tribute to a facility designed in Mexico City for use on the frontier. Plan 6 hours for the round trip, unless you are fortunate enough to catch a ride with the lighthouse tending crew. The remains of vehicles used in this service through the years are scattered along the road exactly where they gave their last gasp.

PUNTA HUGHES & BAHIA SANTA MARIA ANCHORAGE (Looking N) -- The level point of land to the left-center of the photo is Punta Hughes. Bahia Santa Maria is to the right of the point. Most vessels anchor near the upper portion of the bay off the right side of the Punta Hughes promontory.

ESTERO SAN LAZARO (Looking NW) -- Note the breakers at the mouth of the estero, which make passage difficult except with shoal draft craft with considerable outboard power.

beaches that rim the bay. During the day, the giant globular ammonia storage tank and warehouses on the dock at Puerto San Carlos are in plain view over this same area.

BAHIA MAGDALENA ENTRANCE -- Passage into Bahia Magdalena between Punta Entrada and Punta Redonda (See Photos) is clear, deep, and wide. In this regard it is in marked contrast with all the other coastal entrances to Bahia Magdalena and the Magdalena Lagoons. A substantial tidal current sets between the entrance points and throughout the bay.

WHITE BLUFF -- Approximately 5 miles SE from the Bahia Magdalena entrance is a steep, near-vertical bluff displaying rock of a fairly light hue. It is nearly devoid of vegetation. When well illuminated, it makes a good landmark from close-in.

BAHIA PEQUENA LOWLANDS -- Pequena is the Spanish word for small. But here, near the midpoint of Isla Santa Margarita, even this adjective is an overstatement, for there is no bay at all. What is present is a flat sandy plain about 4 miles in width. This plain lies between the two mountain masses that form the extremities of Isla Santa Margarita. From a short distance at sea, this low land is below the horizon, and the area can easily be mistaken for a bay, or the entrance into Bahia Magdalena. I was led into making such an erroneous decision during a night passage when the radar clearly showed the two mountains but failed to detect the intervening lowland.

The name Bahia Pequena appears at this point in the notes of one of the early explorers. Those of us who decide there is a passage here are thus in historic company. It should also be noted that there is an exten-

PUNTA ENTRADA (Looking N) -- The anchorage off the Punta Entrada fish camp (see text) is located in the cove immediately above the point. Punta Belcher is the low sharp point at the top-center of the photo.

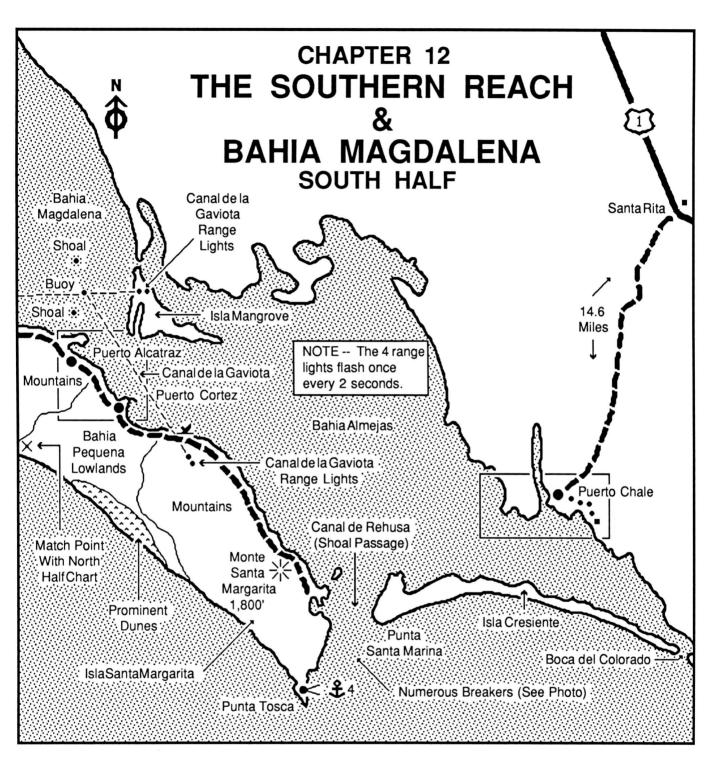

CHAPTER 12
THE SOUTHERN REACH
&
BAHIA MAGDALENA
SOUTH HALF

N

Santa Rita

Bahia Magdalena

Canal de la Gaviota Range Lights

Shoal

Buoy

Shoal

Isla Mangrove

14.6 Miles

Puerto Alcatraz

NOTE -- The 4 range lights flash once every 2 seconds.

Canal de la Gaviota

Mountains

Puerto Cortez

Bahia Almejas

Bahia Pequena Lowlands

Canal de la Gaviota Range Lights

Puerto Chale

Mountains

Match Point With North Half Chart

Canal de Rehusa (Shoal Passage)

Monte Santa Margarita 1,800'

Prominent Dunes

Isla Cresiente

Punta Santa Marina

Boca del Colorado

Isla Santa Margarita

Numerous Breakers (See Photo)

Punta Tosca

sive area of sand dunes along most of the shore of the Bahia Pequena lowlands. This light colored area makes a good landmark. With the aid of field glasses, one may see the Puerto Cortez Naval Base observation hut located on a hill on the eastern side of the low plain.

PUNTA TOSCA -- Punta Tosca is the rocky southern end of Isla Santa Margarita (See Photo in Chapter 13). It provides a home for one of the old original lighthouse structures. The anchorage east of the point is describ-

ed at the beginning of Chapter 13. The high peaks north of the point are visible some 55 miles when approaching from the south in clear weather.

SECTION B
BAHIA MAGDALENA

The overall size and configuration of combined Bahia Magdalena and Bahia Almejas is similar to that of San

PUNTA REDONDO (Looking NE) -- A large area of light colored soil lies immediately inland from Punta Redondo with the navigation light situated at its seaward end.

CABO CORSO (Looking 25 Degrees).

PUNTA REDONDO (Looking 65 Degrees).

Francisco Bay in the United States. The main entrance is bounded on both sides by steep mountains and reminds one very much of the Golden Gate. The main, deep-water portion of the bay lies to the north of the entrance, with the more shallow Bahia Almejas stretching to the south. But here the similarity with its U. S. counterpart comes to an end.

San Francisco Bay is all but surrounded by easy-to-develop hills or plains. At Bahia Magdalena only the outer rim is mountainous. The main peninsular shore is totally flat and rises only a scant few inches above sea level. Urban development is difficult, and fresh water very scarce. Thus, the vast majority of the Bahia Magdalena shoreline is unchanged from prehistoric times.

Without question, Bahia Magdalena offers the best recreational boating waters on the Pacific coast of the Baja peninsula, but this potential is little utilized. A few trailer boaters launch their craft near San Carlos and fish in the bay. Commercial kayaking trips are available into the lagoons at the north end of the bay, and some ocean cruisers spend a day or two here on their way to or from the warmer climates of Cabo San Lucas and the Sea of Cortez. Overall, Bahia Magdalena is seldom visited in relation to its considerable potential.

Bahia Magdalena is the southernmost of the principal calving grounds of the California gray whale. More importantly, it is the only one which

PUNTA BELCHER (Looking NE) -- The partially completed warehouse facilities and circular dock are in view as well as a graded airstrip.

may be entered easily and safely by ocean-cruising vessels. Whales may easily be seen near the entrance to the bay during the calving season.

PUNTA ENTRADA FISH CAMP -- A small fish camp is located inside the bay about 1/4 mile north of Punta Entrada. Behind it is a solitary tamarisk tree shading a diminutive chapel, perhaps a good place to offer thanks for having reached the shelter offered by this fascinating segment of the world (See Punta Entrada Photo).

I have observed vessels anchored off this camp in 6 fathoms in quiet water. This anchorage may offer a convenient place to spend the night for coastal cruisers who do not wish to run further north into Bahia Magdalena. Common sense would seem to indicate that

this spot may be subject to currents passing through the nearby entrance to the bay. The *U.S. Sailing Directions* indicate the Bahia Magdalena currents are in the one-to-two-knot range; thus, this water movement may be of minor importance, particularly to San Francisco Bay sailors where such a flow would be considered as *still water*.

PUNTA BELCHER -- Punta Belcher is a triangular projection of land (See Photo). It is unusual that such a flat point of land would extend from an otherwise steep and rocky shore. This inviting flat terrain was home for a whaling station during the 1850-60s. Previous guidebooks describe a group of black iron tanks, winches, mincing tables, boilers, and trying pots lying on the NW shore of the point. During my visit in 1983 the area's most prominent features were bulldozer tracks. Toward

---

BAHIA MAGDALENA LAND FRAUDS

In 1864, some two thirds of the Baja peninsula was leased to various foreign land speculators by the Mexican government. The initial center of operations for these American "entrepreneurs" was at Bahia Magdalena. In 1870 large headlines in California newspapers advertised "Free land! Free Commerce! Homes for the poor! Riches for the wealthy!" The soil was said to be pure black humus and the grass was higher than the shoulders of a horse. Numerous colonists actually arrived at Bahia Magdalena lured by these fantastic claims.

In due course, the land speculators entered into a legitimate business collecting orchilla plants. Orchilla is a species of lichen which hangs from the branches of

larger desert plants growing in areas along the Pacific coast which are moistened by frequent fog. These plants were combined with indigo for use in dying silk and wool fabrics. The lichens were dried, baled, and shipped to England until German coal tars outmoded them as a dying agent.

This activity caused considerable friction with Mexican authorities and was no doubt the reason for establishment of a Port Captain in such an unlikely place as the village at Puerto Magdalena. Conflict even resulted between the United States and Mexican governments over the orchilla business. All of this subsided about 1872 and Bahia Magdalena settled back into serenity.

PUERTO MAGDALENA (Looking W) -- The mountains shown here are typical of four such highlands that surround Bahia Magdalena and Bahia Almejas.

the rear of the new activity was a pile of rusted tanks, propellers, and various unidentifiable iron objects. The historic artifacts had given way to progress.

The progress above noted is a partially constructed deep-water port facility located on the NW facing side of the point. The intention was to transfer phosphoric sand ore to ocean-going ships. The ore was to have been moved in barges south down the Magdalena Lagoons from a mining area north of Puerto Lopez Mateos. As of 1987 these partially completed port facilities lay abandoned. Future visitors may find them completed and in use.

Water depths of 7 fathoms are present off the above-noted docks. Anchorage may be taken west of these docks in 4 fathoms when the wind is from the south. In contrast, there is an extensive shallow water area south of the point which affords an anchorage in 2 fathoms when northerly winds are present (See Anchorage Comparison Section below). The beach south of the point is encumbered with a group of plywood shacks. These were constructed as part of the port facility but are now used as a fish camp.

And whence cometh the name Belcher, a strange name in this Spanish land? As one would suspect, it is English. Edward Belcher commanded British survey vessels that labored in the area in 1837 and 1839.

PUERTO MAGDALENA -- An indentation in the eastern shore of Isla Magdalena bears the name Man-of-War Cove. Here is situated a village of about 50 modest dwellings (See Photo). This is historic Puerto Magdalena. At one time this remote spot provided headquarters for a Port Captain when it contained only a

scattering of shacks. The place is now considerably larger, and the Port Captain has long ago been replaced by a similar official in Puerto San Carlos.

At the north end of town are three concrete buildings. One of these is a fancy, but abandoned, two-story affair, complete with fireplace. This was no doubt the office of the Port Captain. A long, low, roofless structure is used for town gatherings. The town also boasts a power generator, creosote-treated power poles, and a small salt water desalination plant.

Anchorage is available in Man-of-War Cove off the village in 3 - 6 fathoms. (See Anchorage Comparison below.) A latticework navigation light is located near the old Port Captain's house. An abandoned stone mole extends from the shore nearby. This facility served the 1870's enterprise that gathered and shipped orchilla. The town cemetery adjoins the shore 3/4 mile southward from the town. Its presence is evidence that mankind has labored in this remote location for many years.

PUNTA DELGADO ANCHORAGE -- Good anchorage may be taken in 3 fathoms near Punta Delgado SE of the barrier beach that separates Bahia Santa Maria from Man-of-War Cove (See Anchorage Comparison below). It lies approximately 2 miles NE from Puerto Magdalena and bears 300 degrees from the high point visible at Cabo San Lazaro.

ANCHORAGE COMPARISON -- On one occasion I was able to visit the anchorages at (1) Punta Belcher, (2) Man-of-War Cove, and (3) Punta Delgado in rapid succession in company with 20-knot NW winds. These winds blow directly down the length of Bahia Magdalena parallel to the shore of Isla Magdalena. They generate wind-waves that would make anchoring in modest-size, ocean-cruising sailboats very uncomfortable without protection from some intervening land barrier. Following are additional comments from these visits.

(1) PUNTA BELCHER -- No reduction of wind velocity. Must enter to 2 fathoms to secure significant wind-wave relief from Punta Belcher. Room for only about two vessels in the protected area. Wind blows parallel to the land so that a slipped anchor would probably result in one's vessel going aground. (Unlimited holding ground in calm weather.)

(2) MAN-OF-WAR COVE ANCHORAGE (PUERTO MAGDALENA) -- Some wind reduction afforded by the mountains to the NW. Anchorage depths from 3 to 6 fathoms. Room for 6 or more vessels. Wind blows parallel to the shore. As the shore curves SE south of the anchorage, anchored boats are on a lee shore. This anchorage would no doubt provide good protection in SW weather.

(3) PUNTA DELGADO -- No reduction in wind velocity. Three fathoms 400 yards off the beach. Room for numerous vessels. The only protection here is the low barrier beach between Bahia Santa Maria and Man-of-War Cove, but wind-waves are relatively low as their generation area is only the distance between the beach and one's vessel. Most importantly, the anchorage is not on a lee shore. I recommend this as the best of the three anchorages in strong NW winds.

SAN CARLOS CHANNEL -- Northward from Puerto Magdalena the waters of Bahia Magdalena become shallow. In order to reach Puerto San Carlos one must stay within the confines of a natural channel with a least depth of 29 feet. It is marked by buoys which have small solar-powered lights. The conventional, odd-numbered green buoys (green lights) are located to port going north, and the even-numbered red buoys (red lights) to starboard. The southernmost channel buoys are easily seen from the anchorages at Puerto Magdalena or Punta Delgado.

The buoys are in pairs, although it is sometimes difficult to match up the two due to their irregular spacing. This is particularly true near the two turns, where my notes indicate, "there seem to be buoys everywhere." Red buoy #18 is the marker on the inside of the dogleg turn to the right, and green buoy # 23 marks the inside of the subsequent left-hand turn.

The channel buoys are shown in some detail on Chart 21122. The Port Captain at San Carlos had a copy of this chart. I quote from my notes resulting from a visit to his office. "The Port Captain gave me his chart showing the current (1983) locations of the buoys, many of which he acknowledged were in error. He then proceeded with pencil and eraser to screw things up so badly that the whole mess was worthless." In other words, the buoy positions are changed as necessary to meet current conditions.

The San Carlos channel is a minimum of 100 yards wide, and the buoys are intervisible. They are not difficult to follow if you are alert to the double dogleg bend as noted above. There are fifteen pairs of buoys, although the red buoy of the 14th pair is replaced with a white two-second light atop the grain loading tower at the San Carlos dock. The last pair of buoys is north of the dock and marks the limits of the turning area. Good luck, and drive carefully.

PUERTO SAN CARLOS -- The port facilities at Puerto San Carlos were completed in 1966-67 (See Photos). In Baja, they are exceeded in size only by those at Ensenada. They serve as a shipping point for agricultural products grown in the irrigated farmlands to the east. Principal exports are wheat and cotton. Fish and shrimp are also offloaded here for processing at a packing plant in the adjoining community of San Carlos. Some of these fish are trucked to the packing plant at Puerto Lopez Mateos on the lagoons to the north. A one-lane dirt road connects the two ports. It is a unique experience to have one's camper forced off this lane in the middle of the desert by tractor-trailer loads of tuna fish. Such is life in Baja California.

Puerto San Carlos consists of a 100-yard-wide earthfill mole which projects about 1/2 mile into the bay. Warehouses, grain storage areas, and a large, globular, ammonia fertilizer tank are located on this pier. At its end is an L-shaped dock built on pilings.

PUERTO SAN CARLOS (Looking SE) -- Note the large warehouses and round ammonia tank. The shoal areas which bear at low tide are readily apparent on either side of the pier. Anchoring positions near the pier should be chosen accordingly.

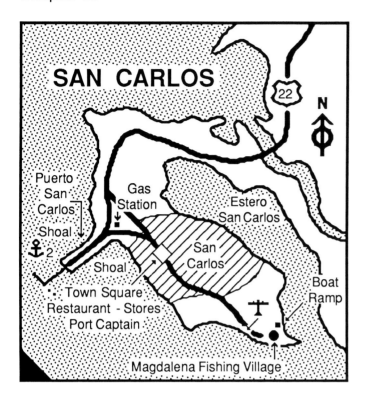

rectly NW of the L-dock in 2 fathoms. I have observed currents of approximately 3 knots at this location (See Puerto San Carlos photo to observe shoal areas near this anchorage.)

From the docking area, it is a walk of about 1/2 mile to the landward end of the mole. A gasoline station is located at this point. It is an additional 1/2 mile journey to the town plaza in the community of San Carlos. The office of the Port Captain is situated on the SW side of this plaza. A small restaurant is on the NE side. Grocery stores and other shops are located nearby. San Carlos is home to more than 5,000 people and one of Baja's five Secondary-Technical schools. There is also a medical clinic and several doctors.

The Magdalena Fishing Village is the main haunt of the few land-based tourists that make their way to Bahia Magdalena (See Photo). It consists of a small restaurant and a group of one-room rental cabins. Travelers with recreational vehicles park in and about the resort area. The water in front (south) of these facilities is very shallow; however, the bay waters may be accessed using a boat launching ramp located to the rear of the resort. It utilizes the slightly deeper waters of Estero San Carlos. The ramp is high and dry at low tide, and flooded at the other extreme. As always in Mexico, patience is a virtue. Also, be careful in camping in this area, as you may awake to find your campsite flooded by the incoming tide.

Recreational vessels are most likely to find dockside space on the inside of the L. I am advised that water is available and that fuel may be purchased. I am not aware of details. Small vessels may also find anchorage di-

SAN CARLOS & MAGDALENA FISHING VILLAGE (Looking NW) -- The semi-circular group of small buildings above the sand spit at the bottom of the photo is the Magdalena Fishing Village. The pier at Puerto San Carlos is out of sight beyond the top of the photo.

SECTION C
BAHIA ALMEJAS

<u>Almejas</u>, the Spanish word for clams, is a good name for a bay that consists largely of shoal draft waters. This is the case with Bahia Almejas. The bay has a shoal draft entrance, Canal de Rehusa, at its SE end. (See description at the beginning of Chapter 13) The deeper water entrance is through Canal de la Gaviota leading from Bahia Magdalena.

As with Bahia Magdalena proper, the bay's inland shores are barely above sea level, while the seaward side is formed by the steep-sided mountains of Isla Santa Margarita. Canal de la Gaviota leads to two communities built on the NE facing shores of this island. These are the fishing town of <u>Puerto Alcatraz</u> and the naval base at <u>Puerto Cortez</u>.

PUNTA REDONDO -- A <u>navigation light</u> situated some 100 feet above the sea near the end of Punta Redondo (See Photo), is at the edge of a small area of gentle terrain in what is otherwise quite steep and rocky terrain. The level segment appears to be a wave-cut terrace resulting from a past geological emergence. Thus, this mountain ridge was at one time rising upward but is now part of an overall region which is clearly subsiding.

CANAL DE LA GAVIOTA -- Canal de la Gaviota has a least depth of 12 fathoms. (See location of the channel center line on the SOUTH HALF Chart in this chapter. Also see Puerto Alcatraz Photo.)

The latticework towers of the two <u>range lights</u> on Isla Mangrove are easy to find. This is not true for the lights at the SE end of the second leg of the channel. There, towers blend in with the steep hillside behind them. From the turning point in the channel, the use of field glasses will disclose that rows of white stones have been placed on this hillside to form an arrow pointing uphill. The upper of the two towers lies near the lower end of the arrow. The lower tower is on the shore below the arrow. The remains of two older lights are still present and serve to confuse matters. The light coloration created by the mouth of an arroyo near the lower light is often the most easily seen landmark during daylight hours.

The *U.S. Sailing Directions* note, "During the ebb, the shoals on the north and south sides of the entrance are clearly marked by heavy breakers even though the sea is smooth and the swell barely perceptible."

PUERTO SAN CARLOS (Looking W) -- Close-up of the dock and warehouse area at Puerto San Carlos. Tie-up space for yachts may sometimes be available along the inside of the L-shaped dock area.

PUERTO ALCATRAZ -- The community at Puerto Alcatraz (See Photos) is one of the few coastal towns where there has been little growth in recent years. The original cannery adjoining the town has been closed for some time and now is used as a shop and warehouse. A new and much larger plant which processes fish fertilizer is constructed on Punta Lengua, the flat spit of land lying in front of the community.

A <u>100-foot dock</u> extends from the cannery with 4 fathoms of water at its outer end. A considerably longer dock projects from the old cannery, but it is in poor repair and its walking surface unusable. There are 1 1/2 fathoms of water at its outer end at low tide.

PUERTO ALCATRAZ Looking NE) -- The odd-shaped segment of land lying off the village is Punta Lengua. The area is actually an island at low tide. Note the cannery and its adjacent dock. Canal de la Gaviota lies between Punta Lengua and the low sandy island at the top of the photo.

PUERTO CORTEZ (Looking SE) -- No naval vessels were present at the dogleg pier when the photo was taken. Anchorage may be taken between this dock and the adjacent shore.

NAVAL BASE HEADQUARTERS AT PUERTO CORTEZ.

PUERTO CHALE (Looking NE) -- The secondary road from Highway 1 to Puerto Chale may be seen in the photo's upper portion. The village lies on the shore of the narrow lagoon to the left of the road, with the shrimp propagation ponds to the right.

Very good anchorage may be taken in 4 fathoms 100 yards SE from Punta Lengua, and in front of the new cannery. This anchorage is the best available inside Bahia Magdalena-Bahia Almejas as it offers protection from prevailing weather wind-waves that have been generated within the bays.

The town has a school, power generator, and many power poles. Fresh water is delivered through a pipeline leading from the saltwater desalination plant at the Puerto Cortez Naval Base to the SE.

PUERTO CORTEZ -- Throughout the world, the military is prone to locate bases in relatively isolated places, perhaps for security reasons, perhaps to keep the personnel separated from temptation. But at Puerto Cortez, they seem to have gotten carried away, for this is seemingly a strange and isolated place for a naval base. I am advised by the base commander, that positioning a military base in this area in 1936 was a reaction to the long-standing interest by various foreign powers (particularly the United States and Japan) in Baja California in general, and Bahia Magdalena in particular. It is somewhat of a "keep out" sign.

In any case, the Mexican navy has one of its four Baja California bases located at Puerto Cortez. The base has flagstone streets and is neat and well maintained. In front of the headquarters building is a fort-like wall with two naval guns pointing toward the bay (See Photo). A church is located about 1/2 mile north of the base. Its two steeples could be mistaken for the Canal de la Gaviota range lights by a nervous skipper who has forsaken finding the real ones. Fresh water is available from the base's salt-water desalination plant.

A 200-yard-long <u>rock jetty</u> is constructed in an east-west direction from the southern end of the base (See Photo). At its outer end is an additional 150-yard-long <u>concrete pier</u> with 3 1/2 fathoms of water at its outer terminus. <u>Good anchorage</u> is available SW of the jetty in 2 fathoms. As at Puerto Alcatraz, there is good protection from any NW wind-waves generated inside Bahia Almejas.

Rocks painted white spell out the word "Bienvenito" (welcome) on a hill inland from the base. I asked the base commander if they really meant what the sign said, and did they really wish to be visited by Norteamericano yacht crews on a regular basis. The answer was an emphatic "yes". Any vessel anchoring at the base can expect to be boarded by naval personnel for a review of the ship's papers, and perhaps a brief look around. But following this, a request to visit the installation will in all probability be honored. The commander advised me he frequently invites visitors to dinner. So if you don't mind the boarding process, go ashore and and foster good relations with the Mexican Republic. The base also has good maintenance shops where emergency repair assistance may be obtained.

PUERTO CHALE -- A good, level, secondary road leads 14.6 miles from Highway 1 to Puerto

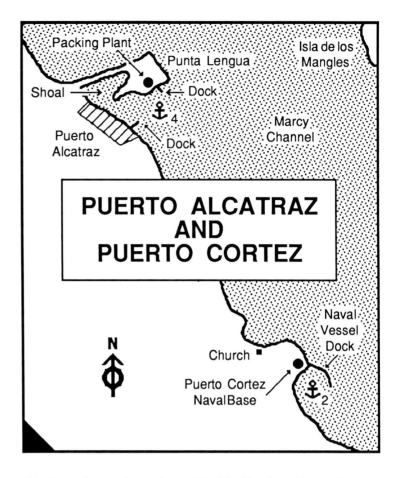

Chale on the northern shore of Bahia Almejas. Here is located a modest fish camp and a shrimp propagation facility (See Photo). There is no launching ramp, but small car-top boats can be manhandled into the water.

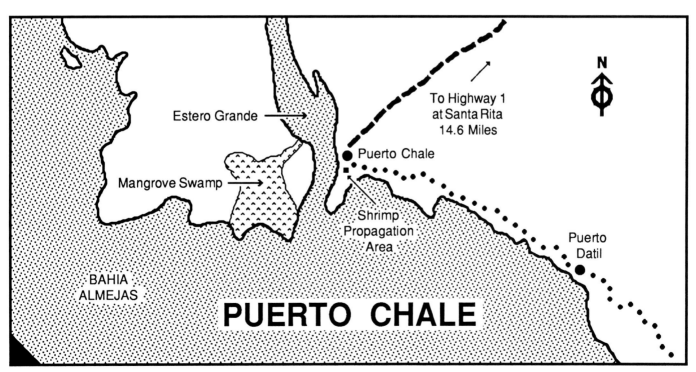

PUERTO ALCATRAZ & PUERTO CORTEZ (Looking SE) -- The naval base at Puerto Cortez is located on the small point of land near the upper-right portion of the photo.

THE AUTHOR AND BASE COMMANDER
Posing together at the base of the flagpole
at the Puerto Cortez Naval Base.

CHAPTER 13
THE SOUTHERN BIGHT
PUNTA TOSCA TO CABO SAN LUCAS

CHAPTER SUMMARY

It was noted in Chapter 11 that the Middle Bight was a little visited segment of the Pacific coast. Now Chapter 13 describes the Southern Bight, which is without question the area least visited by boaters in the entire Baja peninsula. At the northern end, a modest bay is formed south of Punta Tosca. With this exception there are no significant bays, prominent points of land, or protected anchorages.

Coastal cruisers plot their courses on a straight line from off Punta Tosca to the southern tip of the peninsula. The southern portion of the bight (Section C) offers many fine camping sites for land-based campers, but there are no boat launching ramps or protected beaches where small boats can be easily entered into the water.

In spite of this gloomy boating picture, the Southern Bight will be described in sufficient detail so offshore cruisers can identify shoreline features that are in view from the sea.

SECTION			DESCRIPTION
NO.	FROM	TO	
A	Punta Tosca	Boca del Colorado	Very low coastline backed by Bahia Almejas and lagoons. No anchorages except at Punta Tosca.
B	Boca del Colorado	Punta Lobos	Coastline is straight and mostly a sand beach backed by low-lying terrain. No coves or anchorages.
C	Punta Lobos	Cabo San Lucas	Coastline contains only minor points, but is steep faced and backed by mountains. No coves or anchorages until Cabo San Lucas.

SECTION A
PUNTA TOSCA TO
BOCA DEL COLORADO

The coastline from Punta Tosca to Boca del Colorado is a continuation of the submerged seacoast that started many miles to the north. Section A is approximately 22 miles in length. It is backed by the shoal draft waters of Bahia Almejas and a lagoon that lies behind Isla Cresiente. The only anchorage is immediately east of Punta Tosca.

PUNTA TOSCA AREA -- In November of 1539, the vessels of explorer Francisco de Ulloa found excellent protection in the bight formed east of Punta Tosca. His vessels also entered Bahia Almejas through Canal de Rehusa and referred to this entrance as "wide and deep." (See a more detailed account in Chapter 4 MARITIME HISTORY.)

After the passage of approximately 450 years, conditions are somewhat different. These changes are the result of the relentless work of the ocean in attempting to close off estuaries formed along a subsiding seacoast. (See the Coastal Geology Section of Chapter

PUNTA TOSCA (Looking 95 Degrees)

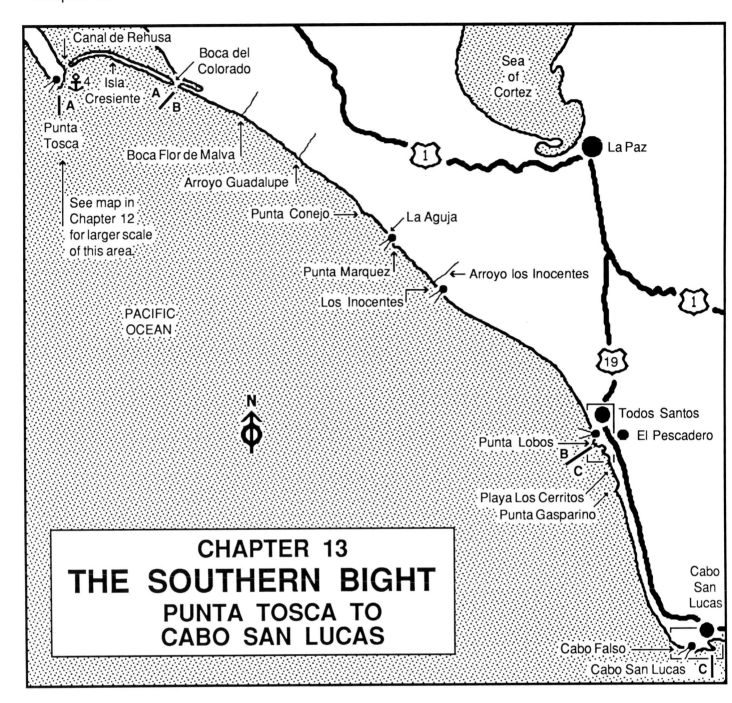

CHAPTER 13
THE SOUTHERN BIGHT
PUNTA TOSCA TO CABO SAN LUCAS

5.) Today a 20-mile-long, crescent-shaped barrier beach (Isla Cresiente) forms the southern boundary of Bahia Almejas. Possibly this bar was partially, or totally, absent in Ulloa's time and the explorer's anchorage was at, or north of, present-day Canal de Rehusa.

So much for speculation. Today's mariner is confronted with Canal de Rehusa as a shoal draft passage some 300 yards in width. It is fronted by swells or breakers which vary in intensity with the state of the weather and tides (See Photo). Mexican fishermen enter through this channel in their pangas by reducing speed and riding in directly behind the crest of a swell. The U.S. Sailing Directions notes that currents through this channel are strong and give rise to tide rips and overfalls.

Water depths between Canal de Rehusa and Punta Tosca are also shallow. I have taken anchorage directly east of the Punta Tosca lighthouse in 4 fathoms. Swell intensities at this location are greatly reduced from those present in the sea to the west of Punta Tosca, but the area is affected by currents passing through Canal de Rehusa. Also, extreme care must be taken not to venture further northward than abeam the light because of the numerous breakers lying off Canal de Rehusa. Charts 21120 and 21121 show these breakers as "Reported 1928." Reference to the photo in this chapter will show that they are present without question. Charlie's Charts guidebook shows Punta Tosca as an "emergency anchorage." I believe it to be acceptable provided due regard is given to the breakers.

PUNTA TOSCA (Looking NE) -- Note the lighthouse on the crest of the narrow ridge which forms the point. Canal de Rehusa is at the photo's top left. The extensive breakers which lie off Canal de Rehusa greatly limit the area available for anchoring east of Punta Tosca (See text).

ISLA CRESIENTE -- When a crescent-shaped sandbar bears the name Cresiente, no translation of the Spanish name appears necessary. Isla Cresiente has already been noted above. Near its eastern end it is separated from the peninsular shore by a narrow channel named Boca del Colorado (See Photo). From close offshore this channel is not visible. One might readily predict that it will not be many years before this passage is fully enclosed with sand, and that Canal de Rehusa will soon suffer the same fate. The sea will thus transform two islands, Isla Santa Margarita and Isla Cresiente, into one peninsula.

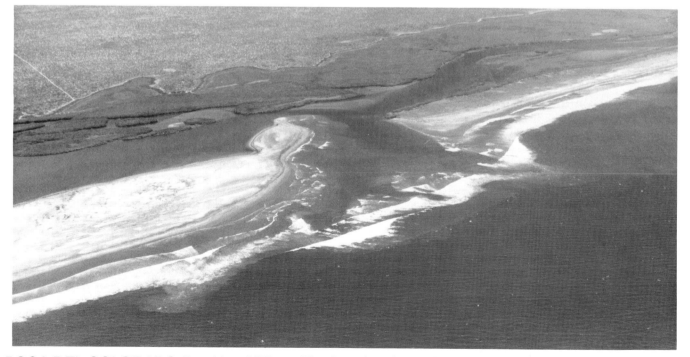

BOCA DEL COLORADO (Looking NE) -- The low, level terrain seen along the top of the photo is typical of that found inland from Bahia Almejas, Bahia Magdalena, and the Magdalena Lagoons.

PUNTA CONEJO (Looking N).

SECTION B
BOCA DEL COLORADO
TO PUNTA LOBOS

The terrain begins to rise gradually starting a short distance east of Boca del Colorado. (This is in contrast to the totally flat plain easterly from Bahia Magdalena and Bahia Almejas.) At this point, the land steepens to form 100-foot-high bluffs a short distance behind the beach. There are extensive stands (cardonals) of cardon (giant cactus) in this general area.

The Boca del Colorado area is the approximate southern end of the zone of coastal subsidence. I say "approximate" because there are some small esteros and low areas farther to the south. However, for the most part, the coastal beach to the south is backed by the above-noted bluffs and low plains that rise gradually to the main stem of the Sierra Giganta far to the east. From the water, one can thus see land immediately behind the beach, in contrast to the nothingness of the subsiding coastal area to the north.

MISCELLANEOUS LANDMARKS -- From Boca del Colorado SE to Punta Lobos there are a scattering of man-made objects and two very indistinct points of land. These are described briefly below. Each landmark

PUNTA MARQUEZ (Looking N).

is referenced to its approximate straight-line distance SE from Punta Tosca. These distances are taken from Mexican topographic maps and not the U. S. Nautical Charts. The latter charts poorly depict the features in this area.

It is interesting to note that I have found this most uninteresting section of coast to be the most difficult and time consumptive writing assignment in this entire book. It is of course hard to make something out of very little; but more importantly, it has been a demanding task to match actual places on the ground with my coastal observations. There are few distinctive landmarks along this section of coast. I have done my best, but perhaps I need to hoist a *small craft advisory* over the balance of Section B.

BOCA FLOR DE MALVA (27 Miles) A break in the coastal bluffs marks the place where a sizeable arroyo joins the sea. There is a lagoon behind the beach but it is not visible from the sea.

ARROYO GUADALUPE (35 MILES) Another low spot in the coastal terrain indicates where Arroyo Guadalupe meets the the coast. There are 2-3 shacks near the mouth of the arroyo. There are also shacks at the mouths of the next two minor arroyos to the SE. The coastal dirt road is occasionally in view. On clear days, one begins to see the Sierra de la Laguna mountains that dominate the peninsula's Cape Region.

PUNTA CONEJO (46 MILES) The Punta Conejo (See Photo) area offers a ranch and windmill nestled between two groups of trees. There is a group of shacks on the beach. Also nearby is a concrete light tower toppled over on the beach, no doubt undercut by high seas. Its red and white horizontal stripes are now vertical stripes. Several other buildings may be seen a few miles inland. Power poles and a microwave tower are visible on the horizon with the aid of binoculars. All this is quite impressive after 46 miles of almost nothing.

The fallen light tower marks the very slight bight formed NW from Punta Conejo. The point and bight are not easily distinguished from the sea.

LA AGUJA (54 MILES) At this point is a ranch near the mouth of a broad arroyo (Arroyo La Aguja - The Needle). NW of this ranch is a round, thatched roof building fronted by a rock wall. It appears to be some type of tourist facility which beckons to be investigated in the future.

PUNTA MARQUEZ LIGHT (55 Miles) A latticework light tower is located near the beach at this point. Approximately 3/4 miles SE of the light is a very undistinguished bluff which is Punta Marquez (See Photo).

LOS INOCENTES (70 Miles) A 30-foot-tall <u>concrete light tower</u> with horizontal red stripes is constructed directly back of the beach. One wonders how long it will survive in an upright position. A short distance NW of the light is the difficult-to-distinguish broad mouth of <u>Arroyo Los Inocentes</u>.

LOS INOCENTES TO PUNTA LOBOS It is 33 miles between these two points. The NW portion of this area is a segment of apparently subsiding seacoast. The beach is backed by an extensive low area which is subject to inundation. Behind are level plains covered with cardon. The land is slightly higher along the SW segment and is of sufficient elevation to be visible behind the beach.

TODOS SANTOS -- The mouth of a broad valley meets the sea about 2 miles north of Punta Lobos. The town of Todos Santos may be seen 1 mile inland on a bench south of this valley, with the lesser community of Cardonozo on the north side. The flat valley lands are fully planted with agricultural crops, but rows of palms and other trees along the roads and fence lines make them look heavily forested when viewed from the sea.

Todos Santos is one of Baja's most charming towns. It was also the site of one of the principal Jesuit missions founded early in the 18th century (1734). There are no protected anchorages in the area, so few if any coastal cruisers visit the town; however, be sure to savor its charms should you travel this way by land on Hwy. 19.

PUNTA LOBOS -- Punta Lobos is a substantial rocky point which projects seaward some 200 yards (See Photo). It is an <u>unmistakable landmark</u>, not because of its size or prowess as a promontory, but because it is the northernmost of many similar hills that lie at or near the coast from here south to Cabo San Lucas. The low-lying Llano de Magdalena to the north has finally come to an end. (There is one low hill 1 1/2 miles north of Punta Lobos but it falls just short of meeting the sea.)

Between Punta Lobos and the above-noted low hill is a red-striped concrete light tower. It is constructed on a 20-foot-high bluff of sand 100 yards back from the beach. A sizeable warehouse lies on this same bluff between the light and the point. The light provides guidance to the panga landing located at the head of the small bight formed north of Punta Lobos. This landing is fully open to NW winds, but is no doubt sheltered from southerly seas which prevail in summer months. I have observed a coastal fishing vessel at anchor off this landing.

SECTION C -- PUNTA LOBOS TO CABO SAN LUCAS

Much of the immediate shoreline between Punta Lobos and Cabo San Lucas is a sandy beach. However, from

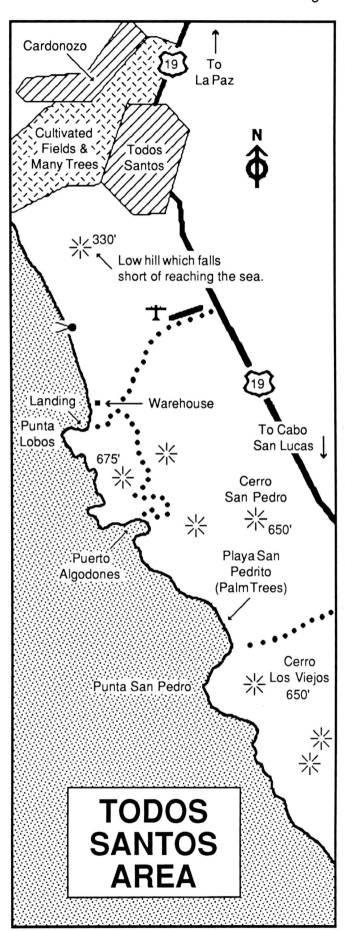

PUNTA LOBOS (Looking E) -- Note pangas on the beach immediately to the left of the point. The Punta Lobos navigation light is out of the photo to the left.

PUERTO ALGODONES (Looking E) -- Note the steep road approaching the cove on its left side.

PLAYA SAN PEDRITO (Looking NE) -- Note the extensive group of palm trees growing inland from the beach. Highway 19 may be seen near the top edge of the photo.

the sea, the coastal topography is dominated by numerous points and hills that lie at or near the shore. These features are in fact the foothills of the Sierra de la Laguna, the topographic feature most in evidence from the sea along this section of coast.

PUERTO ALGODONES -- Approximately 3/4 miles south of Punta Lobos is the only cove in Section C. It is only 200 yards wide and 300 yards deep (See Photo) and may provide NW swell protection for small boats. I am not aware if the cove is clear of dangers and have not ventured within its headlands. It should be entered with caution. A road of equally unknown characteristics switchbacks down to the head of the cove. Algodones thus offers the potential of a small boat launching site.

PLAYA SAN PEDRITO -- One mile SE of Puerto Algodones is a fine 1/2-mile-long beach with steep rocky points of land at either end. This is Playa San Pedrito (See Photo). It is closely backed by a dense stand of palm trees which provide a distinguishing feature from the sea. Playa San Pedrito is a popular camping area for tourists traveling on Highway 19. Look for recreational vehicles near the south end of the beach. Almost certainly this idyllic spot will fall victim to hotel builders, and coastal cruisers will have a new landmark.

The series of rocky hills and points that began at Punta Lobos comes to an end 1 1/2 miles SE from Playa San Pedrito. To the south, the coast becomes low and sandy.

PLAYA LOS CERRITOS -- It is 5 1/2 miles SE from Punta Lobos to a point where the low

PLAYA LOS CERRITOS (Looking E) -- The trailer court noted in the text may be seen inland from the beach immediately above and to the right of the small point of land.

sandy coast is interrupted by a 350-foot-tall hill (Cerro El Gavilan). The NW end of this hill forms a very slight seaward projection shown as Punta Pescadero on Chart 21120. The southern portion of this same hill forms a more pronounced but low-lying point. Extending many miles south from this low point is an outstanding sand beach named Playa Los Cerritos (See Photo).

The above-noted low point provides modest protection from NW winds and swells, and the beach in its lee is thus heavily used as a camping spot. About 200 yards SE of the point is one of the many trailer courts built by the government in Baja California. From a distance, its white concrete utility structures give the impression of cemetery gravestones. It therefore makes a very good, although low-lying, landmark. This trailer court is approximately 6 miles SE from Punta Lobos.

PUNTA GASPARINO -- Playa Los Cerritos stretches southward for 4 miles. At the 4-mile point the beach is interrupted by an inconsequential 150-foot-high hill. Although this hill projects seaward only a few yards beyond the general line of the coast it is honored with the name Punta Gasparino. It is noted only because of its being indicated on Chart 21120.

There are no readily distinguishable coastal features between Punta Gasparino and Cabo Falso.

CABO FALSO -- The name Falso, meaning false, is applied to a variety of geographic features which may be mistaken for the place that is actually being sought; in this case, Cabo San Lucas. However, a substantial case can be

CABO FALSO (Looking SE) -- The old lighthouse may be seen near the end of the point above and to the right of the extensive sand dunes that lie to the north. A portion of Bahia San Lucas is visible near the top left portion of the photo.

CABO FALSO (Looking NW).

SIERRA DE LA LAGUNA

The Sierra de la Laguna is a chain of mountains that runs from La Paz south to Cabo San Lucas. Several peaks exceed 6,000 feet in elevation. The range is in clear view from the sea and is the dominant topographic feature of the Cape Region of the Baja peninsula. The main peaks lie from 20 to 23 miles inland from the Pacific shore.

Laguna is the Spanish word for lagoon, although it sometimes refers to a lake. I could never understand why this name would be applied to a majestic range of mountains where there are no lagoons. Finally, my topographic maps disclosed the presence of a small meadow ESE of Todos Santos within a few feet of the summit of the range's tallest peak (6855 feet). This meadow bears the name La Laguna. These mighty mountains thus appear to be named in honor of what is in reality a most insignificant area of moisture. In an arid land such an oasis gets respect.

Mexico underwent considerable revolutionary activity during the second decade of the 20th century. The result was a new constitution in 1917. In Baja California, Felix Ortega organized a band of armed men who fought with federal troops at La Paz and in the mountains to the south. These actions took place from 1913 to 1915. The Sierra de la Laguna was the locale for many of these battles and served as an area of refuge for the revolutionary forces.

made that Cabo Falso (See Photos) is in fact the *real* cape. It is approximately 500 yards farther south than Cabo San Lucas, as are several places on the beach between the two points. The mountain peak inland from Cabo Falso is also far taller (600 feet) than anything on its more famous competitor. Finally, the cape lighthouse is on the peak inland from Cabo Falso, while there is no navigation light at Cabo San Lucas. But Cabo Falso loses the battle of the capes because it makes very little projection from the general alignment of the coast and offers no bay or protected anchorage. (In rounding the point note the old lighthouse structure located on a flat bench about 150 feet above sea level.)

CABO SAN LUCAS -- It is an exciting and memorable experience when one finally rounds Cabo San Lucas into Bahia San Lucas. I even savor it sitting here in front of a less-than-

enticing computer. The lure of "Cabo" will stay with the seagoing adventurer forever.

Defenders of Cabo San Lucas as the *real* cape would correctly point out that Cabo San Lucas has an un-

CABO SAN LUCAS (Looking SW) -- Note the cruise liners lying at anchor in the outer harbor.

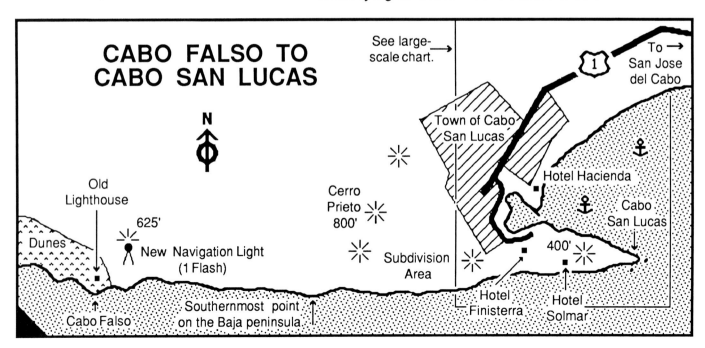

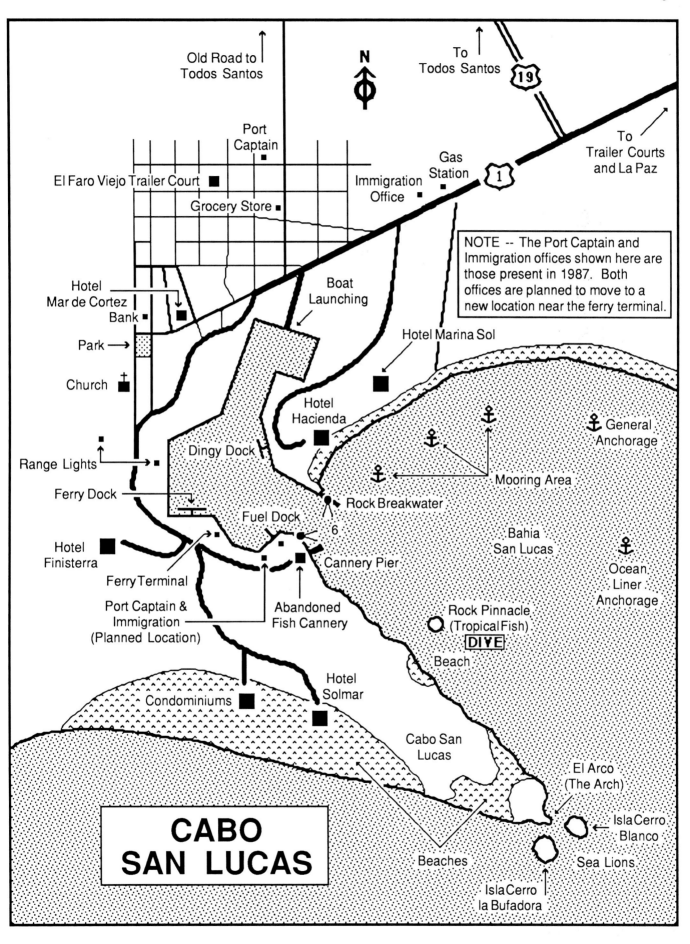

Old Road to
Todos Santos

To
Todos Santos

N

19

To
Trailer Courts
and La Paz

Port
Captain

Gas
Station

El Faro Viejo Trailer Court

Immigration
Office

Grocery Store

1

NOTE -- The Port Captain and
Immigration offices shown here are
those present in 1987. Both
offices are planned to move to a
new location near the ferry terminal.

Hotel
Mar de Cortez
Bank

Boat
Launching

Hotel Marina Sol

Park

Hotel
Hacienda

Church

General
Anchorage

Mooring Area

Range Lights

Dingy Dock

Ferry Dock

Rock Breakwater

Fuel Dock

6

Bahia
San Lucas

Ocean
Liner
Anchorage

Hotel
Finisterra

Ferry Terminal

Cannery Pier

Port Captain &
Immigration
(Planned Location)

Abandoned
Fish Cannery

Rock Pinnacle
(Tropical Fish)

DIVE

Beach

Hotel
Solmar

Condominiums

Cabo San
Lucas

El Arco
(The Arch)

Isla Cerro
Blanco

Beaches

Sea Lions

**CABO
SAN LUCAS**

Isla Cerro
la Bufadora

CABO SAN LUCAS AREA (Looking NE) -- Note the subdivision roads in the photo's lower left section (See text). This photo was taken in April. During the heart of the winter cruising season there are many more vessels anchored in both the inner and outer harbors.

mistakable profile, and that it comes complete with two off-lying pinnacles of rock (Isla Cerro Blanco and Isla Cerro la Bufadora), a perfectly shaped sea level archway, and a colony of sea lions. Furthermore, there is no need for a lighthouse. Our proud cape has two outstanding hotels which provide all the lights which even the most demanding skipper could require. Hotel Solmar and adjoining condominiums are the first major structures to come into view when rounding Cabo Falso from the west. They are located on the beach about 1/2 mile west of the cape. As one proceeds easterly, Hotel Finisterra displays three horizontal rows of lights from its perch atop the cliffs westerly, and farther inland, from the Solmar.

Much of the land lying inland from the beach between Cabo San Lucas and Cabo Falso has been subdivided (See Photo). A a result, the buildings and lights in this area are the first items of significance to greet vessels rounding Cabo Falso from the Pacific.

But regardless of whether you arrived from north, south, or east, CONGRATULATIONS TO ALL HANDS, you have reached Finisterra (Land's End).

CABO SAN LUCAS AREA -- "Fabulous Cabo San Lucas." That is how this area is described in television and newspaper advertisements. The winter weather, sportfishing, and hotels really are outstanding in my view, but one needs to keep in mind that much of the community of Cabo San Lucas is a dirt-street fishing village struggling with its transformation into a tourist mecca. If you will not hold this against the community, you will find that it really is fabulous.

Winter season prevailing NW winds pass over Bahia San Lucas and the adjoining community. These winds are a

daily occurrence with velocities at their height in the afternoons (normally in the 10-15-knot range).

THE OUTER HARBOR -- Scores of vessels anchor or moor for extended periods during the winter season in the area NE from the entrance to the inner harbor (See Photo). This outer harbor area is now largely occupied with fixed moorings available on a fee basis. They tend to be occupied mostly by sportfishing powerboats. It is difficult to anchor immediately seaward of the moorage area due to steep water depths. A deep underwater canyon proceeds SE from the inner harbor entrance.

The area SW from the moorage area must be left clear to allow passage of the Cabo San Lucas-to-Puerto Vallarta ferry which docks in the inner harbor.

Usually there is ample space to anchor near the eastern end of the moorage area; many vessels are positioned here. If you are coming into port late at night, or for the first time, here is the best place to settle until you have a chance to checkout the neighborhood. Water depths are in the 6-to-12-fathom range. This area is somewhat subject to Pacific swells refracting around Cabo San Lucas so it can be a bit rocky even in fair weather. Also, water depths are deeper here than in the moorage area. In summary, the moorings take up the best anchoring area.

THE CAPE'S NE FACE -- Note the rock pinnacle shown on the CABO SAN LUCAS Chart. The waters around this rock are the home of thousands of colorful tropical fish. It thus makes a fine area for diving and snorkeling. Ship's tenders and trailer boats may be landed on the small beach south of the pinnacle and this area used as a base for visiting the fish.

CABO SAN LUCAS INNER HARBOR (Looking N) -- The elongated light-roofed structure on the low ridge at the photo's left center is the Hotel Finisterra. The ferry dock is situated immediately to its right. Vessels in the outer harbor occupy a portion of the area supplied with fixed moorings.

The picturesque beach near the end of the cape is a good spot for sunbathing. The nearby arch and sea lion colony are also worth a visit.

A few skippers choose to anchor close to the shore SE from the abandoned cannery pier. I have also observed several boats end anchored off the pier itself.

THE INNER HARBOR -- Dredging of the inner harbor (See Photo) commenced about the same time as completion of the Transpeninsular Highway in 1973. During 1987 it was being redredged. The process may be self-perpetuating. The eventual plan is to fill the northern portion of the basin with an array of floating docks. However, the years continue to pass without this being accomplished. I suspect that the Mexican government is having difficulty finding private interests willing to invest in marina facilities that would probably be converted to a pile of rubble during the first hurricane. My best counsel is that marina facilities here are a matter of "what you see is what you get," and don't count on seeing the same thing two years in succession.

While a marina is still in the offing, some ocean cruisers choose to bow-stern anchor in the inner harbor in company with many local small sportfishing vessels. The location is close to town but I suspect that the use of onboard heads results in water quality that leaves something to be desired. Anchored vessels must also leave a path for boats using the launching ramp at the north end of the basin.

The southern portion of the inner harbor must be kept clear to allow the entrance and turning of the Cabo San Lucas-to-Puerto Vallarta ferry which is scheduled to depart on Wednesdays and Sundays. On my most recent visit, yachts were permitted to anchor in this area immediately after the ferry's departure. The resulting influx of sailboats with anchors dangling from their bows may best be described as an anchoring frenzy; something like a department store exchange counter the morning after Christmas.

Two bright range lights are located on tall latticework towers as shown on the CABO SAN LUCAS Chart. These flashing white lights stand out well even though surrounded by many other lights. Shorter latticework towers with red (right) and green (left) lights mark the entrance to the harbor.

THE COMMUNITY -- The small park shown on the CABO SAN LUCAS Chart is more or less the center of the town's business section, although many businesses lie on the main street between here and the gasoline station to the east. All of the four hotels shown on the chart are worth a visit. If one had to name *the* place to see, it would be the Whale Bar at the Hotel Finisterra.

There are a variety of restaurants, shops, grocery stores, and small motels. Walk around and enjoy. To tell you more would be just filling up space.

IN CLOSING -- Should you have been so kind as to use these pages as your guide along Baja's Pacific shore, I sincerely hope they have not led you too far astray, and that your boating adventure has been a safe and memorable experience for all hands. VOLUME II of the *Baja Boater's Guide* stands ready to assist in the Sea of Cortez. It would be a pleasure to hear from you should you be so inclined. -------- Jack Williams

BAJA BOOKSHELF

The BAJABOOKSHELF offers the Baja Buff an array of publications concerning Baja California. Some were written specifically about the peninsula. Others are the best available books dealing with subjects related to Baja such as wildlife, Spanish, etc. Each represents my choice of the best title available on the subject.

Order books directly from the BAJA BOOKSHELF. On request we will send you more complete information and prices on any book, including new titles that were not available when the BAJA BOATER'S GUIDE was published.

NUMBER	TITLE	AUTHOR	PRICE	AD PAGE
1	The Magnificent Peninsula	Jack Williams	$14.95	6
2	Baja Boater's Guide - Volume I - Pacific Coast	Jack Williams	$24.95	----
3	Baja Boater's Guide - Volume II - Sea of Cortez	Jack Williams	$26.95	15
4	The Baja Catch	Niel Kelly & Gene Kira	$15.95	177
5	Diver's Guide to Underwater Mexico	Michael & Lauren Farley	$14.95	24
6	Airports of Baja California & NW Mexico	Baja Bush Pilots	$24.95	25
7	A Field Guide to the Plants of California	Norman C. Roberts	$18.00	51
8	Field Guide to the Gray Whale	Oceanic Society	$ 3.95	52
9	The Elephant Sea	Burney J. Le Boeuf	$ 4.50	56
10	A Field Guide to the Seabirds of the World	Peter Harrison	$24.95	60
11	Cave Paintings of Baja California	Harry W. Crosby	$27.50	146
12	Friendly Neighbors	Alan Riding	$ 4.95	205
13	Back Country Mexico - Guide & Phrase Book	Burleson & Riskind	$12.95	205
14	Spanish Mexican Style	Vern Jones	$ 6.95	205
15	Chart Guide Mexico West	Ed Winlund and others	$41.00	Text - 20

Use order form below, or write your order on any piece of paper. Add 6 % sales tax for books shipped in California, + $2.00 shipping charge for each book except titles 8, 9, & 12, add $1.00.

NUMBER	TITLE	PRICE	TAX	SHIP	TOTAL
_____	_____	$_____	$_____	$_____	$_____
_____	_____	$_____	$_____	$_____	$_____
_____	_____	$_____	$_____	$_____	$_____
_____	_____	$_____	$_____	$_____	$_____

GRAND TOTAL _____

Make checks or money orders payable to H. J. Williams Publications. (U. S. dollars only.)

Mail your order to:

H. J. Williams Publications
P. O. Box 203 - A
Sausalito, CA 94966

INSTRUCTIONS FOR COMPLETING
MEXICAN ENTRY PAPERS

Sample forms are shown on the following pages. Feel free to make photocopies for your use.

FORM 1 (ROL DE TRIPULANTES)

Present 4 copies of this form to the Mexican Consul. (See additional discussion on page 22 in Chapter 2.)

LINE 1 --
    First Blank -- Name of the city where the Mexicam Consul is located. In most cases San Diego, CA
    Second Blank -- The registration or document number of the vessel.
LINE 2 -- Name of the vessel.
LINE 3 --
    First Blank -- Name (City, State, Country) of the home port of the vessel.
    Second Blank -- Gross tonage of the vessel.
LINE 4 -- Captain's name.
LINE 5 -- First port-of-call in Mexico where it is planned to present the ROL DE TRIPULANTES to
    Mexican authorities.
THE CREW LIST --
    NOMBRE -- Name of each person aboard the vessel.
    NACIONALIDAD -- Nationality of each person.
    TITULO -- Title of each person. "Capitan" for the skipper, and "Marinero" for crew members.
    EDAD -- Age of each person.
LINE 6 -- The total number of persons aboard the vessel.
BOTTOM LINE --
    La Fecha -- The date when the form is presented to the Mexican Consul.
    Por el Capitan -- The Captain's signature.

FORM 2

Present approved Form 1 (ROL DE TRIPULANTES) and filled out Form 2 to the Immigration Office at the first port-of-entry in Mexico.

LINE 1 -- Captain's name.
LINE 2 --
    First Blank -- Vessel's name.
    Second Blank -- Home port of the vessel.
LINE 3 --
    First Blank -- The Vessel's gross tonage.
    Second Blank -- The vessel's net tonage.
LINE 4 -- The principal port in Mexico which is the vessel's destination.
LINES 5 & 6 -- List intermediate ports, or state "puertos intermedios" (intermediate ports).
THE CREW LIST -- Same as for Form 1.
LINE 7 -- Total number of persons aboard the vessel.
LINE 8 -- Date when Form 2 is presented to the Immigration Office at the first port-of-entry.
LINE 9 -- Captain's signature.
That portion of the form below the Captain's signature will be filled in by Mexican authorities.

ESTADOS UNIDOS MEXICANOS

SECRETARIA DE AL MARINA NACIONAL

DIRECCION DE MARINA MERCANTE

ROL DE TRIPULANTES

PUERTO DE _____ NUMERAL _____

Rolde los personas con que navegal el_____

matricula de _____del porte de _____ toneladas

brutas de arqueo, al mando de su Capitan, _____

que zarpa para el puerto de _____

_____

NOMBRE	NACIONALIDAD	TITULO	EDAD

Comprende este Rol los asientos de _____ individuos, y siendo de mi
satisfaccion como Capitan que soy,me obligo al exacto cumplimiento de cuanto
disponen las leyes y reglamentos del legitimo comercio nacional y de mas
disposiciones vigentes que me sean provenidas por las Autoridades Maritimas de
los puertos nacionales.

_____ _____
la fecha   por el Capitan

C. Capitan de Puerto
PRESENTE:

_____, Capitan del yate de placer
_____ , de la matricula de _____
del porte de _____ toneladas brutas y de _____ netas de arqueo, declara:
Que el dia de hoy zarpara con destino al Puerto de _____
con escala en los siquieentes puertos: _____
_____
siende la tripulacion de este yate como sique:

NOMBRE   NACIONALIDAD   CARGO A BORDO   EDAD

Comprende este Rol los asientos de _____ personas y es de mi satisfaccion,
como Capitan que soy, manifestar que me obligo al exacto cumplimiento de todo
cuanto disponen las Leyes y Reglamentos actualmente en vigor.

_____ de 19 ____

El Capitan

_____

Visada de conformidad por esta Oficina de Migracion con _____
tripulantes inclusive su Capitan; se hace a la mar con destino a _____
_____ escalando puntos intermedios.

_____ de 19 ____

El Jefe de la Oficina, de Migracion

_____

Habiendo cumplido su escala en este puerto, el yate _____
en este fecha despachese para _____escalando todos
los lugares que se mencionan. Con _____ tripulantes inclusive su Capitan.

_____de 19 ____

El Capitan de Puerto

_____

INDEX BY PATTY

Bold Type indicates the principal references
to places found in PART II Sailing Directions

COMMON SPANISH TOPOGRAPHIC TERMS

Arroyo	Stream Course	Cerro	Hill	Piedra	Stone or Rock
Bahia	Bay	Estero	Estuary	Playa	Beach
Bajo	Shoal	Isla	Island	Puerto	Port
Boca	Mouth or Entrance	Islote	Islet	Punta	Point
Cabo	Cape	Laguna	Lagoon	Rio	River
Caleta	Little Cove	Mar	Sea	Roca	Rock
Campo	Camp	Mesa	Flattopped Hill	Sierra	Mountain Range
Canal	Channel	Morro	Knob or Knoll	Valle	Valley

Index

A GREAT COMBINATION

① MEMBERSHIP IN THE VAGABUNDOS DEL MAR
Baja / Mexico's First & Foremost Travel Club.

② MAJOR SAVINGS IN MEXICAN INSURANCE
For Vagabundo members only.

THE PRICE OF BOTH IS LESS THAN THE COST OF MEXICAN INSURANCE ALONE AT MANY OTHER PLACES

The VAGABUNDOS DEL MAR is a non-profit social club of nearly 5,000 members who have joined together for recreational boating and travel. The club organizes many activities each year in Alaska, the U. S. and Canadian Pacific Coasts, and western Mexico. Many take place in Baja.

Join now. 12 month membership includes newsletters, decals, the opportunity to make new friends, to participate in all activities and programs, and to enjoy many discounts.

VAGABUNDOS DEL MAR
MEMBERSHIP APPLICATION
Mail to P.O. Box 824 Isleton, CA 95641

☐ Please enroll me (and my family) in the Vagabundos del Mar. First 12 months (includes $30.00 annual dues) $40.00.

_____
Name (include name of spouse)

_____
Address

_____
City - State or Province - Zip

☐ For a subscription to the Bi-monthly magazine "Western Boatman" add $6.50

☐ For your Vagabundos membership book, club flag, and 4 inch multi-colored jacket patch ($25.00 value) add $10.00

Enclosed is my check for $_____

☐ Include application for auto insurance.

ANNUAL AUTO & RV INSURANCE

Current Market Value	Premium**
FULL COVERAGE	
$ 5,000 thru $ 9,999	$144.00
$10,000 thru $14,999	$165.00
$15,000 thru $19,999	$181.00
$ 20,000 thru $ 24,999	$198.00
$ 25,000 thru $ 29,999	$213.00
$ 30,000 thru $ 34,999	$229.00

Includes liability. No extra charge for trailers or other towed vehicles.

LIABILITY ONLY $ 60.00

ANNUAL BOAT INSURANCE

Hull   -- $1.50 / $100 coverage
Liability   -- $ .20 / $100   "
plus fees and taxes.
Example   -- $20,000 Hull and Liability
$448.50 / year.

** Rates subject to change